POLISH SOCIETY UNDER GERMAN OCCUPATION

POLISH SOCIETY
UNDER GERMAN OCCUPATION

The Generalgouvernement,
1939-1944

Jan Tomasz Gross

PRINCETON UNIVERSITY PRESS

PRINCETON, NEW JERSEY

Copyright © 1979 by Princeton University Press
Published by Princeton University Press, Princeton, New Jersey
In the United Kingdom: Princeton University Press,
Guildford, Surrey

All Rights Reserved
Library of Congress Cataloging in Publication Data will be
found on the last printed page of this book

Publication of this book has been aided by a grant from
The Andrew W. Mellon Foundation
This book has been composed in Linotype Caledonia

Clothbound editions of Princeton University Press books
are printed on acid-free paper, and binding materials are
chosen for strength and durability

Printed in the United States of America by Princeton
University Press, Princeton, New Jersey

To my parents

Contents

Tables and Figures

Preface

THIS work is a study of a society under occupation. Its subject matter stands at the crossroads of history and sociology. Though I deal with a historical phenomenon in an individual country—the occupation of Poland by the Germans during the Second World War—the choice of the subject was motivated by my belief that the occupation of Poland has a universal significance. It lasted longer than the occupation of any other country during World War II. It was also the most severe, as the result of the racial conceptions held by the Germans, who made an absolute distinction between Jews and Slavs on the one hand, and the nations of Western Europe on the other. Such views allowed little room for either compromise or accommodation between the occupier and the occupied. What happened in Poland between 1939 and 1944 provides an exemplary case for studying the impact of a prolonged disaster on various forms of societal life.

In this study I shall analyze the occupation of Poland in the framework of sociologically significant questions. My main purpose is to identify the alternative forms of collective life that emerged in response to the social control exercised by the occupier. Thus the study will focus on two interrelated sets of factors: the model of German occupation and the way it was realized in practice; and the patterns of collective behavior in which the Polish population engaged as a result of the occupier's policy. The main orientation of my analysis is to identify the peculiar processes of reconciliation among various groups acting in pursuit of incompatible and mutually exclusive goals.

The original intention of the German occupiers was to set

up a social system geared entirely to the possibility of unlimited exploitation of the subjugated populace. My contention is that such a model of social control cannot work. Or, to put it differently, a social system cannot be based on the total exclusion of the majority of the population from the benefits of social cooperation. Contrary to the occupier's intentions, there emerged in Polish society alternative forms of collective life that allowed for at least a minimal satisfaction of social needs, including the need for a normative order to determine the rules of social organization. When the occupier has no explicit policy of providing institutions through which the local population can satisfactorily pursue its interests, then such institutions, or substitutes, are built spontaneously on the remnants of previous forms of collective life. The occupier, if he wishes to achieve his own goals of exploitation, must in some way adjust to these forms of societal "self-defense." My hypothesis is that a *society* cannot be destroyed by coercion, short of the physical extermination of its members.

Since a variety of strategies aiming at the restitution of the nation-state and the preservation of national life were worked out and put into action in Poland during the nineteenth and twentieth centuries prior to the Second World War, I think it necessary first to devote some space to a presentation of certain central themes from Polish history. Such a brief discussion, I hope, will introduce the main actors to those unfamiliar with Polish history and provide sufficient background for understanding the developments in the years 1939-1944. It was, after all, around the nucleus of various prewar organizations that the underground network was set up and developed.

It seems appropriate also to inform the reader at the beginning about two subjects missing from this text. I do not offer a sociological interpretation of life in the Jewish ghettos. It is a subject for a separate book, not only because of the sheer amount of existing evidence and documentation that bears on it, but also because the Jews were *separated* from the rest of the population and treated differently by the occupiers.

The other omission derives from the methodology of presentation. I am aware that an analysis of the German occupation of Poland is not complete without giving some attention to the threat of a Communist takeover, which became more and more unavoidable as the end of the war drew near. I have purposely omitted this issue, however, because it would demand an extensive presentation of the political history of the underground and would frustrate my effort to give a sociological orientation to my analysis. Besides, omitting the problem of the Communist underground does not make it impossible to give a satisfactory description of the processes of adjustment of Polish society to German occupation. In the first place, the Communist underground was born very late, after all other underground institutions were already well established; second, it never grew to sizable proportions. A recently published chronicle of life in Cracow under the occupation (Wroński, 1974:433-440) lists the underground publications in that city. Of 137 titles, only 9 are Communist papers. In fact, a closer scrutiny reveals only 4 different titles, since the same paper reappeared at different times but was listed separately each time (see entries 46 and 119; 77 and 93; 51, 105, 106, and 107). Only one of the four Communist journals was published for longer than a year. If proof of the relative obscurity of the Communist underground by a not unfavorably biased source is needed, Wroński's list provides it. Thus, by omitting from this analysis the problem of the Communist underground, only a very marginal area of society is left out; at the same time, we avoid a more detailed political history than a sociological presentation can support. Finally, I would argue that the threat of the Communist takeover and the Communist takeover itself belong, or rather, constitute, the next period (following the German occupation) in contemporary Polish history. I think that one can speak about a distinct *process of transition* from the German-occupied Poland to the Soviet-imposed People's Poland, a process taking place between, say, mid-1944, when the Red Army crossed Polish prewar eastern boundaries, and, say, December 1948, when the Unification Congress of the Polish Socialist Party and the Polish Workers' Party took place. This, incidentally, accounts for "1944" rather than "1945" in the book's title.

This book was, three drafts ago, a doctoral dissertation written under the direction of Professor Juan Linz, whose help was invaluable to me. Also, I am particularly indebted to Professor David Apter for his criticism at the early stages of the writing. To Professor Piotr Wandycz and Dr. Lucjan Dobroszycki I wish to express my gratitude for their guidance and advice concerning the history of Poland. I would also like to thank Professors Allan Silver and Andrzej Korboński for having given their time generously in reading the manuscript. Finally, I wish to thank my copyeditor, Gretchen Oberfranc, for her thoughtful professional assistance.

A grant from the Foreign Area Fellowship Program of the American Council of Learned Societies enabled me to carry out research in the archives of the General Sikorski Historical Institute and the Underground Poland Study Trust in London.

Abbreviations and Acronyms

Archives and Collections

(Most of the archival collections I consulted are not catalogued. Full identification of each document therefore requires that I provide, in addition to the name of the archive and collection, the title or number of the file in which the document is kept and, wherever possible, the date that appears on the document.)

GSHI   Instytut Historyczny Imienia Generała Władysława Sikorskiego (General Sikorski Historical Institute), London
        PRM   Kolekcja Prezydium Rady Ministrów
        A   Unnamed Collection

HIA   Hoover Institution Archives, Stanford University
        PGC   Polish Government Collection

HL   Hoover Library, Stanford University
        PUC   Polish Underground Collection
        MSW Ministerstwo Spraw Wewnętrznych (Ministry of Internal Affairs)

UPST   Studium Polski Podziemnej (Underground Poland Study Trust), London

Published Documents

IMT   International Military Tribunal, *Trial of the Major War Criminals Before the International Military Tribunal*, 42 vols. (Nuremburg, 1947-1949)

Polish Political Parties and Organizations, 1919-1939

BBWR Bezpartyjny Blok Współpracy z Rządem (Nonpartisan Bloc of Cooperation with the Government) (Sanacja)

COP	Centralny Okręg Przemysłowy (Central Industrial Region)
ONR	Obóz Narodowo-Radykalny (National Radical Camp) (also ONR-Falanga)
OZN	Obóz Zjednoczenia Narodowego (Camp of National Unity) (also OZON) (Sanacja)
PPS	Polska Partia Socjalistyczna (Polish Socialist Party)
SN	Stronnictwo Narodowe (National Democratic Party)

Polish Underground Political Parties and Organizations, 1939-1944

AK	Armia Krajowa (Home Army) (earlier SZP and ZWZ)
AL	Armia Ludowa (People's Army) (Communist)
BIP	Biuro Informacji i Propagandy (Bureau of Information and Propaganda) (AK)
BP	Biuro Polityczne (Political Bureau)
CKON	Centralny Komitet Organizacji Niepodległościowych (Central Committee of Organizations for Independence)
CKRL	Centralne Kierownictwo Ruchu Ludowego (Central Leadership of the Peasant Movement)
GRP	Głowa Rada Polityczna (Main Political Council)
KON	Konwent Organizacji Niepodległościowych (Committee of Organizations for Independence) (Sanacja)
KRN	Country's National Council (Communist)
LSB	Ludowa Straż Bezpieczeństwa (Peasant Party)
NLOW	Narodowo-Ludowa Organizacja Wojskowa (National People's Military Organization) (SN)
NOW	Narodowa Organizacja Wojskowa (National Military Organization) (SN)
NSZ	Narodowe Siły Zbrojne (National Armed Forces)
ODB	Obozowe Drużny Bojowe (SN)

OPW	Obóz Polski Walczącej (Camp of Fighting Poland) (Sanacja)
OUN	Ukrainian Nationalists
PKP	Polityczny Komitet Porozumiewawczy (Political Consultative Committee) (later RJN)
PPR	Polska Partia Robotnicza (Polish Workers' Party) (Communist)
PPS	Polska Partia Socjalistyczna (Polish Socialist Party)
PS	Polscy Socjaliści (Polish Socialists)
RJN	Rada Jedności Narodowej (Council of National Unity) (earlier PKP)
SL	Stronnictwo Ludowe (Peasant Party)
SN	Stronnictwo Narodowe (National Democratic Party)
S.O.S.	Samoobrona Społeczna (Societal Self-Defense)
SP	Stronnictwo Pracy (Labor Party)
SZP	Służba Zwycięstwu Polski (Service for the Victory of Poland) (later ZWZ and AK)
TWZW	Tajne Wojskowe Zakłady Wydawnicze (Clandestine Military Printing House)
UPA	Ukrainian Insurgents' Army (OUN)
WRN	Wolność, Równość, Niepodległość (Freedom, Equality, Independence) (PPS)
ZO	Związek Odwetu (Association of Revenge) (AK)
ZWZ	Związek Walki Zbrojnej (Association of Armed Struggle) (earlier SZP, later AK)

Polish Welfare Organizations, 1939-1944

RGO	Rada Główna Opiekuńcza (Main Welfare Council)
SKSS	Stołeczny Komitet Samopomocy Społecznej (Capital's Committee of Social Assistance)

German Administration

DAAD	German Academic Exchange Office
DVL	German National List

ABBREVIATIONS AND ACRONYMS

GG	Generalgouvernement
HSSPF	Higher SS and Police Leader
NSDAP	German National-Socialist Workers' Party
ROA	Russian Liberation Army
RSHA	Main Reich Security Office
SD	Security Police
U.W.A.	Office of the Plenipotentiary for Special Missions
Z.A.M.	Central Registration Office

Russian Administration

NKVD	State Secret Police (earlier ChK)

POLISH SOCIETY UNDER GERMAN OCCUPATION

CHAPTER I

Historical Background

A READER of the underground Polish press during World War II found it largely devoted to Polish history. He was not surprised, because he wanted it to be that way: a people faced with rapid changes, crisis, and, finally, disaster, feels it necessary to interpret events, to understand the new things that are happening, and to discover clues to the solution of its current problem. Its impulse is to revisit history and to draw lessons from the strains already coped with and survived.

Polish history interested the German occupiers as well. Their curiosity also derived from their concern with contemporary problems: they wanted to find the most effective methods to perpetuate Poland's subjugation. Heinrich Himmler, one of the main architects of the new German empire, found it so useful to study nineteenth-century Polish history that he ordered all SS leaders in the Generalgouvernement to read a report he had received on this subject: *Die polnischen Methoden bei der Vorbereitung und Durchführung des Aufstandes gegen die Russen im Jahre 1863. Die Art der russischen Abwehr* (Polish Methods of Preparation and Conduct of the Uprising Against the Russians in 1863. The Manner of Russian Defense).[1]

[1] The document Himmler received in February 1940 (Halicz, 1965:356-368) can be summarized as follows:

The Poles may wish to remind the world of their existence, as they did in 1863, and they might start an insurrection.

Religious differences between Catholic Poles and Orthodox Russians reinforced the patriotic appeals of 1863. Today the situation is similar because Germans are considered by the Poles as Protestant, that is, heretic.

In 1863 the Russians kept the peasants from participating in the

Indeed, a variety of strategies for coping with occupiers had been worked out in Poland during the nineteenth century. For over a hundred years, until the outbreak of the First World War, Poland was occupied and partitioned, and, as Jan Szczepański put it, Poles "proved their ability to endure and their capability to resist" (Szczepański, 1970:20). Thus, when after twenty years of independence Poland was again occupied in 1939 and partitioned by its eastern and western neighbors, Polish society already had considerable experience in living under foreign domination. Some brief comment on the attitudes of Poles vis-à-vis their nineteenth-century occupiers may make clear the kinds of experience they could draw upon when faced with another occupation in the middle of the twentieth century.

The Polish Patriotic Tradition

At the risk of oversimplification, the Polish patriotic tradition forged during the nineteenth century can be said to have two components: a romantic tradition of patriotic

---

revolt by introducing reforms that benefited them. It is perhaps possible today to keep certain parts of the population quiet by meeting their economic demands.

The Russian government employed large numbers of Poles in the local administration. This was a mistake. The National Government in 1863 had some authority over the Poles employed in the Russian administration; as a consequence, the postal service and the railways were often used by the insurgents.

The uprising in 1863 failed militarily because the Poles had not had a standing army since 1831 and because the population was not trained in the art of warfare. Today, after twenty years of the draft in independent Poland, the situation is different.

Since partisan operations cannot succeed without help from the civilian population, close attention must be paid not only to the military but also to the civilian organization of the uprising.

The Russians hesitated in their repression of the uprising in the initial stages; that is why it lasted so long. Repression should be immediate and severe. Collective responsibility should be introduced.

conspiracies and armed insurrections; and a positivistic tradition of peaceful efforts to find a formula that would promote coexistence with the occupier but still allow for the
encouragement of national identity and economic strength.

Insurrections came first. The program of coexistence
gained support only in the last forty years of the nineteenth
century, after the series of insurrections by every generation since 1815 was finally judged to have been too costly.
After a sequence of ruthlessly suppressed uprisings, young
and educated members of the bourgeoisie came forward
with a program calling for "realism." The nation should
build its strength, rather than dissipate it in futile uprisings,
and this could only be achieved by abandoning politics for
the time being and promoting economic development and
education. *Enrichissez-vous* was one of their most popular
catchwords.

In the last twenty years of the nineteenth century, with
the coming of socialism, problems of social reform were
added to those of national liberation or preservation. Socialists opposed the solidaristic vision of the society advocated by the positivists, and they pressed not only for social
revolution but also for independence by force of arms. For
this reason they seemed, in twentieth-century independent
Poland, to be the most legitimate heirs of the romantic tradition. It was only natural, therefore, that a socialist, Józef
Piłsudski, organized the legions that won back independence, and that he was hailed in the aftermath of the war as
the Chief of State (*Naczelnik Państwa*).

Although the romantic revolutionary period was succeeded by "Warsaw's positivism," the program of "organic
work," or Galician loyalism,[2] it remained the more important and somehow more treasured inheritance in the eyes

[2] Under the Hapsburgs the patriotic program of accommodation
went even further and called for political cooperation. But in the
Austro-Hungarian partition of the province of Galicia, where far-
reaching autonomy was granted, loyalism without apostasy was possible.

5

of later generations, perceived in brighter colors and treated more extensively in literature and education. Let us
therefore examine in detail the heritage from the nineteenth
century that was most meaningful for the active participants in the anti-German conspiracy one hundred years
later: the tradition of opposition and insurrection, or as it
was later called, romantic messianism.

Deep commitment to freedom and liberty has roots in
Polish tradition that reach back to the sixteenth century
and the so-called "golden freedom."[3] The golden freedom
was conceived of as a symbol for the special quality embodied by the Polish state, indeed, as the highest value that
can be achieved in the life of a society, more important
even than political stability and economic prosperity. This
value could not be compromised or traded for any other.
Furthermore, it was viewed as indivisible: a society, a nation, or class, the Polish gentry believed, was either entirely
free or was, of necessity, enslaved (Hernas, 1974:5, 6).

This notion turned out to be a self-fulfilling prophesy:
in defending the total freedom embodied in the institutions
of the "gentry's republic," the gentry lost its freedom completely when internal anarchy weakened Poland to the
point where it could not but yield to foreign domination.
It is important, however, to note that nineteenth-century
Polish patriots drew upon this tradition of freedom and
consequently professed libertarian beliefs of a universal
character. Accordingly, the watchword of the Polish legions
that fought in the Napoleonic wars was "for your and our
freedom and for future brotherhood" (Szczepański,
1970:17). As the poet Adam Mickiewicz wrote: *"Ibi patria
ubi male*: wherever in Europe liberty is suppressed and
fought for, there is the battle of your country" (Namier,

---

[3] During the sixteenth century Poland was probably the freest and
most tolerant country in Europe (Fox, 1924:64-66; Wilbur, 1945:
266; Kot, 1960:22). Even after the Counter-Reformation began, the
Polish gentry continued in what was known as "golden freedom."

1964:58). Thus, after Poland was partitioned its patriots could *again* demand freedom in a radical, unrestrained fashion.

When demands for freedom are raised in the midst of oppression, they may very well be pushed to extremes and still remain unambiguous. Only later does the dialectic develop that demands that freedom in a society be in some way restricted in order to be preserved. While it is still being sought, freedom is a crystal-clear, unadulterated concept; it loses that clarity only when it is actually won and is no longer simply freedom *from* (the oppressor), but must be translated into freedom *for* (and freedom for *what* may be subject to the widest disagreement). As has been repeatedly demonstrated in many parts of the world, the struggle for liberation is capable of arousing incomparably more enthusiasm and hope than the actual exercise of liberty, and the struggle is further ennobled by the symbolism of sacrifice. Writing about the nineteenth-century cult of Napoleon in Poland, Jules Michelet remarked: *"Vainqueur, s'etait pour eux un grand homme; vaincu et captif, un heros mort, ils en ont fait un messie"* (Treugutt, 1974:37-38).

The messianic quality of the romantic tradition emerged from this admixture of idealism and historicizing. According to this tradition, Poland's commitment to the ideal of freedom was unconditional, and its struggle for liberation was a selfless effort undertaken on behalf of all mankind. "Poland," wrote Mickiewicz, "will re-arise and free all the nations of Europe from bondage" (Namier, 1964:58). Polish poets and writers perpetuated the image of Poland as the Christ of Nations (Walicki, 1970:57ff.; Miłosz, 1972:88-89). Martyrdom became the key to understanding Polish history.[4]

---

[4] Such an interpretation of history, however, is double-edged: it can be used to rationalize two opposite modes of relation to the world—the most desperate gestures, or lethargy and inaction. A maverick of Polish radicalism, Stanisław Brzozowski, analyzed this double consciousness with particular insight: "always, those who

The heroic interpretation of the martyrdom myth inspired Poles with a conviction that the main component of their "national character" was a unique propensity for desperate actions in defense of such ideals as freedom and independence. From the historical point of view, however, this conception, like many similar constructs, does not stand the test of truth. In fact, many other European peoples also fought for their independence and freedom and asserted their national identity in the nineteenth century. But it is not historical truth that concerns us here. Rather, we are looking for socially relevant history, for what is preserved in the collective memory.

Recognizing a nation's myths about its past may be more useful for an understanding of present-day attitudes than knowing the actual facts behind those myths. The people themselves know the myths better than the facts of history, and not just because they are simpler and easier to remember than the complicated sequence of historical events. For collective memory is not only *less*, but also *more*, than history itself; it serves a people's eternal longing to make sense of its existence, giving intelligibility and meaning to the past. No wonder myths are so difficult to eradicate, and lost myths so quickly replaced by new ones. Collective memory cannot remain empty.

---

survived all miseries and learned nothing, insist that in view of this past misery we show indulgence to them, to all, to ourselves" (Brzozowski, 1937:36-37). The sense of martyrdom nurtured by the Poles, he argued, was a substitute for efforts to deal with the questions of social and political reform that were emerging throughout Europe at that time. Evidently, Poles felt that they had already done their share, through suffering. "From Henryk Sienkiewicz to a Marxist social-democrat, everybody in Poland, with very few exceptions, was convinced that he could once and for all be insulated from the problems of life. . . . Until today, all of us, in the depths of our minds, are convinced that in one or another form we have something that allows us to look calmly and perhaps with a slight contempt at the enormous transformations of human thought and morality in the whole of the big, laborious world" (Brzozowski, 1927:98).

Myths about the past are projections into the future. History is read not merely for information, but for help in understanding present-day situations and their implications for the future. It is recalled when a nation faces a problem, when new, unexpected developments in its life force it to abandon daily routines and reevaluate its behavior. We may hypothesize, then, that when the Poles, threatened with the loss of freedom and independence, recalled their mythologized past, they opted for a radical course of action—the desperate defense of the values of independence and freedom—not necessarily because they had always fought for these values more fiercely than others, but because they *thought* they had.

FRAGMENTATION OF THE POLITY

Division of the territory of Poland among three different countries throughout the nineteenth century left a profound imprint on the twentieth-century Polish society and state. The task of consolidating the reborn state after World War I, when its eastern frontiers remained undefined,[5] was further complicated by the necessity of unifying into one organism territories that during the past century had developed different political traditions, were part of different economic entities, followed different laws, and, last but not least, encompassed a variety of ethnic groups. Altogether, this was a formidable challenge during the difficult interwar years, and it was met with some degree of success.

First, there were significant variations in the political cultures to which Poles had been socialized in different regions. Ferdynand Zweig describes them well:

the political and social education of the Polish people differed greatly as between the three parts of Poland. . . .

[5] Poland was involved in a protracted conflict on its eastern frontiers that developed into a full scale war and lasted until March 1921, when Poland and Bolshevik Russia finally concluded the Treaty of Riga (Davies, 1972; Wandycz, 1969).

9

The citizens under Hapsburg rule were inclined to be democratic and bourgeois in outlook, accustomed to hold the rule of law in great respect, and educated in self-government, which was widely practised with the cooperation of large masses of bourgeoisie. Those under the Hohenzollerns were nationalistic in outlook, liked order and discipline, were much under the influence of the land proprietors, and were very successful in business and trade. Those ruled by the Romanovs were old hands in the underground movement, socially minded, and extremely distrustful of administration in general. (Zweig, 1944:17, 18)

Thus, when referring to the nineteenth-century tradition of insurrections, one should note that the two most important —the November 1830 and January 1863 uprisings—took place in the Russian partition. That the insurrections occurred in this area should not be surprising, since the restitution of Polish statehood could not have *excluded* territories occupied by Russia. By reason of historical geography, if only one partition rose up to struggle for liberation and independence, it would necessarily be the Russian. Thus, it should be remembered, the tradition of armed struggle for independence was associated in the minds of the Polish people primarily with anti-Russian insurrections.

Anti-Russian orientation, however, was by no means characteristic of the entire spectrum of patriotic political movements that played dominant roles in Polish politics during the so-called period of Twenty Years (Dwudziestolecie, 1918-1939). The National Democratic Party, which originally started in the Russian-occupied territory and later found its strongest support in the German-ruled region, actually professed a pro-Russian orientation.[6]

[6] The leader of the party, Roman Dmowski, believed that no realistic Polish statesman could be anti-German and anti-Russian at the same time. He chose the anti-German orientation, speculating that the Central Powers would ultimately lose to the Russian-French-

As another consequence of the nineteenth-century partitions, sections of Poland were economically integrated with Russia, Germany, and Austria, but not with each other. Before 1914, 83.3 percent of all imports into the Polish area came from those countries. At the same time, only 8.2 percent of the total imports of the three sections can be attributed to trade with each other. There was no communication between Pomerania and Warsaw; Lwów had no communication with Warsaw; Silesia was not linked with the sea or with eastern Poland; Wilno had no link with the sea, and so on (Zweig, 1944:13-14).

Poland's economic predicament was intensified by the heavy industrial losses suffered during the military campaigns of World War I.[7] Moreover, as a former part of enemy territory, the newly unified Polish state was given no rights to reparations. It even had to share some of the debts of its former imperial rulers. Economic unification of the country was never completed during the Dwudziestolecie. Legal unification also took a long time. Fiscal laws were unified in the late twenties, but the Code of Civil Procedure did not appear until 1933, and the Commercial Code and the Code of Obligations came out a year later.

The ethnic composition of the country promised further difficulties in the unification of the state. Although state boundaries were drawn by the Versailles Treaty following ethnographic lines, the European problem of national minorities was not solved during the interwar period, and Poland was no exception to this malaise. Ethnic minorities constituted more than 30 percent of Poland's population.

English alliance, and that the boundaries of the Russian empire would shift west, incorporating all Poles into one state. Consequently, since Russia could never cope with the "Polish question," the ethnically Polish territories would have to be granted some kind of autonomy. He therefore did not advance any program for Polish independence, as a dynastical union with Russia would eventually allow for the reconstruction of Polish statehood.

[7] These losses were estimated at 12 million gold francs.

In addition, ethnicity and religious affiliation overlapped, producing cumulative cleavages that effectively introduced subcultural differentiation into the polity (see Table I.1). Compact pockets of minorities further contributed toward strengthening separtist identifications.[8] Clearly, Poland was susceptible to all the kinds of complications that often arise in multinational polities or in polities with large subcul-

TABLE I.1

RELIGIOUS AFFILIATION OF ETHNIC GROUPS IN POLAND, 1939
(In Percentages)

Religious Affiliation	Native Language							
	Polish	Ukrain-ian	Ruthe-nian	Belo-russian	Russian	German	Yiddish and Hebrew	Other
Roman Catholic	92		1	8	1	16		13
Greek Orthodox	2	52	95					
Russian Orthodox	2	47	3	91	72			80
Protestant	1					81		1
Other Christian					25	1		1
Jewish							100	
Other								2

Source: *Petit annuaire statistique de la Pologne*, 1939:26.

[8] The Polish majority was unevenly distributed throughout the country. Poles constituted about 90% of the population in the western vojevodships and then declined to about 80% in the central and only about 60% in the southern (with the exception of the Cracow vojevodship). In the eastern vojevodships Poles were a minority, and a not very sizable one in some: for instance, they constituted only about 14.5% of the population of the Polesie vojevodship and slightly over 16% of the Wołyń vojevodship.

12

tural cleavages that have not developed an accommodating approach to politics (Lijphardt, 1968).[9]

The strains of economic recovery, millions of landless peasants awaiting land reform, a mixed national composition, economic and legal fractionalization accompanied by different political traditions—all these pressures put a heavy burden on the system and produced, to no one's surprise, a very fragile and divided polity.

DEMOCRATIC INSTITUTIONS IN A TRADITIONAL SOCIETY

"It is doubtful," wrote Leonard Schapiro (1969:99), "if in the world that emerged after the First World War any legitimacy other than democratic (or pseudo-democratic) legitimacy could have been successfully asserted in the 'climate of opinion' then prevailing." Indeed, the first constitution enacted in twentieth-century Poland was most democratic in spirit, established a weak executive, and gave predominance to the legislative branch of the government. This was due in part to the prevailing "climate of opinion," but it also reflected the fear, particularly by National Democrats, that Józef Piłsudski might take power into his own hands (Polonsky, 1972:46). In reality, this institutional setup, rather than helping to avoid difficulties, created them.

The purpose of those who shaped the world's order after the First World War was to establish in the new nation-states an institutional framework for representative, democratic government. This intention, however, was not necessarily consonant with the character of "civic culture" in

[9] Arend Lijphardt (1968) formulates a set of conditions that have to be fulfilled in a subculturally divided society in order to produce a stable political democracy. Among others, he mentions commitment to the preservation of the system by all participants, permanent minority position of all blocs, overarching cooperation at the elite level, habits of pragmatism and prudence in politics, proportionality, and depolitization of issues.

13

those states. The rapid introduction into Europe of the new formula of legitimacy produced strains between the political institutions it created and the societies those institutions were supposed to serve.[10] Peter Gay characterized this phenomenon in his *Weimar Culture* (1968) by describing supporters of the Weimar Republic as *Vernunft Republikaner*, thus emphasizing the ambiguity of their commitment. In Poland, additional strain was put on new institutions by the presence of the towering figure of Piłsudski, who by his charisma embodied still another, competing principle of legitimacy of authority. Naturally, this produced further disequilibrium in the democratic institutions of the new country.[11]

Before long, it became clear that a stronger executive power was necessary to cope effectively with the long agenda of pressing issues, to order priorities among them, and to allocate scarce resources. In 1926, the year of Piłsudski's coup, even such committed parliamentarians as the socialist Ignacy Daszyński and the peasant leader Wincenty Witos were demanding a stronger executive. The ease with which Piłsudski's coup was legitimized post factum indicates, it seems to me, not only that politicians were dissatisfied with the performance of the system, but also that the legal-rational formula of legitimacy had rather weak support even among the ranks of the parliamentarians.[12] Evi-

[10] "Europe, like Asia, is still a monarchic continent," wrote Guglielmo Ferrero in 1941 (1941:172).

[11] After the May 1926 coup, when the National Assembly elected Piłsudski president of Poland, the two principles of legitimacy—legal-rational and charismatic—could have been brought together and could have reinforced each other, but Piłsudski declined to take the job (Próchnik, 1957:237-240). For a brilliant analysis of the process of institutionalization of legal-rational authority in a new nation by a charismatic leader, see Seymour Martin Lipset's (1967:21-26) comments on George Washington's role in establishing national authority in the United States.

[12] As noted above, Piłsudski was subsequently elected president. He grasped the paradox of this situation when he stated that for the

dently, the Polish public could still identify more easily with a person than with abstract philosophical formulas, and they were better prepared to rely on the wisdom and benevolence of a leader than on the justice and impartiality of the law.

ECONOMIC GRIEVANCES AND SOCIAL UNREST

Statistical yearbooks list Poland in a section entitled "Agricultural Europe," together with Spain, Portugal, the Baltic countries, Hungary, Rumania, and the Balkan states.[13] Poland was indeed one of the rural countries of Europe. More than two-thirds of its GNP came from agricultural production, and about 60 percent of the country's population earned its livelihood from the land.

The agrarian reforms enacted soon after the reestablishment of the state went far toward improving the lot of destitute peasants. But even the redistribution of 200,000 hectares of land a year from the largest estates, as stipulated by the reform, could not solve the problems of the overpopulated rural areas. In 1937 there were more than 5 million "superfluous" people of working age in the countryside, and each year their ranks were increasing.[14]

---

first time in history a revolution had been made without revolutionary consequences (Próchnik, 1957:238). Piłsudski let the public know that his coup was not made "in the name of a social program, but in the name of public morality." "My program," he said, "is the eradication of thievery and the pursuit of the path of honesty" (Polonsky, 1972:172-178). The name *Sanacja*, denoting the government establishment in Poland during the period 1926-1939, is derived from the Latin root *sanus*. It was intended as a declaration of commitment by the new government to bring "health" to a deteriorating political system.

[13] There were 10 cars per 10,000 inhabitants in Poland in 1938, as opposed to 13 in Rumania, 63 in Portugal, 69 in Czechoslovakia, and 100 in Italy. Production of electrical energy in Poland was 10% lower than in Czechoslovakia, which had 3.5 times less population.

[14] According to estimates by J. Poniatowski, a noted agricultural expert and a minister in one of the interwar cabinets, 42% of the

15

The international scale of the great depression condemned each country's economy to dependence on its own internal market. The volume of Polish international trade, for example, was two and a half times smaller in 1938 than in 1928 (*Petit annuaire statistique*, 1939:163). Immediately after the crisis began, "price scissors" for agricultural and industrial products opened, and they did not close until the end of the Second Republic (see Table I.2). This, of course, implied contraction of the internal market and a relative worsening of the material conditions of the peasant population. Not surprisingly, it was accompanied by a political

TABLE I.2

Price Scissors in Poland, 1932-1938
(1928 = 100)

Year	Prices of Industrial Articles Purchased by Farmers	Prices of Agricultural Articles Sold by Farmers
1932	81.0	48.9
1933	72.6	42.6
1934	70.3	37.0
1935	66.3	35.8
1936	64.6	38.7
1937	66.2	49.2
1938	65.0	43.8

Source: Drozdowski, 1963:18, 196.

rural population was "superfluous." He estimated that on January 1, 1937, there were 5,346,000 unemployed or partially unemployed persons of working age in the countryside. Similar results were obtained using methods of calculation by G. Zalecki, M. Szawlewski, B. Stolarski, T. Oberlander, and S. Antoszewski. Of the annual increase of rural population from 1935 to 1939—estimated by the Institute for Social Problems at 230,000—around 30,000 were absorbed by industry, and about 50,000 received land through the agrarian reform. Thus, every year an additional 150,000 people of working age compounded the burden in the already critically overpopulated countryside (Drozdowski, 1963:199-200).

radicalization of the peasants, who, Witos reported, pressed the leadership of the Peasant Party for an all-out confrontation with the government (Witos, 1963:171). Dating from the period of agricultural unrest in 1933, when scores of prominent peasant community leaders were arrested, censorship and social ostracism no longer extended to the families of people in jail as a matter of course. Instead, a spirit of solidarity spread throughout agricultural communities, and help was given to the families of those who were arrested (Witos, 1965:352-354). It was a significant change, indicating a potential for more unrest in the future. In fact, that potential was realized a few years later in a rather unusual form of protest—peasant strikes—which were brutally put down by the government.

Needless to say, the working class also suffered economic hardships in the thirties and signaled its dissatisfaction on many occasions. The number of industrial strikes remained high from 1932 to 1939 (*Petit annuaire statistique*, 1939: 146). In 1936, a confidential paper prepared by the security department of the Ministry of the Interior estimated the number of urban unemployed at one million ("Sprawozdanie referatu," 1961). Although urban unemployment included others besides industrial workers, most of the jobless in the cities belonged to the working class. In 1938, employment in large and medium enterprises (small enterprises were similar to craftsmen's shops, and their employees should be classified on the fringes of the working class) reached 784,900, compared with 809,000 ten years before.

But in truth, not all the blame for the economic difficulties lay in the international scope of the crisis. The government was at first reluctant to abandon its orthodox, deflationary monetary policy. Poland was among the last countries to impose restrictions on monetary exchange and to suspend payment of its debts. Only in 1936 did the government decisively step into the economy by proposing a large investment plan and by undertaking a huge project

17

to construct a new industrial region (Drozdowski, 1963: 68ff.). These were indeed important and successful measures. But they came rather late, and people accustomed to seeing the government intervene in every sphere of life could not easily be persuaded that the international scope of the crisis relieved the government from at least some of the responsibility for domestic economic problems. In any case, by the late thirties Sanacja had succeeded in so alienating the political parties of the pre-May coup era and the social forces that stood behind them, that a full stomach was no longer the key to political stability.

ETHNIC MINORITIES

In addition to conflicts among social classes and the political parties representing them, the government could not solve the problem of coexistence of the Polish majority and the ethnic minorities that constituted one-third of the country's population. Indeed, nationalism, on the rise in the interwar years in Europe and gathering strength in Poland, was adding urgency to the problem of minorities while it prevented a reasonable formula for solution that would take into consideration the interests of all concerned parties.

The first important political crisis in Poland following independence highlighted the issue of the minorities. The country's first president, Gabriel Narutowicz, was assassinated by a fanatic nationalist shortly after being sworn into office. This act was applauded by the National Democratic Party (SN), which previously had denounced his election because they attributed it to the votes of minorities. While the Nationalists subsequently grew in power, the minorities still comprised more than 30 percent of the total Polish population, and the relationship between the ethnic minorities and the Polish majority continued to worsen.

As early as 1923, a center-right coalition government under the premiership of Witos formulated a program, the so-called Lanckorona Pact, around the issue of preserving,

18

defending, and strengthening the rights of the Polish majority in the areas of economy, education, and government.[15] The implementation of the agrarian reform, for example, illustrated the antiminority bias of the government. The full burden of land redistribution fell on the western territories, even though rural overpopulation—that is, the very problem the reform was intended to solve—was lowest in that area. The result was that two-thirds of the land owned by Germans in 1918 had been redistributed by 1939. At the same time, only 11 percent of the large estates in Polish hands came under the reform.[16]

The educational policy of the government was discriminatory as well. Numerous difficulties were created by the authorities for the Ukrainians in the east and the Germans in Upper Silesia who wanted their children educated in schools with Ukrainian or German as the language of instruction. The number of Ukrainian elementary schools in Eastern Galicia declined 80 percent between 1921-1922 and 1934-1935. At the same time, as a result of *numerus clausus*, the number of Jewish students at the universities decreased from 9,576 (24.9 percent of the total student population) in 1923-1924 to 4,791 (9.9 percent) in 1937-1938 (Horak, 1961:129, 144; Bergmann, 1935:120-122, 162).

In the opinion of the government, the only loyal ele-

[15] The major points of the agreement were that in "local and state government the Polish national element must be preserved. The Polish majority must be the basis of any parliamentary majority and the government should be formed only by Poles. . . . Polish youth must have the opportunity to be educated at the universities, in professional and high schools, according to a fair nationality percentage . . . the Polish population must be given an adequate share of government contracts, jobs and concession . . . the government administration in border territories should try to bring change in the direction of strengthening national and governmental spirit [w duchu państwowym i narodowym]" (Witos, 1965:36-37).

[16] The reform fixed the maximum size of permitted landholdings at 180 hectares in the western areas and 300 hectares in the east, where most of the landowners were Poles (Horak, 1961:138-140; Drozdowski, 1963:209).

ment in the country was the Polish majority: of 120,705 employees of the state administration in 1923 (including teachers, judges, and police), 111,332 were of Polish nationality. Most of the remaining 10,000 were teachers in minority schools (Żarnowski, 1964:216, 233, 267-268).

Understandably, the minorities returned these hostile feelings. Sometimes their hostility was translated into acts of terrorism, the best known of which was the murder of the Minister of Interior, Bronisław Pieracki, by Ukrainian nationalists. More important, the hostility and tension led to a weakening of the loyalty of the minorities toward the state: national-socialist propaganda found many listeners among the German minority in Poland, and when the Russians occupied the eastern half of the country in 1939, it was primarily from among the Jews that they managed to enlist collaborators to set up the new administration.

THE POLITICS OF INTIMIDATION

Beginning with Piłsudski's May 1926 coup, a process of intimidation in Polish politics resulted in the gradual alienation of political parties from the system. The parties *were* the system until 1926, but from then until 1930 they were pushed into the opposition, although they could still be considered the loyal opposition. From 1930, however, following the center-left platform and the Brześć trial of principal opposition leaders, the parties were maneuvered into semiloyal opposition, which remained their posture until 1935, when they abstained from participation in the elections. The last four years before the war were a period of radicalization, confrontation, and social unrest. There was an atmosphere of anticipation of some critical development.[17]

[17] The "young" of the SN were calling for a takeover from Sanacja; Sanacja was trying to mobilize support through OZON (Camp of National Unity); the Peasant Party was expecting delegalization and preparing a semiclandestine network of activists who would take over

Sanacja, as the Socialist leader Niedziałkowski perceptively observed, was only a system of government, never a
mass movement. It did not succeed in building a reasonably strong organization that could mobilize public support
behind it, nor did it succeed in formulating its own distinc-
tive ideological appeal. (Nationalists ridiculed Sanacja for
adopting their programs—but always ones already outdat-
ed.) It was lifted to power by an almost legendary figure,
a man whose talents as an administrator, however, could
not match his talents as a conspirator and a military commander. Thus, although Sanacja effectively curbed political
pluralism, it never succeeded in eliminating it completely.
Sanacja did not become a one-party system. If anything, it
was a no-party system, a kind of benevolent authoritarianism.[18]

I think it is particularly appropriate to speak of a politics
of intimidation when describing Sanacja's challenge to political parties. The challenge was very often stated in abu-
sive and threatening rhetoric, but it was never followed by
all-out repression of the opposition. Sanacja's leaders did
not destroy their opponents, but they managed to alienate
and offend them. A few days after the May coup, when the
politicians had already demonstrated their willingness to
accommodate and the center-left had called for Piłsudski's
election to the presidency (only two days before he was,
in fact, elected to that post by the National Assembly),
Piłsudski addressed a gathering of politicians:

When I came back from Magdeburg I had power that
no one else in Poland could match. . . . I did not have to let
you into the National Assembly and could have mocked

in the event the present leadership was arrested (interview with F.
Wilk, London, 1972); and the left, in revolutionary rhetoric, was
warning against the fascist danger and promising that it would take
an uncompromising stand against it.

[18] On the concept of authoritarianism see Juan Linz (1964), particularly his definition of the concept of limited pluralism and of
the concept of mentality as distinct from ideology.

you all. But I wanted to see if one could rule Poland without a whip. . . . I warn you that the Sejm [lower house] and the Senate are the most hated institutions in the country. . . . I declared war on scoundrels, rascals, murderers, and thieves, and I shall win that war. The Sejm and Senate have too many privileges . . . you made a laughingstock of this country. . . . My program is to end rascality and to open the way for honesty. I am waiting, and I want to assure you gentlemen that I will not change. I shall go after thieves. (Próchnik, 1957:244)

During the next four years Piłsudski grew increasingly impatient with politicians who apparently could not or did not want to improve sufficiently on their own. But rather than do away with the parliamentary system altogether, Sanacja decided to adopt a moderate strategy for taking over the power of the legislature. It created an organization called, significantly, Nonpartisan Bloc of Cooperation with the Government (BBWR), in order to gain control of the parliament through the electoral process, change the constitution, and thus legitimately consolidate its power and change the system, all without a revolution.

The final showdown was to take place during the elections of 1930, but the opposition parties were not prepared to yield peacefully. The center-left coalition (Centrolew), including previous supporters of Piłsudski's coup and subsequent sponsors of his nomination for the presidency, attacked Sanacja violently, denouncing the regime as the dictatorship of Piłsudski, declaring that the preservation of democracy is not solely the business of parliament but of the whole society, and threatening that in case of an attempted coup d'état "the society will consider itself free from all obligations" and that "all attempts to use terror will be met with physical force" (Witos, 1965:182-184). The declaration called for the resignation of President Ignacy Mościcki, who, according to its authors, was yielding to the dictator's pressures, and it demanded the end of the dictatorship so that urgent domestic and economic problems could be solved.

The opposition formed an electoral bloc around this platform, designed to be a serious challenge. Sanacja took it as such and responded with determination. Leaders of the opposition were summarily arrested in September 1930.[19] They were kept in preventive detention for several months in a military prison in Brześć, where they were beaten and humiliated.[20] All but one were subsequently convicted of conspiring to abolish the government and were given short prison sentences. Their trial, known as the Brześć trial, was a cause célèbre.

Starting in mid-September, the government also carried out a brutal pacification in the east, which lasted for ten weeks. Finally, many irregularities occurred during the elections. Electoral lists of the opposition were invalidated by district electoral commissions, and the German minority was exposed to extreme pressure to vote for Sanacja's candidates during the elections for the Silesian parliament.[21]

[19] Among those arrested were: Barlicki, Lieberman, Pragier, Ciołkosz, and Mastek of the Polish Socialist Party (PPS); Putek and Bagiński of the Liberation (Peasant) Party; Kiernik and Witos of the Piast; Popiel of the National Workers' Party; Dąbski of the National Democratic Party; and several minority deputies.

[20] One of the arrested, Professor Adam Pragier, a socialist deputy known for his wit, remarked later that they were all lucky to have been put into Brześć near Bug (a nearby river) rather than into Bug near Brześć.

[21] District electoral lists had to be scrutinized by commissions. The chairman, appointed by the administration, was empowered to declare invalid those lists submitted by illegal political parties or those lists of a "doubtful" nature. District commissions made wide use of their powers, accepting only 485 of the 690 lists submitted to them. Of 37 lists submitted by Poalej-Sion, only 27 were accepted; of 58 lists of the center-left, 10 were found unacceptable. The Ukrainian-Belorussian Electoral Bloc submitted 21 lists, but only 14 were accepted. However, all 64 lists of the BBWR passed the scrutiny of the electoral commissions. On the pressures to which the German minority was exposed, see Santoro, 1931:27-31, 36.

Nevertheless, Sanacja fell short of its goal of a two-thirds majority in the legislature. The BBWR secured a clear and comfortable majority of 26 seats (248 of 444) in the Sejm, but this was not enough to accomplish constitutional changes single-handedly.

Following the 1930 elections, however, supporters of democratic institutions were fighting a losing battle in Poland. In 1934, through an illegal maneuver, Sanacja managed to have a new constitution enacted (Polonsky, 1972:386-387). Political parties, protesting the new constitution and the new electoral law, called for a boycott of the 1935 elections. In a spectacular demonstration of the public support for the parties, 54 percent of the electorate stayed away from the polls, despite government pressure.

Why Not Fascism?

After Piłsudski's death in 1935 Sanacja tried to salvage the remnants of his charisma by building a hero-cult around his chosen successor, Edward Rydz-Śmigły, a general soon given a marshal's baton. In spite of all the effort,[22] Rydz-Śmigły lacked popular appeal. Thereafter, in 1937, a period when nationalist emotions were rampant, Sanacja launched a new mass organization—the Camp of National Unity (OZN; also OZON)—designed as an instrument for institutionalizing public support behind the government. OZON was intended to supersede all political parties in order to create "in Poland a new democracy . . . in which the interest of the individual and that of the State will be indissolubly

[22] On July 16, 1936, *Gazeta Polska* published a circular of Prime Minister Felicjan Sławoj-Składkowski stating that "general Rydz-Śmigły, designated by Marshal Piłsudski as the first defender of the Fatherland and as the first collaborator of the President in ruling the country, is to be regarded and respected as the first person in Poland after the President of the Republic. All state functionaries, with the Prime Minister at the head, are obliged to show him respect and obedience" (Polonsky, 1972:412).

united" (Polonsky, 1972:426). But OZON was recognized, and ridiculed from the start, as a mere continuation of the unattractive BBWR (Jędruszczak, 1961).

When there was talk of fascist danger in 1937, it was not because of Sanacja's activities. Speaking at the Twenty-Fourth Congress of the Polish Socialist Party, Niedział-kowski pointed to the National Democratic Party as the chief quasi-fascist political movement in Poland. He argued that the SN was the enemy of socialists because it was a mass movement, while Sanacja was merely a "system of government" (Żarnowski, 1961:103-105). It was the youth of the SN and the National Radical Camp (ONR)—a radical right splinter organization with an openly fascist program—who were screaming nationalistic slogans most loudly and committing acts of physical violence, mainly against Jews. The "young" of the National Democratic Party, who as a group were beginning to take over the leadership of the party, did not hide their admiration for fascism. "Fight with Germany but not with Hitlerism" was one of their slogans, and a resolution of the Supreme Council adopted in February 1936 called for "using the same method which led National Socialism to power in Germany" (Terej, 1971:72-73).

Of course, neither the nationalists of the SN nor the fascists of the ONR were in power in Poland. Although the government shared some of their ideas and, according to some indications, might have been willing to share power,[23]

[23] There is some evidence that Rydz-Śmigły planned a coup d'état in collaboration with the ONR. Witos tells an interesting story explaining why the coup did not take place (1965:457). It is based on testimony of Colonel Grzędziński, a former confidant of Piłsudski. When Rydz-Śmigły was coming back from a state visit to Rumania, he was joined at the border station by Bolesław Piasecki, the leader of the fascist ONR-Falanga. Everything was ready for the coup, and crowds were prepared to meet the two men at all railway stations on the way to Warsaw. Demonstrators were supposed to demand that Rydz take dictatorial power. But at that time Falanga published an article insulting President Mościcki, which was confiscated by the

it was nevertheless wary of them and firmly decided not to let control of the situation slip out of its hands. Some of the activists of the National Radical Camp were sent to the concentration camp at Bereza Kartuska, where in the late thirties the government kept a wide array of its most radical political opponents—Communists, members of terrorist Ukrainian organizations, and fascists. At the same time, it declared illegal some of the bolder initiatives of the National Democratic Party, for example, the creation of the Camp of Great Poland, an organization that, like OZON, was supposed to unite the whole nation into one "camp." Despite the government's antiminority bias, the powerful apparatus of repression available to a twentieth-century state was never at the disposal of radical nationalists in Poland.

Democracy in Poland was de facto replaced in 1926 and de jure limited by the new constitution of 1935, and a similar process was occurring in Europe during the 1920s and 1930s. One can justifiably ask, then, why the breakdown of democracy in Poland did not result in fascism. That is, no doubt, a theme for a major book, but a tentative answer may be sketched briefly. Late nineteenth- and early twentieth-century Polish history could be written largely in terms of the controversy between the Socialist and Nationalist parties. However, a characteristic of Polish history later reduced the usefulness of nationalism as a theme around which the right could be mobilized: namely, the tradition of fighting for independence was associated with the Socialist Party. Conversely, the goal of independence was originally excluded from the program of the National Democratic Party. Owing to this "nationalistic" tradition, socialism could not be blamed later for the alleged lack of patriotism and internationalism that were offensive to the

censorship. Mościcki summoned the minister of interior, General Składkowski, who ordered the arrest of the editorial board of the paper—the very team that was supposed to carry out the coup in Warsaw. Since they were locked up in jail, the action was called off outside of Warsaw as well.

growing nationalistic mood of the population. Nor did Poland suffer from the "defeated nation" syndrome in the aftermath of the First World War,[24] for it had no stratum of frustrated and discontented army officers and NCOs after the war ended. Instead, it was widely felt that the Polish military effort during the war had contributed strongly to the establishment of the status quo that persuaded the Versailles Conference to reestablish independent Poland. Moreover, everyone agreed that the effort of arms had saved the new-born country in the 1920 war with the Bolsheviks. Polish military men were held in high esteem, and it was not an accident that the unquestionably charismatic leader of this period, Józef Piłsudski, was, in his own pronouncements and in the public mind, the most eminent military commander.

Traditional, deep-rooted hostility toward Russia, and the war with the Soviet Union in 1920, which was viewed as a continuation of the war for independence, mitigated possible fears that a new Soviet republic would be established in Poland. Paradoxically, the experience of actual confrontation with the Bolshevik revolution restrained fear of it. In addition, the image of the Socialist movement as one supporting independence rather than international revolution helped to reduce fears about the ultimate loyalty of the left.

The drift toward an authoritarian style of government after the May 1926 coup, and particularly after 1930, made it less likely that fascism could win in Poland. Totalitarianism is more likely to subvert democracy once democracy begins to break down than it is to emerge in the context of an authoritarian society. It may simply be that an authori-

[24] Strangely, a country did not have to be on the losing side to suffer from that syndrome. In Italy, for instance, the anti-interventionist position of the left meant that many returning soldiers were greeted with little sympathy, resulting in frustration among the combatants. Also, there was dissatisfaction with postwar territorial arrangements. D'Annunzio's escapade at Fiume and the government's hesitation in bringing about its end were indicative of that dissatisfaction.

27

tarian regime does not allow enough freedom for a fascist movement to build up, consolidate, and, finally, to take over successfully.

Both the Italian and German cases provide sufficient data to support the contention that a fascist movement is built and picks up momentum through a mixture of legal and extralegal tactics. There must be the opportunity for an opposition party to be elected to the parliament and for the *squadristi*, SA-men, or their equivalent to come out into the streets. But authoritarianism limits participation in government to the point of excluding de facto opposition from effective access to official institutions. Furthermore, it does not hesitate, to the degree democracy often does, to use coercion against anyone who attempts to exert pressure on the government through the use or threat of violence. The fate of political leaders who participated in the Centrolew agreement in 1930 and the repression of peasant strikes in the late thirties may serve as examples here. In this perspective, Piłsudski's coup can be seen as a move that prevented the emergence of fascism in Poland. Last but not least, Poland was a Catholic country, and as we know from the German and Italian experiences, Catholicism was a barrier to the emergence of fascism. None of these factors would suffice alone as a deterrent to fascism. Taken together, however, they present a strong set of circumstances that prevented the emergence of fascism in interwar Poland.

I have deliberately stressed the divisive elements of the polity and the sources of conflict in interwar Poland because, despite these conflicts, the nation managed to resist the enormous pressures brought to bear on it by its occupiers. It did not disintegrate. The resistance of Polish society to the German occupiers appears as an extremely puzzling phenomenon precisely in the context of its fragmentation before the war.

CHAPTER II

New Order and Imperial Ideology

NAZI domination of Europe is most often referred to in the literature of the period as the "New Order." That is was "new" is beyond dispute, but one should note that there was hardly any order in it. Already in their own country the leaders of Nazi Germany deliberately pursued a policy of constant revolutionary change. Their hostility to previously existing forms of societal organization found expression in their attempt to destroy the plurality of social life. Political parties, unions, and other socioeconomic organizations disappeared from the surface of life in the course of the 1934 *Gleichschaltung* with little resistance. Presumably, these organizations counted on a short life for the Nazi regime, and above all, they wanted to preserve their own structure and assure their own continued existence. This urge to "survival" led them to pledge loyalty and cooperation to the hostile regime until they were too weak to resist the final stroke. Subsequently, they were outlawed or incorporated into some new organization that the Nazis created to replace them.

Although the Nazi revolution took place in a modern society equipped with institutions designed to handle social change, it aimed at the destruction of the existing institutional framework. It could not, then, be accommodated by institutional provisions for social change in the Weimar Republic. We know that the Nazis made use of the institutions of constitutional democracy in order to gain access to power, but they did so, as they openly admitted, only to destroy the system later.

The Nazi revolution explicitly rejected the legal-rational basis for legitimization of authority. What it subscribed to —the centralization of political power and the establishment

29

of personal loyalty as the basis for authority—are anachronistic features, characteristic of traditional societies that had never based their authority on legal-rational principles. A traditional society maintains the stability of its institutions only so long as social change is absent. The stability of institutions born under charismatic authority, as we know from Weber, can be established through the process of routinization only after the transfer of power from the founding leader to his successors has taken place in an orderly manner. German society under Hitler did not fulfill those requirements; not surprisingly, it lacked institutional stability.

Some students of National Socialism have stressed the feudal components of the system (Koehl, 1960; Parsons, 1942; Orlow, 1968). Its most important features—authority based on personal loyalty, and the area of competence defined by personal "gifts" rather than by the office itself— were the very expressions of the institutional chaos of Nazi Germany. Hitler's interest in increasing his personal power —imitated by all subleaders in their domains—led to a blurring of the lines that divided the government from the party. The Nazis' disdain for impersonal traits and for the anonymity of a legal-rational bureaucracy led to the rediscovery of *loyalty* from subordinates and honest acceptance of *responsibility* by superordinates as the only legitimate modes of exercising political power (Koehl, 1960:922). The *Führerprinzip* was born out of these circumstances.

Since in key appointments bureaucratic power in Nazi Germany was assigned by the Führer not to an office but to a man, the division of the spheres of responsibility among different agencies could not be clearly maintained. There is abundant evidence of constant friction between offices and agencies, with each trying to expand the areas of its competence. Had they not tried, they would have shrunk into oblivion, for they never had any firm guarantees of their existence, and their more energetic colleagues would have eliminated them. Just as the regime could not stop its expansions, which ultimately led to war, so internal wars also were fought continuously. The result of those conflicts were *Personalunionen* and arbitration by third parties, which summarily defined new spheres of competence. "One of the most amazing similarities to the feudal system in Nazi administration is the nominal subordinate who acquired power to give his superior orders through appointment by a still higher superior as his 'personal agent'" (Koehl, 1960:926). In such a situation, because of the criss-crossing web of personal loyalties, it very often became difficult to determine who ought to obey whom and why. The system's response to this institutional vagueness conformed to its very spirit: in order to fulfill high priority goals, additional special agencies typically were created with powers that enabled them to cut through red tape (Milward, 1965:9ff.). The perpetrators of the "new order" themselves recognized that the efficiency and centralization of the new setup was a myth (Speer, 1970). A definition of National Socialism popular in Prague in 1939 stated that it was a mixture of "Austrian efficiency and Prussian charm" (Kennan, 1968: 11).

Paradoxically, however, the institutional and bureaucratic chaos that hampered the effective accomplishment of any matter through the bureaucratic routine also provided for unusual speed and efficiency in the realization of matters that were given priority by the Führer. The creation of new, powerful agencies by the Führer's commands not only added to the already existing bureaucratic jungle but also permitted bypassing of this "jungle." Thus, Milward notes, the blitz military campaigns suited the Nazi German system very well. The thrust of Milward's analysis suggests the possibility of sociological generalization: *the Nazi power system and its institutional setup permitted very effective mobilization for short-range goals on short notice.* That is, the anomie (Parsons, 1942) that characterized the system and meant that no stable institutional patterns existed nevertheless permitted fast mobilization of whatever re-

31

sources were available, on condition that the initiative was the Führer's. The low level of institutionalization gave the system a certain elasticity that allowed it to shift priorities and gear its efforts toward their achievement much faster than would have been possible under a stable institutional pattern. On the other hand, any sustained effort or long-range planning was impossible, or at least extremely difficult, within this framework.[1]

Nor can we find much "order" in Hitler's Germany in the sense of regularized, patterned forms for the exercise of authority in a social system. Citizen obedience was, in fact, the sole indicator of "order" in Nazi Germany, but we know that the arbitrary exercise of power can elicit the same response from people through fear. A more appropriate focus for the study of the German polity at that time would be an analysis of the methods of terror used rather than an analysis of institutional patterns. This focus applies particularly when we begin to study German policies of occupation in Europe during World War II.

I think it is neither possible nor fruitful to devise a systematic conceptual framework and typology for the study of regimes of occupation in Europe. They escape typology because the Germans lacked a systematic plan for governing the countries they conquered. Individual variations among occupation regimes far exceeded their similarities, and the personality differences among the local German officials who exercised power in the name of the victors were more important than the affinities of the institutional setups. Did the Nazi elite ever work out a coherent project for the German empire? If so, did the reality of German rule in Europe reflect that? These questions, generally, can be answered in the negative, in part because of the institutional characteristics of Nazi society already mentioned: feudallike relationships and the network of vested interests that nat-

[1] In any case, there was no long-range planning: "The lack of documentary evidence on economic and military planning before 1942 indicates how little of such planning there was" (Milward, 1965:25).

urally sprang from them could not find a better environment in which to proliferate than in the occupied countries;
and agencies and individuals that had disputed one another's
authority in Germany proper did so even more vigorously
when operating in new territories. However, one must also
look elsewhere to find the reasons for the Nazis' inability
to plan and to realize a project for the creation of an empire.
It seems to me that certain elements of their doctrine could
not be easily matched with the character of the movement
when its area of operation was extended beyond the borders
of Germany.

IDEOLOGICAL PREMISES OF IMPERIAL EXPANSION

Florian Znaniecki has argued that all modern "national
culture societies," as he calls them, have a tendency to
expand. Their very formation, he says, is a dynamic, expan-
sive process, and he singles out creative and popular expansions as particularly important.[2] These two processes
represent the intensive and extensive aspects of the growth
of nationalism in whatever organizational form it might
appear. As it happens, however, neither of the two necessarily takes place in a friendly environment. Popular and/or
creative expansion may encounter the hostility of various
socioeconomic, religious, and political groups and, ultimately, of other "national culture societies" as well. From
that moment, further expansion of the given nationality may
proceed only at the cost of interfering with another society's
expansion. Znaniecki calls processes originating in this stage
"aggressive expansion," and he groups them into four dis-

[2] Creative expansion, says Znaniecki, "consists in the conscious
striving of group members to enrich national culture by creative
activities" and popular expansion in efforts to "raise membership in a
national culture society from a relatively small nucleus of intellectuals
to hundreds of thousands or millions of people who, according to the
ethnic standards of historians and ethnologists, should belong to the
same cultural society" (Znaniecki, 1952:114).

tinct categories: geographic, economic, assimilative, and ideological expansion (Znaniecki, 1952:115). German occupation regimes during the Second World War were a mixture of all four processes, shaped (though never becoming a very specific policy) by such ideological elements as the *Völkisch* concept of the state, Social Darwinism, and the sense of the special destiny and the special mission of the German nation.

The *Völkisch* theme, the idea of reforging an allegedly lost unity of the people, is only one of the many variations of the arguments constructed in reaction to rationalism and the ideals of the French Revolution (Mellon, 1958; Szacki, 1965; Baldensperger, 1968). Jerzy Szacki's brilliant analysis in *Counter-Revolutionary Paradoxes* (1965) shows that after the revolution, conservatives could not simultaneously satisfy two of their most important claims: they could not demand that the *ancien régime* be restored and, at the same time, oppose the revolution as a form of social change on the grounds that it was a noncontinuous process involving a radical break with existing conditions and the past. Thus, they could either maintain opposition to revolution—conceived as an instance of discontinuous social change—and accept the new society, or they could continue to believe in the *ancien régime* and become, in the context of the new society, advocates of a *counterrevolution*. Neither solution suited them well. That is why, de Maistre proposed, the dilemma for opponents of the French Revolution was to invent a *contrary of a revolution* rather than to opt for a counterrevolution. But the contrary of a revolution was never invented. Instead, nationalism in the nineteenth century acquired the radical orientation, and, as Bracher succinctly put it, "International revolutionary socialism found itself face to face with the national-revolutionary idea of an all inclusive people's community-*Volksgemeinschaft*" (Bracher, 1970:13). It is of primary importance that this development coincided with the emergence of Social Darwinism.

34

Indeed, Social Darwinism suited the enemies of the French Revolution because it expressly denied egalitarian beliefs in an open, mobile society and rejected the notion of the educability of men.[3] As a logical culmination of Social Darwinism came a reflection upon the relative qualities of various races. Chamberlain's *Grundlagen des 19. Jahrhunderts*, on which Rosenberg later largely based his *Mythos des 20. Jahrhunderts*, expanded this theme. The notion of "racial purity" belongs to ideological constructs based on Social Darwinism. The idea that nations are not only distinct units, but that they also can be ranked as "better" or "worse," carries an implicity negative evaluation of racial mixing, at least from the viewpoint of the superior race. By the time Hitler began to propagate his ideas, the proper climate for their reception had already been created.

IMPERIAL STRATEGY

The specific character of imperial doctrine and strategy is not decided solely upon the basis of broad ideological principles. It is also a product of ideas held about the character of the movement and the principles of the polity-to-be. Broad ideological principles are of predominant importance in the early stages of elaboration of the doctrine, when justification of conquest must be articulated. Once expansion begins, notions entertained about the rules of the polity and the character of the movement acquire decisive importance, because the patterns of coexistence between conqueror and conquered are worked out in accordance with these notions. A comprehensive imperialistic doctrine must state both the

[3] The antiliberal, antimodern, anticapitalist thrust of Social Darwinism can be observed best in the variations that it offered on the theme of virility and strength: democracy favors the mass over the heroic, noble, and virtuous few; Christian morality preaches compassion, offering protection to the weak at the expense of the strong; capitalist economy favors "unproductive" businessmen over "honest workingmen"; the migration of the rural population into cities and foreign lands depletes the reservoir of the strong and the healthy, etc.

justification for conquest and the rules of coexistence. In the Nazi case, the second part of the doctrine could not be formulated satisfactorily because the character of the one-party system introduced by Hitler was revolutionary rather than exclusionary.[4] What I am referring to is a specific application of a general distinction between two opposing patterns of sociation: "on the one hand, there is the principle of including everybody who is not explicitly excluded; and on the other, there is the principle of excluding everybody who is not explicitly included" (Simmel, 1964:369).

Hence, the effort to build an empire can follow either one of these two paths, or it may at least come closer to one than to the other. Ancient Roman imperial tradition from the time of the Republic, for example, was closer to the exclusionary pattern of empire construction[5] than was the proselytizing zeal expressed in religious conquests of Christian European monarchs centuries later.[6] Outside of Europe,

---

[4] I am referring here to the conceptual distinction between exclusionary and revolutionary one-party regimes introduced by Huntington (1970). Revolutionary systems, according to Huntington's definition, aim at the assimilation or liquidation of all social forces and groups that at one time or another are outside of the movement. A revolutionary one-party system does not intend to restrict politics to any particular group of people. It desires that all citizens participate, but only as supporters. Exclusionary systems, on the other hand, are characterized by the adoption of a strategy that aims at securing political power. They do not attempt the conversion or annihilation of those who do not support them; they simply want nonsupporters to avoid politics. Opponents are permitted to cultivate their own ways and opinions in all others spheres of life on the condition that they accept the restrictions on access to politics.

[5] "C'est la folie des conquérants de vouloir donner à tous les peuples leurs lois et leurs coutumes: cela n'est bon à rien, car, dans toutes sortes de gouvernement on est capable d'obéir. Mais Rome, n'imposant aucunes lois générales, les peuples n'avaient point entre eux des liaisons dangereuses; ils ne faisaient un corps que par une obéissance commune" (Montesquieu, 1964:449).

[6] The emperor, in the Hohenstaufen tradition, was the *dominus mundi*, and his aspirations were by no means limited to the frontiers

Latin colonial empires were typically closer to the revolutionary pattern than were those of the British or Dutch.[7] Other European nationalities lived a different life under the Hapsburgs (exclusionary pattern and also associating pattern with respect to the Hungarian part) than did their eastern neighbors under the Romanovs (Russification resembled a revolutionary pattern, although an exception can be noted in the formerly Finnish territories, which enjoyed a considerable degree of self-government).

Empire building is seldom pursued with a uniform policy. Different territories are usually appraised by the conqueror in terms of the potential threat each constitutes and the capability of each for self-government. Local customs and institutions, and the intensity with which the local population adheres to them, will also demand different policies for different areas. The two strategies of empire construction lie at opposite ends of a continuum of imperialistic policies

---

of the empire. His concept of universal monarchy was captured in a phrase from a decree of Barbarossa—"One God, One Pope, One Emperor"—or, for example, in the preamble to the Great Charter of the Teutonic Order: "God had established our Empire above all the kings of the earth and extended Our dominion over diverse climes in order that We may set Ourselves to magnify his name down the centuries and spread the faith among the Gentiles" (Bloch, 1969:35).

[7] "The exploitation by the Latin colonial powers of the natives was no less brutal than that practiced by the colonizers from northwestern Europe, but it was justified by different premises. The Spaniards, for example, justified their exploitation of native peoples on the basis that these people were pagans and therefore outside the pale of Christian ethics and consideration. It might be argued that since the result was the same, whether exploitation was justified on a racial or religious basis had no significance for the modern world. The difference of religion could be overcome by conversion, and in Spanish, Portuguese, and French colonies, amalgamation was usually strongly discouraged. . . . This is one of the most important facts which explains why the race problem is being solved through amalgamation in such countries as Brazil, while it is perhaps more acute than ever in such countries as South Africa" (Jonassen, 1951:159).

that, on one extreme, are guided by limited and pragmatic goals, and, on the other, by diffuse and ideological objectives.

The Nazi movement in itself was revolutionary: that is, it did not tolerate even neutrals within the polity. But once Nazism spilled over the boundaries of the ethnically German territories, this aspect of the movement could not be made consistent with its fundamental doctrinal principle that race is the element upon which inclusion in, or exclusion from, the system is decided. Interestingly enough, Hitler himself, in conversations with Chamberlain, formulated the imperialistic dilemma of National Socialism. Fears in the West that his "appetite is growing with eating" and that after the attainment of one objective he would make fresh demands resulted, he said, from "a complete misunderstanding of the National Socialist doctrine. . . . The racial basis of the National Socialist Party and with it of the German people . . . excluded any form of imperialism" (Ulam, 1973:497). To say this to Chamberlain was a deceit on Hitler's part, as we know. But, characteristically, he presented an argument that he thought was *rational*, and therefore, convincing.

Logically, only two procedures could accommodate both revolutionary strategy and the adoption of race as the qualifying characteristic for membership in the polity: genocide, or a redefinition of the concept of race. The choice of strategy depended largely on one's understanding of the concept of "Germanic." Some Nazis became advocates of the policy of assimilation and "Germanization" of racially "worthy" elements among conquered peoples. Rosenberg's statements and, curiously enough, Himmler's recruitment policy in the later period of the war, when he became an advocate of a united European effort against Bolshevism, showed that, with the exception of Jews, no population was a priori excluded from reappraisal by Nazi ideologists. Unfortunately for the peoples of Europe, Hitler's understanding of "Germanic" was very narrow, and he was skeptical even about Himmler's "fishing expeditions." As for Rosenberg, neither he nor his ideas were taken seriously by the party leadership after 1932 (Kluke, 1955).

Both genocide and manipulation of the definition of race (Germanization) were practiced by the Nazis. At the outset of the war, it seems, the Nazis were not cold-blooded enough to contemplate and openly elaborate a theory of empire based on genocide. They tried isolation and resettlement of the racially "inferior." It was not until the early forties that they began systematically to apply the theory of the "final solution," although even then they attempted to conceal it from the public. Originally, extermination related to Jews only, but undoubtedly, other "inferior races" would have been treated similarly if time had allowed.

As the number of people to be annihilated increased, creating almost insoluble practical problems, the Nazis proceeded to formulate racial theories that permitted them to resolve practical and theoretical problems simultaneously by reducing the ranks of potential victims while at the same time preserving the revolutionary strategy and racial purity of the empire-to-be:

> Racially valuable are those inhabitants of the Protectorate in whom or in whose ancestry Slavic racial characteristics do not predominate. . . . Slavic racial characteristics, apart from Mongol types, are for instance a markedly disorderly and careless family life, demonstrating a complete lack of feeling for order, for personal and domestic cleanliness, and of any ambition to advance oneself. (Mastny, 1971:130)

These guidelines for determining race were elaborated in the office of the Protector of Bohemia and Moravia, but they were not different in spirit from the criteria used for compiling German National Lists (DVL) in other territories occupied by the Nazis. Clearly, no racial theory of empire was available that would dictate unequivocal occupation policy to the German administrators of conquered terri-

39

tories. A policy would eventually have emerged in the form of a mixture of genocide and flexible definition of race. However, during the five and a half years of the war, the Nazis were constantly changing their plans for the different parts of conquered Europe.

They were similarly vague about geopolitical projections where they foresaw intercontinental strife,[8] and they were indecisive in their efforts to mobilize Europe against Bolshevism. Their projections did not result in a coherent doctrine, and their efforts were merely a practical, immediate reaction to an approaching military crisis. The only concrete outcome of these considerations was the Waffen SS, which (an exception in the German military establishment) took in volunteers of various nationalities, who were recruited precisely for the purpose of the all-European defense effort against Bolshevism. It is an interesting and curious fact that this same elite organization, which originally required of its prospective members proof of several generations of pure Germanic breeding, later became the sponsor of an international, European solidarity.[9]

[8] "Europe, organized according to the policy laid down by National Socialism long before the war, has openly aggressive aims towards the U.S. The conception of 'rival continents,' the claim of the historical, cultural and political predominance of Europe over any other part of the globe is primarily directed against the U.S. of America" (Worsley, 1942:26; see also Weinberg, 1964). Placing the U.S. at the top of the "enemies list" was related to Nazi *Völkisch* ideology. In the estimates of Nazi statisticians, about 27.5% of the entire population of the U.S. was *Volksdeutsche* (H. Kloss, ed., *Statistischer Handbuch der Volksdeutschen Ubersee*, quoted in Znaniecki, 1952:122). Znaniecki also reports German estimates from around 1900, indicating that 25,477,-583 persons living in the U.S. were of German origin. Clearly, America should be Germanized, concluded Colin Ross (*Unser America*) in 1936 (Znaniecki, 1952:122).

[9] Looking closely at these developments, perhaps we should reexamine commonly held views on the nature of the two twentieth-century totalitarian movements. Fascism was widely believed to be a violently nationalistic movement, while Communism was successful in putting forward its international orientation; yet in time the systems

The Nazi leadership was unable to commit itself to any kind of settlement in Europe. They responded negatively to Quisling's proposals and, more importantly, to Vichy's overtures indicating willingness to join Germany militarily in her war effort in exchange for a peace agreement ending the nominal state of war between the two countries (Paxton, 1972:309-326, 109-131). But the shape of the European "New Order" was not settled in their minds, and, willingly or not, they had to keep a completely free hand to decide what would emerge. As a knowledgeable student of the subject has put it, "between Minsk and Calais lay an immense administrative and political *tabula rasa*" (Orlow, 1973:286). The ideology of aggressive nationalism did not dictate any specific colonial policy when expansion beyond ethnically German territories began.

---

seemed to develop in opposite directions. Nazi overtures at the end of the war and the *Ordine Nuovo, Neue Ordnung, l'Ordre Nouveau* brand of contemporary neofascist movements clearly indicated a potential for the international integration of the movement, while at the same time the crisis of the Communist International and the shaping of "national roads" to socialism, with hidden or half-open use of nationalistic appeals, were characteristic of the development of the Communist movement. For an excellent insight into this subject, see Eli Halevy's (1938) comments made in 1936.

CHAPTER III

The Pattern of Unlimited Exploitation

RELIABILITY OF SOURCES

Before proceeding with the description and analysis of conditions of life in the Generalgouvernement (GG), we must become aware of the extreme difficulties connected with obtaining reliable data on almost any subject during this period. These difficulties arise not because documents and statistics were irretrievably lost or destroyed during wartime, nor because people had more serious preoccupations than putting figures and recollections on paper. A large quantity of data is available, but most of it is false and unreliable.

Indeed, much information concerning the buildup of the underground was never recorded at the time. Some data have occasionally surfaced in memoirs written after the war. Following the Communist takeover of Poland in the aftermath of the Second World War, no effort was made to gather information about the anti-German conspiracy. Because the role of the Communists in the underground struggle was much less prominent than that of the so-called "London Underground," the Communists have tried to falsify history and to destroy or suppress the witnesses and records of contemporary events.

Wartime records must be also scrutinized for intentional distortions. Colonel Iranek Osmecki, the last Chief of Intelligence of the Home Army, told me (interview, London, 1972) that those in the headquarters of the Home Army were aware that they could not rely on data reported by field commanders concerning such important matters as the numbers of enlisted soldiers or armaments in stock. Unit commanders often cheated in those two areas because there was an acute shortage of weapons, and everyone exaggerated shortages in the hope of getting more. There was a shortage of everything during the war, and we may rightly suspect that any reports sent up within any organization were purposely colored in order to get more of whatever resource the organization controlled.

There is a methodological problem in general as to the reliability of data reported by subordinates to superiors, and accounts are particularly susceptible to "error" in times of shortages. Superiors to whom reports are forwarded usually have control over the allocation of some resources that are necessary, or at least useful, for the functioning of the lower echelons of the organization. It is a very plausible assumption that those reports will be written in such a way as to make sure that needed resources will be made available by superiors. Or, in another version of the same problem, the lower echelons may be interested in concealing that they do have certain resources, so that their superiors will not ask for them or will not set performance standards at a higher level. Particularistic goals will often take precedence over the overall goal of an organization, and unless there is a truly independent agency collecting data, we shall always have to deal with biased information.

How reliable any information is must be decided by the social scientist in each separate case, because it is an empirical question. There is perhaps one general rule of thumb: the less free expression and pursuit of individual interests allowed within the institutional framework to independent groups, the more inaccurate will be the data, since these groups will try to pursue their interests even by illegitimate means and, to cover and make possible their illegal activity, will falsify data.

Data from German sources probably was slanted as well. First, we certainly cannot trust the official publications designed for the Polish public; they were intended to sell a certain picture of life in the GG as painted by officials in the propaganda office. Nor is it likely that secret German reports, circulated internally, will provide full and reliable information about the conditions of life in the GG. As we shall learn later, the German administration was utterly corrupt on all levels. Without an adequate system of control—and there was none in the Generalgouvernement—most German officials were interested in making their reports in a manner that would cover their misconduct. It was also in the interest of the GG's administration as a whole to keep Reich officials unaware of the full extent of available resources in the GG, in order to be spared additional requests for deliveries. There were, finally, powerful animosities within the German apparatus in the GG and therefore only a slight sense of common purpose. Local bosses were primarily interested in protecting their own domains and their particular interests. Therefore, the material in their official documents is most likely distorted or falsified and hence unreliable.

It would be too difficult to check each figure quoted in this study and impossible to discard all those that we find questionable. No history of this period would ever be written if one insisted on using only materials of irreproachable veracity. What I am attempting to do is to use a wide variety of sources—underground reports, memoirs, letters, newspapers, and official documents—in the hope that the result approximates reality. Fortunately, different people and organizations had contradictory interests and therefore stressed different aspects of the case. Naturally, we shall never know how well one bias compensates for another.

The task that lies ahead of us is to reconstruct the process by which a society was destroyed and to offer an analysis of the forms of collective life that appeared in its stead. Substitute forms of collective life are of interest to us, since the destruction of Polish society did not mean the literal extermination of every one of its members (which would have meant ipso facto the elimination of all forms of collective life). Although extermination was an important part of the German policy of occupation (some selected groups —the Jews and, to a lesser degree, the Polish intelligentsia —were particularly affected), millions of men, women, and children survived during the five years they were deprived of their state, schools, political organizations, voluntary associations, and viable economic system. They suffered under the constant threat of death on food rations that at best would have permitted them to die of starvation within a few months. We want to find out how they managed to live through this.

Our analysis will focus on the Generalgouvernement. By the end of October 1939, Poland already had been divided: the USSR took 50 percent, Germany 48.4 percent, and Lithuania 1.6 percent.[1] The Generalgouvernement was located in the center of Poland, covering roughly one-third of the country's former territory and containing 45 percent of its former population. In 1941, after the outbreak of Russo-German hostilities, the district of Galicia was added to it. The Germans considered the GG as *the* occupied territory of Poland—*Generalgouvernement für die besetzen Polnischen Gebiete* was its original name—and they transferred to the GG large numbers of Poles and Jews from the Polish territories incorporated into the Reich. Various forms of Polish collective life, be it the underground, the black market, or local government, flourished in the GG to a greater extent than in the western or eastern part of occupied Poland, and the information we have about it is more complete.

BEGINNINGS OF THE ADMINISTRATION

The most important decree regulating the legal status of Poland after Germany's victory was issued by Hitler on October 12, 1939. The occupied territory of Poland was defined as a residual category—territories occupied by the

---

[1] In August 1940 Lithuania was incorporated into the USSR.

German army and *not* incorporated into the Reich. Dr. Hans Frank, former president of the German Academy of Law, was nominated to the post of governor general. In this capacity he was subordinate only to Hitler.

The formula of Führerprinzip was adopted for the organization of authority in this territory: all branches of the administration were to be directed by the governor general rather than by parallel Reich ministries from Berlin. The Polish government administration and practically all voluntary associations were dissolved. Polish law was to remain in force except when it conflicted with the taking over of the administration by the German Reich. The occupied territory itself had to cover the cost of its own occupation. The Generalgouvernement was separated from the Reich by customs laws, financial barriers, and passport control. Although the GG did not have its own armed forces or foreign ministry, it did have a quasiambassador in Berlin. Frank liked to think of himself as a head of state.

On October 20, six days before the official inauguration of the GG took place, a conference was held between Hitler and the high command of the Wehrmacht (IMT, v.26:378-383). The basic outlines of German policy toward Poland were formulated during that meeting:

1. The Germans did not intend to incorporate the Generalgouvernement into the Reich. The GG was to be given some sort of "independent" status. The justification for this decision was the anticipation by German leaders that "a period of tough struggle between nationalities was to come and that it could not be fought successfully had the German authorities been bound by any legal norms." If the GG were completely independent of the Berlin administration, the local authorities would be free to do what they must, even if their actions conflicted with some of the rules that the Reich administration legally had to follow.

2. Essentially, only two goals were to be accomplished:

first, the Polish intelligentsia was to be prevented from taking a leadership role in the future;[2] second, communication lines were to be kept in good condition so that the occupied territory could later be used for mobilization of the armed forces in anticipation of future conquests. In addition, the administration of the GG was to help the Reich authorities in their task of "cleansing" the Reich of Jews and Poles.

Instructions on how to accomplish these goals were primarily negative in nature: prevent the rebirth of any forms of national life; avoid rebuilding the economy or finances; encourage *Polnische Wirtschaft*[3] as much as possible; and make sure that the standard of living remained low. The only role assigned to the Poles was to provide the Reich with manpower.

What these enigmatic instructions really meant is revealed more explicitly in Goering's directive for economic exploitation of the occupied territories, issued on October 13, 1939, in his capacity as deputy for the Four Year Plan:

> there must be removed from the territories of the Government General all raw materials, scrap materials, machines, etc., that are of use to the German war economy. Enterprises that are not absolutely necessary for the meager maintenance of the naked existence of the population must be transferred to Germany, unless such transfer would require an unreasonably long period of time and would make it more practical to exploit those enter-

[2] By this euphemism was designed the policy of extermination of the Polish intelligentsia in the framework of the so-called AB-Aktion. The social category of "intelligentsia" was rather broadly defined as Polish "teachers, clergy, medical doctors, dentists, veterinarians, officers, ranking bureaucrats, big merchants, big landowners, writers, journalists, as well as persons who had university or high school diplomas" (Frank, 1970 v.1:133).

[3] A derogatory expression in German, denoting lack of organization, clumsiness, and stupidity in the conduct of one's economic affairs.

prises by giving them German orders to be executed at their present location. (United States, 1946 v.7:467; original translation)

On October 26 Frank took over from the military administration and began his tenure with a proclamation announcing the creation of this new "legal person," the Generalgouvernement. The mechanics of the operation of the new administration were explained, but not its goals. Prospects of a happy future for the Polish population under the new rule were sketched, with a promise to let Poles cultivate their "Polishness" in a new atmosphere, under the protection of the Great German Reich.[4]

But what lay behind the facade of official declarations? What was in fact the program of occupation that Germany devised for Poland? Despite occasional changes of course that took place at various times during the occupation (usually following changing German military fortune), the basic goals of occupation, as I see them, changed little if at all. There were shifts in priorities, but the range of alternatives to choose from remained, I think, limited to four. All were derivations from the principal concern of the Nazis: to establish a racially pure empire.

In the first place, then, the territories located to the east of the German border were to serve as a dumping ground for all "undesirable elements" from the Reich, and subsequently also from those parts of newly conquered territories that were incorporated into the Reich. A difficulty of this program lay in the absence of a decision about where the German expansion should stop. Since no definite limit to the expansion could be deduced from the doctrine, what

---

[4] Ludwik Landau reports in his *Chronicle* that as soon as the proclamation containing Frank's speech was posted all over Warsaw, slips of paper were glued to it reading: "As Commander Piłsudski would say: 'Kiss my ass' " (Landau, 1962 v.1:54). They expressed very well both the reaction to Frank's speech and the style of Piłsudski's rhetoric.

seemed a suitable dumping ground at one time later had to be cleaned of the same, and more, "undesirable elements" as expansion continued.

These difficulties, among others, led the Germans to adopt another policy: the extermination of non-Germans. Obviously, extermination was the only foolproof method of accomplishing the goal of a racially pure state. There is little doubt that the Poles would have become victims of genocide, in turn, if time had allowed.

But even this remarkably simple policy was not free from ambiguities, because of technological problems and because the Nazis were also committed to the principle of *Wieder-eindeutschung*, that is, to salvaging and returning to "Germandom" all precious drops of the German blood that could be found. The latter called for careful screening before the "final solution" was applied. Unavoidable complications arose because eligibility for obtaining Germanic status through inscription onto a German National List (DVL) was determined arbitrarily. Different ethnic groups were assigned quotas more in accordance with Hitler's personal whims than with any systematic criteria. Thus, for example, only 3 percent of the population of the Generalgouvernement was considered fit for Germanization (Madajczyk, 1961:87), while at the same time 50 percent of the Czechs were classified in that category (United States, 1946 v.3: 618-619). In specific cases, it was the top local official who decided who could join the DVL and who could not.[5]

[5] In March 1941 the *Reichsgesetzblatt* published a decree on that matter, stating that revocable German citizenship was to be given to those "citizens of foreign race who are particularly designated as a result of directives by the Reichsführer SS, Reich's Commissar for the consolidation of German race and culture" (United States, 1946, v.5:589). That these decisions depended on official whims is well documented by the situation in the incorporated Polish territories. Several Polish families were split and living in different *Gaue*. And it was not unusual that children of the same parents were considered Poles when living in Warthegau but were put on German national

Finally, the last goal that the German administration wanted to accomplish in occupied Poland—the utilization of non-Germans as a slave labor force—was a residual goal, adopted as a temporary measure, in view of unavoidable delay before reaching—through resettlement, extermination, or Germanization—the final desired state of the intended polity: the racially pure Great German Reich. In its extreme form, employed in the concentration camps, this goal was known as the policy of "extermination through labor."

Before we proceed with an examination of German policy during the occupation in the GG, one more note of caution is appropriate. Such terms as "occupation" and "colonial or foreign domination" imply that there is essentially only one deep cleavage in the societies in which they occur: that between the occupier and the occupied. Implicitly, the subjugated society and, to a greater degree, the occupying power are represented as monolithic social systems united behind one well-defined goal: exploitation, or resistance to it. This is far from the truth. Just as there are differences in responses to occupation by different groups within the subjugated society, there are also a variety of interest groups in the administration of the occupying power. I hope that this study will serve, additionally, to document this point.

ORGANIZATION OF THE GERMAN ADMINISTRATION

From the beginning of the occupation, Governor General Frank was caught between two contradictory courses of action. On the one hand, he wanted to establish the presence of the German Reich in the Generalgouvernement, but at the same time, he wished to maintain the independence of his administration from Berlin. The first concern

---

lists when living in Danzig-West Prussia. In still other cases, parents living in Pomerania were treated as Germans, while their children in the Poznań province were treated as Poles (Madajczyk, 1970 v.1:445; Orlow, 1973:293).

led him to model his administration on that of the Reich government itself, which in turn made it impossible to fulfill his second goal of autonomy.

In other occupied territories the administration typically consisted of only four departments, but Frank's administration was divided into twelve (later fourteen) main departments (*Hauptabteilungen*) and a Secretariat of State with several offices. In addition, there were eleven plenipotentiaries of various Reich ministries in the GG and one plenipotentiary—the aforementioned "ambassador"—of the GG in the Reich. The bureaucracy of each district administration was a copy of the one just described, with one difference—each consisted of only ten departments. On all territorial levels, whether it was a county (*Kreis*), city (*Stadt*), district (*Distrikt*), or the GG itself, the Führerprinzip was adopted, that is, all authority was concentrated in the hands of one man, the head of the administration at the given territorial level. Exceptions were the Reich Ministry of Communication and the Reich Ministry of Posts, each of which had direct links with the Main Departments of Railways and Posts in the Generalgouvernement.

The close resemblance of Berlin's and the GG's bureaucracies encouraged the Reich ministries and made it relatively easy for them to bypass the governor general in their contacts with corresponding main departments in the GG administration. If such contacts were sporadic in the first years of the war (they were by no means nonexistent [Frank, 1970 v.1:265]), they became much more frequent between 1942 and 1943 (Madajczyk, 1970 v.1:119), after it had become apparent to some segments of the German leadership that a large-scale coordination of effort was necessary to conduct total war (Milward, 1965).[6]

Simultaneously, the Führerprinzip, which was supposed

[6] For example, Dr. Blaschek, who visited Cracow for a few days in August 1942, observed that at that time the Main Department of Construction kept in direct contact with Speer's ministry in Berlin, bypassing the office of the governor general (Blaschek, 1965:144).

to have unified the administration, had a devastating effect on all the comprehensive policies that should have been implemented in the GG. Since in each district, in each Kreis even, functionaries responsible for all branches of the administration were fully subordinate to a *Kreishauptmann* or a *Gouverneur*, no instructions from, for example, an economics department in the government of the GG could be carried out by the lower echelons of economic administration unless the local leader agreed with it. On the local level, however, local interests often prevailed over the commitment to the "general" goal of the occupier. Sometimes the German administration would side with the Polish interests in the area in opposition to the government in Cracow.[7] The Führerprinzip assured effective regional centralization, but there was no institution that could ensure the amalgamation of various regions (Kula, 1947:148).[8]

Administrative chaos was compounded by the fact that offices of the State Secretariat (created in March 1941) in many instances duplicated the work of the main departments. There was, for instance, an Office of Price Setting in the secretariat, while at the same time there were five main departments concerned with economic affairs. To make things worse, some of these departments deliberately

[7] Such, for example, was the case of the financial department of Warsaw's city administration in arranging, with the cooperation of German supervisors, that all revenues from various taxes collected by the Polish government in Warsaw before the war should go to the city administration. According to the new law, this tax revenue actually belonged to the government in Cracow (Ivanka, 1964:410-413).

[8] As an unanticipated consequence of the Führerprinzip, numerous "consultative bodies" emerged and cumbersome consultative procedures were adopted. Since a local leader technically had the authority to make binding decisions but in fact was afraid to take responsibility for those decisions, he usually contacted various "bodies," sought their opinion, and hoped to share the burden of responsibility and blame with the "experts" (Kłosiński, 1947). This practice both prolonged the decision-making process and rendered its results totally unpredictable, since they depended on a wide variety of standards.

tried to cripple and eliminate Polish elements that had remained economically sound, while others favored economic reinforcement and consolidation of the Poles in their jurisdiction. Similarly, there was a Legislative Office in the State Secretariat and a parallel Main Department of Justice. A visitor from a neighboring protectorate, Dr. Blaschek, could not hide his bewilderment at such a criss-crossing network of organizations (Blaschek, 1965:142, 149).

The administration was overblown, and as a result, many trivial matters were decided at the central level. During a meeting on June 18, 1942, someone suggested that the complicated administrative structure of the GG be simplified. In support of this proposal he cited tasks that could be handled perfectly well on the middle and lower levels of the administration. For example, only the government of the GG was empowered to decide what brands of sausage were to be produced, what was the proper time for the delivery of carp, or how the nurseries for young trees should be organized. Frank's only reply was that in the Reich also, decisions about sausages were made by the central authority, the Ministry of Food and Agriculture (Frank, 1970 v.1:641). A direct consequence of centralization was, paradoxically, the inability of the central authorities to provide overall guidance or to shape binding policies. They were, instead, lost in a maze of detail (Blaschek, 1965:150).[9]

[9] The general framework of the administration underwent a few changes during the time of its operation in the GG. In December 1940 the Office of the Governor General was renamed the Government of the GG. In May 1942 the Secretariat of the State for Security Matters was set up, following a long period of bitter conflict among Frank, the police, and the SS. The territory was originally divided into four districts: Cracow, Warsaw, Lublin, and Radom. The district of Galicia was added later, with its capital in Lwow. Districts, in turn, were subdivided into smaller territorial units—town and rural *powiat* (*Kreis*). The districts' chiefs held the title of governor from September 1941. Kreis- and Stadthauptmanns headed town and rural powiat.

THE CADRES

The quality of the German personnel employed in the administration was low. There were exceptions, of course, but it seems that better qualified people, as a rule, were sent to the West (Madajczyk, 1970 v.1:497). Hitler insisted that "strong personalities," that is, fanatic Nazis, go East. As a result, many of Ley's Ordensburg graduates,[10] who were known for their incompetence and total unsuitability for occupying leadership positions, found employment in the GG (Orlow, 1973:202, 288).

Goldfasanen, the derogatory nickname with which employees of Rosenberg's Ostministerium were christened, indicates that German administration further east was not much better:

> the German government in occupied Poland was from the beginning ineffective, both politically and administratively. The Eastern territories not only were rampant with corruption, but quickly lost their political glamor as well. Instead, they achieved the reputation of being *areas to which one sent PL's* [political leaders] *who could not be used anywhere else.* The Nazi administration in the East very rapidly became the byword of a colonial regime run amok. (Orlow, 1973:297)

Along with party-selected personnel, we find many retired lawyers, mayors, and civil servants in the German administration of the Generalgouvernement. They usually aimed at high posts in the occupation administration and quite often got them. In Warsaw, for example, thirty-nine of ninety prominent employees of the German civil administration had doctoral degrees (Madajczyk, 1970 v.1: 497-498). Several Austrian Nazis were also employed in Po-

---

[10] The Ordensburgen, literally "order castles," were training institutes for the party's cadres and were conceived by Ley as "finishing" schools in the pedagogical system devised for future political leaders of the NSDAP (Orlow, 1973:188-192).

land at that time. In some cases, the administrators of smaller German towns took over duties in the occupied areas. The team that came to Częstochowa, for example, consisted of the former employees of the town of Hof in Bavaria and its "over-mayor" Wendler (who was, incidentally, Himmler's brother-in-law) (Rybicki, 1965:58).

Not surprisingly, the governor general's subordinates were not well qualified, and he knew it. Roughly one year after a brilliant start, Frank was already complaining about the catastrophic lack of middle-level civil servants (Frank, 1970 v.1:262). Many of those who came to serve in the East did so in anticipation of large and attractive spoils. It was neither time nor the brutalizing arbitrariness of the occupation regime that made these employees corrupt; they were so from the beginning.[11] Unwilling to press charges against their own countrymen, administration officials would remove functionaries and transfer them to other places, or to the army if things were really bad and it was impossible to cover up their crimes.[12]

Corruption permeated the whole administrative hierarchy. The governor of the Radom district, Dr. Lasch, died in prison after being arrested for corruption and sentenced to death; Frank's brother-in-law, Beyer, was also arrested

[11] There is nothing easier, wrote Landau in the *middle of December 1939*, than to bribe a German. Not only would they take bribes, but they would also steal "hot" items—gasoline, for example—and sell them illegally. Two months later Landau speaks again of corruption, noting that for a bribe one could get anything—a foreign passport, release from labor conscription, waiver from wearing a yellow armband, information about arrested relatives, etc. (Landau, 1962 v.1:36, 270).

[12] In September 1940 Landau noted an unusually high rate of turnover in the German administration. The reason, he speculated, was that they perhaps wanted to give a chance to as many of their pals as possible to participate in the plunder of the Polish population. This, at any rate, was the explanation popular around town at that time (Landau, 1962 v.1:703, 704), and it implies that the behavior of a new administrator was typically not so different from that of his predecessor.

and sentenced for illegal trade in garments. And these two were not isolated cases (Madajczyk, 1970 v.1:500). By 1943 the situation was already so bad that one of the governors, Kundt, raised the issue, in a peculiar way, at a meeting of the GG government. Since, he said, there seemed to have developed a tendency to prosecute the *Reichsdeutsche*, it was of utmost importance that only those persons against whom the evidence was absolutely conclusive be brought before the courts: "We have very few employees left on the district level and we can't afford to be fussy" (Frank, 1970 v.2:91).[13] The lack of qualified personnel, not only in the GG but also in the incorporated territories, led to desperate attempts to recruit new employees. In April 1940, for example, advertisements were placed in a Silesian paper by the Łódź city administration, inviting any and all candidates to apply for any positions they wanted (Landau, 1962 v.1:443).

The situation steadily grew worse in the first half of 1943, when it became increasingly difficult to maintain draft-exempt status and many administrative employees went into the army. New replacements, whenever they were sent in, were even more incompetent than their predecessors (Rybicki, 1965:204), but even they were not always available. Frank's request at the beginning of 1943 that the Wehrmacht send him some disabled war veterans was answered in the negative (Frank, 1970 v.2:52-53). We can imagine how drastic was the manpower shortage if the administration was denied personnel, even though it put forth basically only one condition—that the men be physically disabled and unfit for military service. As a conse-

---

[13] Inasmuch as the concept of "victim" did not apply in the new law to Poles who were dealing with Germans, the only accusation that would bring a *Reichsdeutsch* before the court would be "economic" in nature. The only "victim" acknowledged by the law was the Reich, and it might very well be victimized by its functionaries if they used their official positions for private gain.

quence, stated Dr. Bühler, "we must employ more people of foreign nationality" (Frank, 1970 v.2:52-53). Indeed, the number of Germans in that administration was not very large; of the 22,740 German men and 7,184 German women employed by the GG on September 1, 1943, 15,880 men and 2,980 women worked in the railway and postal services (Frank, 1970 v.2:264).

The NSDAP in the Generalgouvernement

Curiously enough, the NSDAP in the Generalgouvernement did not develop into a significant contender for power, although ideological politics were pursued both in Poland and in the territories further east at the expense of pragmatic, bureaucratic rationality. One could argue, perhaps, that the task of carrying ideology into the occupied territories was left primarily to the SS, and indeed, we can verify on the basis of available data that all over the newly acquired lands the SS and the police built an empire independent of the civil and military authorities.

Party organization in the GG had been set up by Frank in May 1940. Its organizational structure was rather vague, something between district organization in the Reich and abroad (*Heimatsgau* and *Auslandsgau*). Appropriately, a special name was invented for it: *Arbeitsbereich GG der NSDAP* ("area of work activity").

A close *Personalunion* between the government and the party structure existed in the GG: Frank, the district governors, and the powiat chiefs were at the same time leaders of the respective territorial organizations of the party. But this complete fusion was not indicative of the party's complete control in the area. The government came first for the Generalgouvernement, so to speak, and party positions were acquired by government employees rather than the other way around. Indeed, party functionaries had a tendency to handle most problems in their capacity as government employees, that is, through government rather than party channels. Because problems were handled in this manner, the NSDAP could not fulfill its function of informal control over the administration. District governors tried to secure titles of *Gauleiters*, but they did not succeed. In general, Dr. Blaschek observed, political work was not the first priority of the GG's administration (Blaschek, 1965:154-156; IMT, v.12:57; Frank, 1970 v.1:533).

The party's position in the incorporated areas was radically different. Greiser in Warthegau and Forster in Danzig-West Prussia, notwithstanding their mutual dislike, were united in their efforts to avoid the introduction of any vestiges of the *Rechtstaat* that still prevailed in the old *Gaue*. Indeed, they consistently overruled appointments of the Interior Ministry and staffed their administrations with party officials rather than civil servants (Orlow, 1973:291; Madajczyk, 1970 v.1:78-79). "The immediate results," noted Orlow,

> were administrative chaos and political catastrophe. As a group, the new PL [political leaders]—county executives constituted a very unqualified administrative team that had little experience in governing large scale territorial units and even less inclination to acquire such knowledge. Rather, the party functionaries regarded themselves as pioneer *Herrenmenschen* whose behavior and success could not be judged by the normal standards of efficient administration. (Orlow, 1973:292)[14]

[14] It may be interesting to note here that the Gauleiters, who were committed to establishing party predominance over governmental administration and who were operating in the occupied territories, had both very good and very bad relationships with the SS. Greiser's relationships with the SS were excellent, while Forster's were not, perhaps because of his rather unorthodox strategy for making his Gau *Polenrein*. Instead of resettling the Poles to the GG on a mass scale, as Greiser did, he would have had them sign DVL and, by their national "redefinition," avoid the problem. This rather carefree attitude toward proper race selection set him against Himmler and the SS (Orlow, 1973:293).

THE ADMINISTRATION VERSUS THE SS AND THE POLICE

The two leading pillars of the German rule in all occupied territories were the administration and the police. Relationships between the German administration in the GG and the SS and the police stationed there, or, to put it more directly, conflicts between Frank and his higher SS and police leader (HPSSF), Krüger, belong in a special study of the emerging pattern of interrelationships among institutions of the Nazi state. They constitute an exemplary case of what seems to have been the pattern everywhere, in the Reich as much as in the occupied areas: the emergence of an SS state within the Nazi state, which can, perhaps, be interpreted as a further step in the Nazi revolution, coming after *Gleichschaltung*.

Differences in Ideology

The buildup of the SS-*Staat* in Nazi Germany should be viewed, I believe, as an indication of a continuing effort on the part of a segment of the Nazi leadership to discard what was left of the *Rechtstaat*, the laws that survived the Nazi seizure of power in the Third Reich and provided it with the regularity, predictability, and appearance of legality that were needed to run the state bureaucracy and administration. This task was undertaken by the SS, the only "political" nucleus of power in the state capable of simultaneously validating and realizing the revolutionary and totalitarian claims of National Socialism: "Police power became political power, its protective role was transformed into a "positive" claim to make policy beyond the "legitimate" state power. Behind the pseudo-legal disguise, police power represented the *permanent revolution*" (Bracher, 1970:354).[15]

[15] In Italy, as early as 1925-1926, one could see that ideas of constitutional reform or definite organization of the state were regarded by radical fascists as antipathetic or at least irrelevant. Camillo Pellizzi wrote at that time: "Fascism fought for a principle of au-

Nothing could be more irritating to Hans Frank. As the president of the Academy of German Law and Rechtsführer der NSDAP, he was obsessed with his personal responsibility for safeguarding the law of the Third Reich. The whole of his active life in the service of the Reich was devoted to the task of "coordination," "reformation," and "supervision" of the law.[16] He thought that the revolution was over long ago, that it was time for harmonious consolidation, and that the new society could be framed in new legal formulas. Apparently, he even insisted that he "preferred a bad constitutional state to the best conducted police state" (IMT, v.12:132). Not surprisingly, he was severely disappointed with the new course of events indicating that respect for law—the new law, as he saw it—was not held in the highest esteem by the Reich authorities.

Despairingly, he expressed his views in a dramatic memorandum to Hitler when the Führer appointed Himmler's favorite, G. Thierack, to the post of Minister of Justice, and at the same time dismissed Frank from all his "legal" assignments (hence the mysterious repetition of "1942" as the terminal date of all his long-term legal appointments). The memorandum accompanied Frank's resignation from the post of governor general. He felt that he no longer

---

thority. . . . Authority: but not that of a written law or a constitutional system . . . the genuine fascism has a divine repugnance for being crystallized into a state. . . . The fascist State is, more than a state, a dynamo" (Lyttelton, 1966:77).

[16] Frank's career under National Socialism was as follows: between April 1933 and December 1934, he had held the post of "Reich Commissar for the Coordination of Justice in the States and for Reformation of the Law" (Reichskommissar für die Gleichschaltung der Justitz und für Erneurung der Rechtsordnung) in the Ministry of Justice; March 1933–December 1934, Bavarian Minister of Justice; 1933-1942, president of the Academy of German Law; 1933-1942, leader of the National Socialist Lawyers Bund; 1941-1942, president of the International Chamber of Law; 1930-1942, "editor or author" of *Deutsches Recht, Magazine of the Academy of German Law*, and *National Socialist Handbook for Law and Legislation* (United States, 1946 v.5:684-685).

enjoyed the Führer's trust and that he therefore could not continue on the job as his plenipotentiary in the newly acquired territories. By promoting Thierack, wrote Frank, the Führer

> indicated that he wanted to eliminate from the German legal system the position that I [Frank] am advocating once and for all. I anticipated such a turn of events and thus it does not really hurt me. I do not think of it as if it were a crisis of the legal system but rather a crisis of the state, and from the depth of my heart I beg God that the unavoidable consequences of this action be not very damaging. . . . As for myself, what is actually happening does not make me change my point of view in the smallest detail. I firmly believe that the legal idea of our nation [Rechtsidee] is immortal and that it cannot be destroyed by any order within the state. As an unappreciated clairvoyant, who fell into disgrace with the magnates of his epoch, I look from my spiritual position at the coming events. . . . I hope that after the war the accumulated experience will let another point of view win —totally opposed to the one presently held that it is necessary to destroy the existing legal system. This new point of view will be able to demonstrate that in order for our nation to achieve a favorable internal situation we must put into realization the legal program that I have sketched before. (Frank, 1970 v.1:529-530)

Not many people in their right mind would dare to address Hitler from such a position of superior wisdom. If anything, this domain was reserved exclusively for the Führer. But Frank was desperate and obsessed. Evil was epitomized for him by the increasing domination of the SS and the police over all other institutions of the Reich, and the threat to the authority of all other governmental agencies, he felt, could only imperil the unity of the Reich and of the movement.

His top advisers might be suspected of sharing similar views. A scrutiny of short biographical sketches about some of them, published in *Das Deutsche Führerlexikon* (1934),[17] reveals one characteristic peculiar to this group: all of the men who had completed a university education—six out of the total of eleven[18]—held degrees in law, and a seventh, who apparently did not graduate from a university, had *Juristische Ausbildung* (*Das Deutsche Führerlexikon*, 1934: 123, 129, 130, 160, 190, 270, 363, 457, 498, 541, 548). Naturally, such a saturation of top administrative positions with trained jurists might have accounted for the administration's leaning toward a formalistic and bureaucratized, as opposed to content-oriented and revolutionary, interpretation of legal order. Holding such views, Frank and his administration could not have had harmonious relations with the SS.

But caution is necessary here. Although at times Frank's administration, in a unique blend of grotesque and horror, appeared devoted to upholding the "legality" of its actions,[19] Frank's conception of the "legal state" could not be

[17] Of the 47 Nazis prominent in the Generalgouvernement (Madajczyk, 1970 v.1:106-112)—members of the government, heads of main departments, governors, and higher SS and police leaders—only 11 are mentioned in *Das Deutsche Führerlexikon* (1934).

[18] This proportion is not unusual in the Nazi leadership; in 1934 60% of the Nazi elite had attended the university (Lerner, 1951:21).

[19] In December 1941, one of Frank's governors, Kundt, complained that the procedure for validating death sentences passed on Jews caught outside of the ghetto was cumbersome and should be simplified. He proposed that the governors, rather than Frank himself, be empowered to validate them. Also, he said, the concept of a "borough designated for Jews" should be specified more clearly because judges in his district sometimes found it difficult to decide whether a Jew had actually been caught outside of the area where he could legitimately dwell (Frank, 1970 v.1:409). If one did not already know better, one might infer from this discussion that Frank's signature was necessary in order to kill a Jew in the GG and that before a Jew was actually executed, the courts weighed carefully whether he indeed was caught outside of the ghetto. Another example, this time rather

stretched far enough to admit Poles under the protection of its laws. As far as the Polish out-group was concerned, *Juristische Ausbildung* dictated to the governor that he had to establish a legal framework within which *anything* could be done to its subjects. In this framework it was not the population that enjoyed the protection of the law, but the state, that is, the organizers of the new public order: under the new law no agents of the administration could ever commit excesses or legally punishable acts when dealing with the local population. Since all excesses could be subsumed under some paragraph of the new law, no excess was, by definition, possible. With a stroke of the pen Frank made everything legal, bureaucratic, and routine. Certainly he wanted in this way to preserve the Reich's *Rechtsidee* and the integrity of the German administration working under conditions that required superhuman efforts.[20] What he accomplished instead was appropriately named by Hannah Arendt the "banality of evil."

Without a detailed analysis of specific legal provisions to elaborate this point, let two general pronouncements made by Frank in 1940 stand as proof of the narrowness of his conception of the "legal state." That Poles were excluded from it, he stated openly in December 1940. "In this country," he said, "the force of a determined leadership must

---

innocent, concerns a choice of methods in the struggle against the underground. SD intelligence reports in mid-1942 revealed that sizable shipments of firearms and explosives were sent through the mail to fictitious German addresses and were picked up at their destination by couriers of the underground. Frank questioned whether the supervisors of postal service could not check the content of parcels at their destination points, and Ministerialrat Breithaupt answered that such procedure would be incompatible with the principle of confidentiality of correspondence. This exchange took place during a meeting of GG's government on August 19, 1942 (Frank, 1970 v.1:520).

[20] This is precisely what Himmler once said to the commanders of *Einsatzgruppen* and the higher SS and police leaders: We realize that what we are expecting from you is "superhuman," to be "superhumanly inhuman" (Arendt, 1965:105).

rule. The Pole must feel that we are not building him a legal state, but that for him there is only one duty, namely, to work and to behave himself" (United States, 1946 v.4: 909). This statement was merely a polite rephrasing of what he had stated at a meeting in January 1940:

My relationship with the Poles is like the relationship between ant and plant louse. When I treat the Poles in a helpful way, so to speak tickle them in a friendly manner, then I do it in the expectation that their work performance redounds to my benefit. This is not a political but a purely tactical-technical problem. . . . In cases where in spite of all these measures the performance does not increase, or where the slightest act gives me occasion to step in, I would not even hesitate to take the most draconic action. (United States, 1946 v.4:906)

Though such a concept of colonization in the East must have been to the liking of the staunchest Nazis, it was not enough to improve Frank's relationships either with Bormann or with Himmler (Blaschek, 1965:154-156; IMT, v.12:57; Frank, 1970 v.1:533). Krüger, HSSPF in the GG (handpicked by Himmler) was allegedly sent to Poland with specific orders to "finish off" Frank (Orlow, 1973:322).

The Police

From the beginning of the GG's existence, the position of the police and the SS was not very clearly defined. The governor general was the sole authority in the GG, but the police enjoyed special status in this administration because of the primary importance of security in the occupied territory. Though nowhere was it specifically stated that the police must obey the orders of the governor general, such, of course, was Frank's interpretation of Hitler's decree and his understanding of the leadership principle.

But Krüger, the commander of the SS and the police in the GG, acted as if he were subordinate primarily, if not only, to Himmler, the Reichsführer of the SS and Reich

Commissar for the Strengthening of Germandom. Significantly, Krüger's official title was "HSSPF East" rather than "HSSPF Generalgouvernement." At Nuremberg Frank testified that Krüger did not obey even "a single order" of his, and that Himmler did not seek his approval—"not in a single case"—before carrying out security police measures in the GG (IMT, v.12:10). While we do not have to take this literally, Frank obviously had little control over the police. He could always be rebuffed, and frequently was, with the argument that the GG was only one part of the area where the fight against the resistance movement had to be conducted, and therefore central coordination was necessary—by Himmler, of course (IMT, v.12:11, 65).[21]

Frank was not prepared to yield control over police work to the SS without putting up a fight. He did not emerge victorious, losing almost completely at one moment in 1942. In fact, August 1942 was the lowest point in his career; he later recovered somewhat, but apparently was forced by the course of events to submit his resignation as governor general no less than fourteen times (IMT, v.12:13).

Inability to control the police is bad enough for the head of administration in a given territory, but to be challenged, defied, and opposed by it is incomparably worse. Frank had to suffer both indignities. Employees of his administration were harassed by the police in many ways. Poles were often

---

[21] His inability to control the police led Frank to create a special service, the Sonderdienst, "a formation designed to carry out administrative and technical duties, which, however, *could be called on to perform police duties when police force was not available* (Frank, 1970 v.1:286-287; italics added). A special Referat des Sonderdienstes had been created in the Department of Internal Affairs of the GG government to make it plain to Krüger that the agency was none of his business. It was Frank's pet project, and he dreamed of its becoming a 10,000-man force (Frank, 1970 v.1:405). Of course, the police could not tolerate such a challenge, and during the showdown with Frank in 1942 Himmler obtained his agreement to subsume the Sonderdienst under Krüger's orders in exchange for the formal subordination of Krüger to Frank.

taken into custody without their German superiors being informed of the arrest or of the charges. Since corruption was the accepted standard of behavior in the administration, it was easy to collect incriminating evidence against practically anyone. Thus, corrupt German officials, if the police so desired, could be arrested too. The State Secretary in the GG, Dr. Bühler, who was Frank's deputy after the departure of Seyss-Inquart, testified in Nuremberg that it was difficult and often impossible for Frank or himself to secure the release of arrested officials of the GG administration (IMT, v.12:84).[22]

[22] Frank's negotiations with Himmler, which led to the establishment of the State Secretariat for Security in 1942, for example, had been conducted in an atmosphere of blackmail. Governor Lasch had been arrested by then, as had the administrator of Frank's Warsaw residence, SS-Untersturmführer Lorenz Lov. Frank was easily convinced by Himmler that evidence that had been collected for both trials could be damaging to him and his family. Evidently, in exchange for Himmler's offer not to use the information, Frank agreed to the creation of the State Secretariat for Security in the GG, under Krüger. Krüger, who took the job, became Himmler's deputy for Strengthening the Germandom, subsumed the Sonderdienst under his command, and, with the title of State Secretary, officially became the third person in the GG after Frank and Secretary Bühler. In exchange, it was agreed that all of Krüger's orders would have to be approved by Frank (Madajczyk, 1970 v.1:150-153; Frank, 1970 v.1:571-572). Even before the agreement was officially approved by the Führer, Krüger exceeded his prerogatives: he was not willing, even formally, to clear his orders with GG's government, and he insulted Frank by sending him a memo signed by his aide-de-camp. Frank's position was not yet so weak that he had to bear this in silence. His recent agreement with Himmler, though apparently not softening Krüger's enmity, at least gave the governor general the possibility of calling on Himmler and demanding that he reprimand his subordinate for defiance of the agreement. Indeed, at a government meeting Krüger had to apologize, accept an official reprimand from the governor, and promise that he would neither absent himself in the future from official celebrations organized by the government nor repeat his previous mistakes (Frank, 1970 v.1:456). How short-lived Frank's victory was, we already know; in August 1942, roughly four months after Krüger's formal apology, Frank was

At the local level, districts and below, antagonisms between the administration and the police were as vivid as they were on the leadership level. Sometimes conflicts were mitigated by common practice of corruption. But throughout the occupation the "government" in Cracow was the helpless recipient of an uninterrupted flow of reports from its subordinates, who, although responsible for timely execution of *all* tasks assigned in their areas, according to the Führerprinzip, were repeatedly unable to receive assistance from the local police. At times they were informed post factum about police raids carried out without their authorization in the area under their administration.

Last but not least, the administration was challenged by the police in yet another way, that is, by its direct reporting to Berlin. In the early stages of the administration this procedure seems to have been quite common in the different departments of the Generalgouvernement. In November 1940, however, Frank instructed the heads of all main departments to submit their reports to the state secretary before sending them to Berlin. At the same time, he added that police reports as well must first receive the approval of the governor general (Frank, 1970 v.1:263). As in so many other instances, his instructions in this matter were ignored. Numerous entries in his diaries indicate that he knew that the weekly reports of the SD were being sent directly to Berlin uninterruptedly througout the occupation. He consistently protested against this practice, not only because it interfered with the chain of command and undermined his authority, but also and primarily because he considered the content of those reports unfair and slanderous

---

almost completely destroyed. Himmler himself then committed a far more serious breach of protocol than Krüger ever did. Three weeks before Frank produced the memorable text that I have quoted here, Himmler visited the Lublin district of the GG and issued orders for the construction of a German borough in the district capital. Frank learned about both the visit and the decision from the *Krakauer Zeitung* (Frank, 1970 v.1:498).

toward the GG administration (Frank, 1970 v.1:377, 379). During his premature triumph at the conference of April 21, 1942, when Krüger offered a public apology, Frank pointed out that so much hatred toward duly appointed German authority was expressed in those direct reports that eventually the police and Krüger himself would fall victim to its efflorescence (Frank, 1970 v.1:458).

THE ARMY IN THE GENERALGOUVERNEMENT

During the first year of the Generalgouvernement the confrontation between Frank and Krüger had been attenuated somewhat by the active presence of a third contestant for power in the GG: the army. In a retrospective analysis of the Polish campaign, Heydrich wrote Himmler that the secret orders issued to the *Einsatzgruppen* (which followed each of the five German armies invading Poland) calling for the liquidation of the leading strata of Polish society were too radical to be communicated to military commanders, who, therefore, perceived the behavior of the SS as "brutal and ruthless lawlessness" (Frank, 1970 v.1:111; Madajczyk, 1970 v.1:50). To be sure, at least rear-line detachments of the Wehrmacht participated in the executions that were carried out, often together with the SS and the police squads. Of the 764 executions that took place between September 1 and October 26, 1939, in which a total of 20,000 people perished, the Wehrmacht organized 311 (Madajczyk, 1970 v.1:58).

Notwithstanding this occasional cooperation, the rancor and uneasiness between the army on the one side and police and the administration on the other increased over time. Dr. Seyss-Inquart, the prospective Reichskommissar in the Netherlands and at the moment Hans Frank's deputy in Poland, reported on his early inspection trip in November that in the Lublin district the local commander, Lieutenant General Buechs, "was giving 'the Government' [the administration and police] all possible trouble," while in the district of Radom the newly appointed governor, Dr. Lasch, complained that his predecessor, "Regierungspraesident Ruediger, has put himself into strongly opposed [original translation] the Wehrmacht—and that he had first to bring about a better understanding" (United States, 1946 v.4:953-968). But the conflicts were not easily smoothed. As late as November 1940, Frank reported to his cabinet that Hitler, in Frank's presence, had reprimanded Major General Jodl, saying that the GG was no longer a combat area but an area that belonged to "big politics." "It was high time," commented Frank, "for the Wehrmacht to find out what in fact the Generalgouvernement was" (Frank, 1970 v.1:264).

Indeed, the army's attitude toward the population of the conquered territories was different from that of the police or the administration, partly, perhaps, because its business was with soldiers rather than with civilians. It was not charged with the general maintenance of order, but rather with restoring it whenever there were drastic breakdowns that the police could not handle alone. In addition, the army recruited with less discrimination and less dependence on a strong commitment to Nazi principles. Privates were drafted from the entire population, while the officers corps, as we know, was reluctant to the end to espouse Nazi beliefs enthusiastically. Thus, in a sense, army personnel in the GG was different from that of the administration or the police. In fact, in an underground intelligence report dated October 14, 1940, one finds information about the spread of "Communist" propaganda in the army. While this term was probably used for all the various shades of anti-Nazi opinion tracked down by the Gestapo, nevertheless large numbers of soldiers and officers were imprisoned on related charges (about 800 in Warsaw and about 200 in Cracow), and many of them were shot (GSHI, Kolekcja Kota, no. 25/7: *Raporty "Nur,"* no. 20, Oct. 14, 1940).

From the beginning, the high command of the Wehrmacht opposed police terror. As a consequence of his reluctance to condone police actions, the first commander in the East, General Blaskowitz, was not promoted to marshal, although all other generals who commanded the invading armies were. The army was offended, and it allegedly issued orders that all army personnel behave "correctly" vis-à-vis the Poles.

Polish officers who registered, as requested, with the German military command were not persecuted or arrested, according to another underground report prepared in the beginning of 1941. None of the families of Polish officers or NCOs were evicted from houses or apartments that were under the jurisdiction of military authorities. Furthermore, in the autumn of 1940 German military authorities supplied all those houses with adequate coal, which at the time could not be purchased even on the black market.

In early 1941, when the German armies were concentrated in the GG before the Russian campaign, conflicts with the civilian administration increased somewhat in intensity. Since the war was continuing and the area was in the immediate vicinity of a new front, the military felt that it should be made responsible for administration (GSHI, PRM 46a/41: "Sprawozdanie Antoniego," App. 22). But these were only interludes in the ongoing confrontation between the police and the administration.

Reading about the German occupation of Poland, one is struck by the inadequacy of the portrait of the occupation most commonly held, a portrait that shows the German occupiers, as a bloc, in solid opposition to the Polish population. I say that this is an *inadequate* rather than a false conception of the occupation. Certainly, the deepest cleavage in this society was the one separating the Germans from the conquered population. It is nonetheless puzzling that this rather small contingent of German colonizers was so divided. They lived, after all, in the midst of a hostile population and, after 1942-1943, lost their self-assurance and grew to feel endangered. In spite of the external threat, they did not solidify their ranks, as one would expect. What would explain these internal tensions? Did fundamental differences in their philosophies of conquest and coloniza- tion divide the administration and the police? Before we describe the texture of life in the Polish society under the occupation and reveal characteristic responses to its pres- sures by various social groups, let us try to answer these questions. In order to do so, we must pause to consider three components of German occupation policy: resettlement, ex- termination, and forced labor.

RESETTLEMENT

Resettlement—or rather, unsettlement—from the incor- porated Polish territories began immediately following the end of hostilities in the winter of 1939-1940, and was con- ducted with a brutality and ruthlessness rarely surpassed.[23] The leading concern was always speed and effectiveness. At the beginning, the transports, usually trains, were not sup- plied with food. Several of them arrived without advance notice, and in many cases people were kept in sealed rail- road cars for several days, dying of cold, hunger, exhaustion, and disease. To mitigate the abuse, the Fourth Department of the RSHA issued a directive to the effect that when the temperature dropped to below zero, women and children should, if possible, be shipped in passenger cars so that they would not freeze to death, and that the transports should not contain more than 1,000 people. At one point Frank said that he would refuse to take transports without advance notice and not unless the people in those transports were provided with food rations for eight days (Madajczyk, 1970 v.1:309, 311). According to an underground report, during

---

[23] People were notified ten minutes to one hour in advance that they were being resettled. They were allowed to take only hand luggage—originally 12.5 kg. per person, later 25-30 kg. per person. Each Pole could take along 200 złotych in cash, Jews only 100 złotych per person. Later, the money allowed was made equal for all—10 Reich marks, then equivalent to 20 złotych. For more details on economic exploitation, suspension of property rights, expropriation, and conditions of life, see Chap. IV below.

the first year of the occupation about 1.5 million people were resettled to Generalgouvernement from the areas incorporated into the Reich (GSHI, A 9 III 1/1: "Działalność władz okupacyjnych . . . 1.IX.39–1.XI.40," p. 230). Thus displaced persons accounted for about 10 percent of the GG's population by 1940. It is estimated that, *not counting the Jews,* 1,650,000 people were resettled in Poland during the war, about half a million from Warsaw alone (Madajczyk, 1970 v.1:333).

The Germans showed no concern for the destination of the dislocated families. Trainloads of people were emptied in various places in the GG, and the local population had to take care of them. The Main Welfare Council (Rada Główna Opiekuńcza) (RGO) was created essentially for the purpose of helping these involuntary newcomers. During the course of the war it monopolized all social service functions.

At first the Germans were not concerned with sorting the homeless population and separating out those fit to work. Later, they began to screen them in order to send the strongest and most needed to Germany, often separating children from parents and men from wives. In the most infamous case, scores of children from the Zamość area were sent off to the Reich for Germanization.

Frank was at various times antagonized by resettlements into and within the GG. As long as the GG was being used as a dumping ground for Jews and Poles, Frank well knew that his fiefdom had only secondary status, certainly lower than those of Forster or Greiser, for example. His responsibilities, his political and legal reforms, were only temporary if he could not incorporate in them the program of making his territory *Judenrein* and eventually *Polenrein* as well. He did not object to resettlement, but he was hurt that the GG was chosen as the destination of "undesirables." Thus his anger was understandable when the mechanics of those human shipments were not worked out with him in advance.

The myriad of destitute people brought into the GG on

72

short, if any, notice created additional problems of security, food rationing, etc., for the administration. We can only imagine Frank's relief and satisfaction when the Führer finally decided to proceed with the Germanization of the GG. On March 26, 1941, Frank told his subordinates, with joy, that Hitler had promised to make the GG *Judenrein* in the near future, and eventually to replace its 12 million Poles with 4-5 million Germans (Frank, 1970 v.1:332). Further resettlement (and extermination) was in prospect, and Frank was perfectly happy with it as long as the subhumans were resettled *out of* rather than *into* the Generalgouvernement. Since destination of the undesirables was typically to be further east, it is not surprising that Hitler's communication did not come until the preparations for the Russian campaign had reached their final stages. Although Frank expressed disapproval of resettlement on numerous occasions, he never intended to argue the propriety of the idea. He was, at different times, unhappy with the timing, direction, or speed of the resettlements, but he never spoke against them in substance.

EXTERMINATION

It is unnecessary to reiterate that extermination was one of the most unceasingly pursued goals of the German occupation of Poland. The holocaust of the Jewish population, which took place on Polish land, speaks for itself. I want, however, to dwell briefly on the extermination plans involving the Polish population and on Frank's attitude toward them.

I have already mentioned the secret orders given to special units of the SS operating behind the German armies attacking Poland. They were carrying out the first assignments deriving from the overall plan for the extermination of the Polish leadership stratum. The intelligentsia were their target, with priority given to those who had already distinguished themselves in public life (and to those with whom local active members of the German national minority had scores to settle). According to the plan, the leading strata of Polish society were expendable (Frank, 1970 v.1:104). One of the most spectacular actions—the arrest of professors from Jagiellonian University and other Cracow institutions of higher learning—received so much adverse international publicity that the administration of the GG was forced to release professors from concentration camps, although several of them died in the camps or shortly after their release, and it took a long time before the last ones, the youngest, were finally sent home (Wroński, 1974:401-408).

In a speech of May 30, 1940, Frank ridiculed and rejected the outside pressure that had successfully checked some of the highly publicized German attacks on the Polish intelligentsia:

On the 10th of May our offensive in the West began. On this very same day the peculiar curiosity with which the outside world had been observing what was going on in this territory stopped. It is even hard to conceive the extent of damages done to us by slanderous and patently false propaganda in the world about the methods applied in the GG by our national-socialist authorities. And the truth is that *we could not even let ourselves pursue a bolder course of action as long as the world's public opinion was so much interested in what was going on in our territory*. As of the 10th of May all this slanderous propaganda does not really matter to us any more, we don't have to take it into consideration any longer. Now we must use to our benefit this favorable occasion. And so, in this period I have discussed with comrade Strekenbach, in the presence of comrade Krüger, this special pacification program. I have to admit openly that in its result several thousand Poles, particularly from the spheres of spiritual leaders of the society, will have to die. (Frank, 1970 v.1:193-195)

During this same meeting Frank frequently stressed how much he had to depend on the SS and how unreliable the Wehrmacht was. He was trying hard at this point to attain a better working relationship with the SS and to show them that neither in principle nor in practice was he opposed to pacification. Five months later, Hitler revealed the principle of German policy in the GG: "Poles may have only one master—a German. Two masters cannot exist side by side, and this is why all members of the Polish intelligentsia must be killed. It sounds cruel, but such is the law of life" (Frank, 1970 v.1:309). Ultimately, however, the fate of all, or almost all, other Poles was to be no different. The intelligentsia had to be destroyed before the rest of the nation, but social class was not meant to provide a safeguard. In the official assessment of the peoples living in the territory to the east of the Reich—the area of German *Lebensraum*—Poles were assigned to the third group of racially alien peoples, together with Ukranians, Belorussians, Gypsies, and Jews (Kemenetsky, 1961:83).[24]

In the context of this logic of German expansion, I would interpret the modest estimate in the Generalplan Ost that only 3 to 5 percent of the population of the GG offered suitable material for Germanization as an indirect admission that extermination was the ultimate goal of German policy for that territory.

An Intermediary Solution

Before the final solution of the Polish problem was completed, however, something must be done with the millions of men and women living in the occupied country. That problem had been solved in a simple fashion: the General-

[24] For further documentation of this point and description of various policies advocated by the Nazis for the purpose of the "final solution" of the Slavic problem in the East, see Kamenetsky, 1961: 79, 135, 137, 138, 140, 156, 157, 175, 176.

gouvernement was to become a "gigantic labor camp, a reservoir of labor force on a huge scale," and, more specifically, a reservoir of unskilled labor. Immediate plans for extermination were aimed only at the leading strata of the Polish population, with the specific exclusion of unskilled labor, that is, peasants and workers who, according to a German spokesman, "basically had shown a willingness to work under energetic German leadership" (Frank, 1970 v.1:192, 218, 270, 308).

The plans, as a whole, were future oriented. The education offered the young was designed to make sure that their opportunity to learn was limited: only primary schools were available for the indigenous population; some middle level vocational schools were also open, offering training in forestry, agriculture, and crafts or skills needed in industry. According to the Führer's decision, no Pole would have the possibility of a college education, and none would ever occupy a position higher than foreman. Such subjects as geography, history, and literature, as well as physical education, were excluded from the curriculum (Frank, 1970 v.1:133, 248). A May 1940 memorandum by Himmler on the subject of "treatment of the population in the East" stipulated that schools should have no more than four grades and that the curriculum should cover counting, but only to 500, ensuring only that people could sign their names and learn that it was God's will that they be obedient, conscientious, and polite toward the Germans. It was not necessary that they be taught reading (Frank, 1970 v.1:289).[25]

Just as the subjugated peoples were deprived of oppor-

[25] Goebbels came to the conclusion that the best way to communicate with the subjugated peoples was by a system of radio speakers placed in their living quarters. Indeed, a network of speakers was mounted in the streets of Warsaw, and the population christened them "barking machines." True, there was a short period when ersatz higher education was suddenly opened to a few selected Poles; at one point the Germans permitted students who had only to take final exams to complete their degrees to do so. But this was sporadic, unusual action.

tunities to learn, they were also denied cultural activity. Excellence of mind or soul was not a desired character trait of a conquered people. Furthermore, such excellence was useless to Germany, since the local population was supposed to do nothing but provide manpower for German economy and agriculture. However, the laborers were allowed some entertainment after work. Movie houses were open, and appropriate films were chosen; a gambling casino was opened in Warsaw; theaters and concert halls were closed, but cabarets and a light-opera company were permitted to operate. The productions have not survived, but their titles reveal much about them: "Your wife, my wife," "I love four women," "An F from love," "Folly of bodies," "Underneath a coverlet," "Only for grownups," "Happy harem," "Under a fig leaf," "Canoes and bushes," etc. (Marczak-Oborski, 1967:200). Sex was the common theme here —one of two subjects chosen by the Department of Propaganda in the GG as a suitable pursuit for the Polish population during leisure time. The second acceptable leisure activity was drinking (GSHI, Kolekcja Kota, no. 25/7: "Pismo z wydziału oświaty ludowej i propagandy GG do starostw powiatowych," June 1940). Several theater productions explored this recreational theme: "Cheerio, followed up with a radish," "From nipple to glass," "Drunken Walter," "In a drunken hive," "Humor, charm, bar." Some productions combined both acceptable topics: "Kiss and rum" and "Drinks and kisses," for example (Marczak-Oborski, 1967:59).[26] Obviously, these efforts were a *peché*

---

[26] Altogether, 17 "theaters" operated in Warsaw at various times from the winter of 1940. Although the underground authorities vehemently opposed any form of participation in the performances (according to rules of conduct formulated by the underground, Poles were not supposed to frequent even movies), the 8,000 theater seats seem to have been occupied at most performances (Marczak-Oborski, 1967:66). Similarly, all seats in the light-opera house were usually sold two weeks in advance. In 1941 alone, about 9 million Poles went to the movies (though this number probably includes

mignon compared with many other German deeds aimed at reducing the Poles to the status of intellectually and emotionally castrated working-machines.

Forced Labor

At the end of 1939, Frank's ordinance imposed the obligation to work on Poles fourteen years of age and older and the duty to work on all Jews beginning at age twelve. The Germans had plans to ship a foreign labor force to work in Germany because of the shortage of manpower that had developed there as a consequence of the mass conscription into the army and the pressures put on industry to keep supplying the army and the civilian sector at the same time—the famous policy of guns and butter. The Jews were the only category of the GG population exempt from the threat of shipment to Germany. Rough estimates indicate that the total number of people sent from the GG was between 1.3 and 1.5 million, including about 400,000 Ukrainians. But this figure does not include those sent to concentration camps or the Polish prisoners of war released for labor in Germany. This last category, according to Frank's estimates, numbered 400-480,000 (Pospieszalski, 1958:285). The figures acquire new significance when we compare them with the total GG population of 15 million.

It would be very difficult to estimate correctly the number of workers who went to the Reich voluntarily. Many who did so regretted it afterwards. However, particularly in the first year after the September campaign, many people actually went of their own will. The difficulty of finding jobs in the GG in the first months of the occupation, skyrocketing inflation, and the experience of rewarding prewar seasonal work abroad, very often in Germany, induced people to sign up in the expectation that they would improve their standard of living considerably and be able to help their families

---

those who went more than once) (Madajczyk, 1970 v.2:137, 140). Along with mediocrities, several well-known Polish actors took part in these performances (*Sprawy Polskie*, Nov. 19, 1940).

in the GG as well. These hopes eventually proved to be unfounded. Treatment of Polish workers in the Reich was humiliating, their wages were low and their taxes high. Only in isolated cases did any of these volunteers return to the Reich when they were lucky enough to get a couple of days vacation and go home—another benefit guaranteed to them but very rarely delivered.

I would estimate that no more than 15 percent of all those conscripted went to the Reich voluntarily.[27] The roughly 85 percent who did not want to go were forcibly rounded up—in the streets of the cities, at railroad stations while seeing their relatives off to Germany, in their homes in their villages during early morning hours, on leaving church, in schools (Landau, 1963 v.3:10, 721), that is, in all possible places and under all possible circumstances. Actually, many more people were rounded up and treated like hunted animals than were actually sent to the Reich, as many "conscripts" succeeded in bribing German officials or escaping from transports at the risk of death.

But just as there was a quota for crops and livestock to be delivered by the rural communes, there was also a quota for the delivery of human beings to the Reich. Throughout the war, roundups were the most feared and ever-present danger for the population. Furthermore, it was impossible to guess, on being caught in a street roundup, whether one might be shipped to a concentration camp or to work in Germany. People tried to avoid capture by all conceivable means: in rural areas, for example, they would escape to the forests or neighboring fields, or live for long periods with

[27] Madajczyk estimates that about 100,000 people were in the first wave of voluntary departures, before news of the actual conditions of work in the Reich got around (Madajczyk, 1970 v.1:643). Apart from this first period, when many people signed up in ignorance of the real conditions, there was a constant trickle of people going to Germany of their own free will, perhaps to escape worse troubles in the Generalgouvernement—impossible family situations, impending prosecution for criminal offenses, or the consequences of breach of employment contracts with German armaments establishments in the GG.

friends or neighbors for fear of being caught at home. In the cities, a certificate of employment in the local government or in some industry engaged in the production of armaments was helpful until 1943. Later, the Germans discovered that so many certificates were forged that they ceased paying attention to them.[28] Fortunately for many Poles, the Arbeitsamte were corrupt, and in most cases bribery made it possible to slip through the net. Many people escaped from transports, while others bought the services of a "professional escaper," a substitute who would show up in one's stead and later, knowing how to pull strings, escape.[29]

In spite of all those who avoided seizure, more than a million were caught in the net of the German labor offices. Their capture was not, however, as bad for the Poles as it

[28] Periodically, during "government" meetings in Cracow, an official of the German administration would express indignation at the sight of thick crowds milling in the streets of Warsaw during working hours. Obviously, the crowds were composed of idlers whose time and energy were being lost for the German economy. But the periodic roundups and very careful scrutiny of people caught in them produced disappointing results. In July of 1942, for example, with the help of Waffen SS, 2,000 people were rounded up from Warsaw's streets during working hours and their whereabouts carefully investigated. All but 80 could prove that they were working and attending to some business matter at the time of their apprehension (Frank, 1970 v.1:496).

[29] People tried to avoid shipments to Germany from the very beginning of the occupation. A Kreishauptmann report from June 1940 states that although he delivered the human quota assigned to him, he had to go personally into the fields and work very hard to catch people because entire villages had run to the forests when the police came for roundups (Madajczyk, 1970 v.1:643). In 1942 Frank reported that in a series of interviews conducted with 27,000 workers in the armament industry, only 42 declared that they would voluntarily go to work in the Reich (Frank, 1970 v.2:460). Jastrzębowski reports that only about 30% of all the people caught by the Arbeitsamte eventually arrived in the Reich. Conditions of work there were indeed very difficult: in a 1944 report, a German official stated that Poles were treated worse than other foreign workers in 21 respects (Frank, 1970 v.2:443; United States, 1946 v.5:260ff., 408ff.).

might have been: the original plans had called for the shipment of one million Poles from the GG to the Reich in 1940 alone (Frank, 1970 v.1:145). A comparison of achievements of the Nazi Labor Program in various European countries shows that the GG was given "special treatment" in that matter as well (see Table III.1).

TABLE III.1

CIVILIAN FOREIGN WORKERS EMPLOYED IN THE REICH AS OF NOVEMBER 15, 1943

Country	Percentage of Total Population[a]
Generalgouvernement	7.3
Holland	3.4
Bohemia and Moravia	3.0
Belgium	2.7
France	1.7
USSR	1.2
Yugoslavia	0.7

Sources: Homze, 1967:148; Kirk, 1946 App. II.

[a] The number of POWs released for work in the Reich is not included. If it were added, the percentages for Russia and the GG would increase most significantly (Homze, 1967:65; Pospieszalski, 1958:285).

CONTRADICTORY ATTITUDES TOWARD MASS EXECUTIONS

In a memorandum addressed to Hitler on June 19, 1943, Frank argued for changes in German policies vis-à-vis the Polish population. In this document he presented himself as an advocate of moderation and expressed his opposition to unlawful arrests and public executions of hostages. To show strength is to find and punish the guilty rather than to shoot the innocent, he said. "Mass executions should take place only after passing sentences according to certain procedures that would satisfy at least the most rudimentary understanding of the law. Even if judiciary procedures are most primitive, insufficient and improvised, they remove or soothe adverse consequences of a penal measure which is otherwise considered by the population as arbitrary" (Frank, 1970 v.2:351).

On February 8, 1944, Frank announced that hostages were no longer to be shot. Henceforth, only persons whose membership in underground organizations had been proven would be executed (Frank, 1970 v.2:399). Three days later, "twenty-seven Polish murderers, members of the secret organization PZP and PPR" were publicly hanged in Warsaw from balconies of the court building (Landau, 1963 v.3:625). It is not difficult to guess whether, because the victims were labeled murderers and members of a secret organization, the "rudimentary understanding of the law" had been satisfied.

Did Frank, or the administration, oppose or condone mass executions? Historical evidence indicates Frank's complete confusion on this issue. In the first months of the occupation he was certainly in favor of mass executions. In confrontation with the army at that time, Frank was, so to speak, on the civilian side. He steadfastly defended the right of his administration—and thus, by implication, also of the SS and the police—to carry out orders from the Reich. Then, in March 1940, he informed his personnel of Hitler's decision not to proceed with the Germanization of the GG, and he ordered that mass executions should be stopped in the future (Frank, 1970 v.1:171). But he soon reversed himself. I have already quoted his statement of May 30, 1940, in which he expressed satisfaction that it would finally be possible to carry out pacification programs decisively.

In his memorandum proposing changes in German policies in the GG, Frank was against mass executions without proper legal justification. Only four months later, however, in October 1943, he and his new SS and police leader, Koppe, began a new wave of terror and public executions. In January 1944 Frank demonstrated Weberian insight: "Politics is more than coercion," he said, "coercion is a ridiculous method for beginners. The art of statesmanship begins when coercion ends" (Frank, 1970 v.2:383-384). Nevertheless, a few days later a new wave of executions began (Landau, 1963 v.3:554).

In July 1944 Frank wrote to Kaltenbrunner expressing his opinion that the attitude toward Poles should be reconsidered in view of the failure of the escalation of terror that had begun in 1943 (Madajczyk, 1970 v.1:187). But on July 19, 1944, Himmler, with Frank's concurrence, ordered that in cases of attempted and/or planned sabotage of important installations, not only were the perpetrators to be shot, but also all the males in their families, and all women sixteen years or older were to be sent to concentration camps (Frank, 1970 v.2:602).

In September 1944 Frank again was caught in a desperate effort to accommodate the local population and at the same time to terrorize it. Confused, and faced with the Warsaw uprising, he suggested that talks with the Poles be undertaken, and he added that he did not anticipate great difficulties in conducting the talks, even if it turned out to be necessary to shoot all participants in the uprising. "We could," he said, "maintain that only Warsaw insurgents are to blame, and that the rest of the Home Army is . . . innocent" (Frank, 1970 v.2:549-550).

From this sequence of contradictory policy statements (and they could be multiplied), we can infer Frank's deep confusion as to the feasibility of using brutal repression and friendly offers of cooperation simultaneously as a means to control the population. I think that his confusion originated precisely in the fact that he never opposed extermination in principle. When he did protest mass executions, it was either because they were carried out on somebody else's orders, or because he considered them to be inefficient measures to contain unrest. It should not be surprising, therefore, that the German occupation of Poland stands out as exceptionally ruthless and severe. During the Second World War Poland suffered greater losses of population, through the holocaust of the Polish Jewry and the killings of the Slavs, than any other country in Europe.

TABLE III.2

CIVILIAN AND MILITARY WAR LOSSES

Country	Percentage of Prewar Population
Poland	22.20[*]
	13.60[**]
	17.90[a]
Yugoslavia	10.60
Greece	6.90
USSR	3.90
Holland	2.20
France	1.50[*]
	2.00[**]
	1.75
Czechoslovakia	1.30

Sources: Kirk, 1946; Szafrański, 1960.

Note: I have used two sources in preparing this table. Wherever their estimates disagree by 0.5% or more, I give both percentages, indicating with one asterisk (*) the Polish source, and with two asterisks (**) the American source. In all other cases I have computed averages. The only discrepancy that needs explanation concerns Poland. Part of the difference is the result of different estimates of Polish civilian and military losses during the war. Kirk (1946:69) gives 4,620,000 as the number of casualties, quoting from a report prepared by the International Committee for the Study of the European Question. Szafrański (1960:38, 42), quoting from an official report of the Bureau of War Restitutions (Biuro Odszkodowań Wojennych przy Prezydium Rady Ministrów), gives an estimate of 6,028,000. This, however, does not entirely explain the difference in percentages. The figure of 22% is arrived at because the Polish report uses as an estimates of the *total* Polish population in 1939 a figure that includes only the number of Poles and Jews living within the prewar Polish boundaries (Szafrański, 1960:38), that is, a total of 27 million rather than 35 million—the *actual* total population of Poland in 1939. I suspect that this strange method of computation had something to do with the establishment of new Polish eastern frontiers after the war. But if we compute the percentages using estimated losses of 6 million and total population of 35 million, we arrive at compatible results. Thus, I think we can accept as the rate of population losses incurred by Poland during the war a figure somewhere between 17% and 18%.

[a] Half of all the dead were Jews.

84

INTERPRETATION OF THE GERMAN OCCUPATION

Along with many people employed in the administration of the East, Frank understood that the anti-German activity of the population could not be contained successfully unless Poles were given something to look forward to, and unless some promise of a positive political solution in the future was offered to them (Frank, 1970 v.2:80). Not that he ever meant to fulfill any such promises. At an appropriate moment, *any* program devised by the authorities could, in his opinion, be carried out. But the moment had not yet arrived. Rosenberg's view was that the war had to be won first, Frank's, that at least the end of the war had to be near. These two heads of the German administration in the East were in basic agreement that a comprehensive policy of colonization was necessary for the successful accomplishment of their tasks. But such a policy, as we know, could not be forged.

Once the population sensed that no limit existed to its exploitation by the occupiers, that no consideration was given to any of its needs, that its extermination was the logical and necessary end-product of the occupation, no efficient method of control could be devised, short of putting everyone into a concentration camp. The Poles' spreading conviction about the Germans' intentions was the primary cause of trouble. To counter it, Frank, among others, proposed that some kind of desirable goal for the Poles be advertised as the purpose of German rule in that territory. But the Germans were not prepared to give up anything. Their propaganda campaign for a common fight against Bolshevism, the so-called Project Berta, failed. It is indeed almost surprising that, despite longstanding historical animosities between Poland and Russia, despite the Russian occupation of half of Poland in 1939 and the crimes committed by the Soviets during that time,[30] and despite Rus-

---

[30] In April 1943 soldiers of a communications unit of the Wehrmacht discovered mass graves in a compound formerly occupied by

sia's widely known determination to take over the eastern part of Poland after victory over the Germans, the Poles refused to join the anti-Bolshevik crusade, even though volunteers throughout occupied Europe joined the German side. This single fact reveals, indirectly, the character of the German occupation of Poland.

Thus, I believe that we would be mistaken to think that two separate segments of the German occupation machinery —the police and the administration—were pursuing two basically different policies vis-à-vis the occupied territories. True, the two agencies were fighting one another and denouncing each other to their superiors in Berlin, but this conflict could very well have stemmed, and in my opinion did stem, from the similarity of their general goals and the belief of each that it could handle the situation independently.

---

the NKVD in Katyń, near Smolensk. Altogether, about 4,500 corpses were found in mass graves in the area. They accounted for about one-third of the total number of 15,000 men, mostly officers, who were formerly kept in Soviet POW camps and who could not be located by Polish authorities after the Sikorski-Stalin pact. Repeated requests addressed to the Russians by Sikorski, Anders, and their deputies to provide information about these men were in vain. Once, during a conversation on the subject, Stalin told Sikorski that these men had probably fled to Manchuria. It has been ascertained beyond a reasonable doubt that they were killed by the Russians. The loss amounted to about 45% of the total of the Polish Land Army Officers' Corps at that time (Zawodny, 1963:9). Since many reserve officers were among those captured by the Russians in the eastern part of Poland on this occasion, it meant that many prominent members of the Polish intelligentsia died. Among the bodies identified at Katyń were those of several hundred lawyers, hundreds of high school and elementary school teachers, 21 university professors, over 100 doctors, and many journalists (Zawodny, 1962:22). The fate of the remaining 10,000 who were held at one time in Russian captivity has never been discovered. Zawodny (1962) pieces together carefully all available documentation relating to the case. It is clear that, notwithstanding their denials and subsequent forgeries of evidence, the Russians perpetrated this mass murder.

86

I do not think we can name one single policy item on which there was fundamental disagreement between Frank and the SS. In each case the governor general would have had something to say as far as the implementation of a specific policy was concerned, but his statements were usually so contradictory that, in fact, variation within them could not be explained by overall policy changes. If there were no significant differences in the philosophies of colonization advocated by various segments of the German apparatus employed in the GG, why did they not at least attempt to *appear* to be united in their efforts to implement the occupation?

In general terms, I think, Frank's dilemma can be interpreted as an example of the perennial tension concerning resource allocation within complex social systems or organizations. Within social systems that are composed of a variety of smaller, but still relatively complex, social "subsystems," there are several competing foci of integration; for instance, those of the subsystems themselves frequently compete with the overall social system for allocation of such scarce resources as labor, capital, and political influence. Such competition leads to crisis when goals for which the large system is striving are not set on the basis of conscientious evaluation of the potential of the subsystems but are instead derived according to some ideological principles. The problems intensify when the procedures of overall integration within the system are not firmly institutionalized. Frank's difficulties were, in addition, compounded by the specifics of Nazi racial ideology that dictated total disregard for the welfare of the population inhabiting the Generalgouvernement.

Nazi desire for "New Order" derived from racist ideology, and the conquest of the world was a necessity stemming from this commitment. But when plans for the future are made according to what must be done rather than according to what can be done, and if that "must" has the compelling, sacred character of a doctrinal principle, those to whom specific assignments are distributed in the pursuit of the project cannot possibly refuse to fulfill them. They cannot question feasibility if they do not want to be suspected of unorthodoxy, because no specific assignment, once sent down the hierarchy of the movement, can be distinguished from the overall goal of the movement.

Tensions arise out of incompatibility between the specific requests sent down from above and the demands of integration at the level of subsystem (such incompatibility becomes exploitation at the moment when the subsystems cannot refuse to fulfill or safely attempt to modify the request), and these tensions are reproduced all the way down through the structure of organization. According to the Führerprinzip, all sub-Führers yield not only complete authority in their respective domains but also complete responsibility. They will therefore try to squeeze out of their subordinates what is being asked of them, with the same disregard for integration problems at the lower levels that was demonstrated by their superiors with respect to their own domain.

The farther down the authority structure we descend, the more we encounter discussion, bargaining, and pleading for common sense; for as we approach the lower echelons, we arrive at the level of administration that will ultimately have to deliver whatever has been asked, be it foodstuffs from the peasants, a quota of laborers for forced labor, or a number of converts to join the movement. Here administrators or party members deal with reality on a day-to-day basis, rather than once a month, once a year, or once every five years, when the major report on the fulfillment of the plan is due. They are therefore more inclined to think and act in terms of a "pragmatic" rather than an "ideological" interpretation of a situation. Ultimately, however, the organization is confronted with a dilemma: it cannot re-argue the case, from bottom to top, in terms of feasibility.

Two strategies are typically adopted by the adversaries in this game in order to protect their respective interests: superiors request more of their subordinates than they indeed plan, or need, to collect; reciprocally, subordinates make every effort to convince superiors that they are capable of delivering less than they in fact can. A handsome confirmation of the universality of such strategy is that it appears both under Communist (Fainsod, 1958:90; Berliner, 1957: Chaps. 5 and 7) and under Nazi rule (see Chap. V below).

The ultimate effect of such exploitative relationships is to hinder all efforts at rational planning on the system's level. After a while, even if the pressure of circumstances brings leaders to desire to modify their ideological stance and tailor developmental goals according to a more realistic assessment of the system's capacities, they cannot do so because no reasonably accurate information on key resources is available.

It seems to me that the major problem of Frank's administration derived from the two orientations that were constantly pulling it in opposite directions. The only justification for the existence of the GG was its contribution to the war effort of the Reich. At the same time, however, the GG itself had to function, even if only in order to provide for the Reich's needs. There were, naturally, certain operational costs: a certain percentage of the available resources had to be diverted and exempted from the Reich's claims simply to keep "the organization" going. This was precisely the source of Frank's unresolvable problems: *Under the model of "unlimited exploitation," no method existed for the apportionment of the GG's resources for these two purposes.*

Frank himself fully agreed that the GG had no justification but to serve the Reich, and he was therefore aware of this dilemma.[31] The GG had to deliver foodstuffs to the

[31] In August 1942, on the occasion of a visit by the Plenipotentiary-General for Labor, Sauckel, Frank appraised the situation: "One can say of an area the size of the GG for example—you are the reservoir for a labor force—and then simply draw the labor force from there; or—you are a part of the general industrial complex of the Reich—and then build industrial plants there. But one cannot do

Reich, but it also had to feed the German army, the administration, the police stationed within its boundaries, and, last but not least, the population of potential labor conscripts, the workers in the German armament industry, and the farmers producing food for Germany, that is, the "indigenous" population. Thus,

> The situation in regard to Poland is unique insofar as on the one hand we must expand Germanism in such a manner that the area of the GG becomes pure German colonized land in decades to come; and, on the other hand, under the present war conditions we have to allow foreign racial groups to perform here the work which must be carried out in the service of greater Germany. (United States, 1946 v.4:912)

Frank had to create such conditions in the GG that would permit "foreign racial groups" to perform tasks "in the service of greater Germany," but he could not legitimately refuse *any* request from the Reich. Since he did not recognize any rights of the foreign population vis-à-vis German claims, he could not, even on purely legalistic grounds, oppose the unrealistic demands of the Reich, and it did not help that he was ready to use extreme methods to execute those demands. It is not always true that readiness to use every conceivable method to secure compliance with preconceived goals is a guarantee of success simply because there would be no moral obstacles to the most comprehensive social engineering.[32] Some resources had to be diverted to cover

---

both things at the same time" (Frank, 1970 v.1:513). During a meeting of the GG government in December 1942, Secretary Bühler expressed what already must have been a mood of desperation among his colleagues when he said that they had to keep a "united front against the Reich, which wants to strip our territory of all its labor force" (Frank, 1970 v.1:564).

[32] The effectiveness of coercive power is related to the harshness of the demands made on the subjugated population. If compliance still permits a reduced but tolerable standard of living, the threat of punishment is enough—indeed, it is even more economical than the practice. But if demands are so harsh that punishment for diso-

the costs of the operation, but Frank could not use this as an excuse when it came to discussing the level and kinds of deliveries to be made to the Reich. *He was therefore bound to be manipulated into a situation where he could not deliver what was expected of him and was not able, in principle, to justify his failure.*

Frank had an intuitive understanding of this problem but was in no position to do anything about it. He was bound to be a loser, and no reason was needed for a rival to challenge his power, no actual disagreement about goals or policies in the GG itself. It was sufficient that there was no efficient system of unlimited exploitation. The SS was in the process of a *Machtergreifung* of its own, and Frank's unavoidable troubles indicated that he was easy prey.[33]

---

bedience involves no worse suffering than does compliance, an individual will weigh his chances of being caught if he disobeys. With universal disobedience, universal punishment is impracticable, and any individual's chances of being punished as an example is small. So, with the cost of compliance known and prohibitive, and the cost of defiance uncertain, disobedience is in fact encouraged.

[33] I have already argued that integrative mechanisms were not institutionalized in the Nazi system but instead were created in response to suddenly emerging priority issues that required mobilization across several social groups and organizations. The Führerprinzip was the only permanent principle of integration in the system, and it operated on a territorial basis. But with its stress on a personalized style of exercise of authority and acceptance of obedience, it was highly variable and unpredictable. In addition, inasmuch as some issues were recognized as perennially urgent (e.g., security; since 1942, organization of the economy for the purpose of conducting total war; maintenance of a steady and adequate supply of labor), and inasmuch as authority from the Führer was delegated to people like Himmler, Speer, and Sauckel on a permanent basis, such authority clearly conflicted with that exercised through the Führerprinzip on the regional basis. In addition, those nationwide, or rather, empirewide, frameworks for integration conflicted with one another. Speer, the rational pragmatist, did not get along well with Sauckel, an ardent believer in the necessity to continue the National Socialist revolution in Europe (Milward, 1970:149). These leaders sooner or later were bound to come into conflict with the SS, which was building a state within a state (Milward, 1965:169).

CHAPTER IV

The Economy

PLANS FOR ECONOMIC EXPLOITATION

I have argued that the Germans did not prepare in advance any political or administrative policy for occupied Europe. The "New Order" had no order. Similarly, in the economic sphere, there appears to have been no systematic planning beyond the limited goal of "preserving the Greater Reich as the heavy industrial and manufacturing center of Europe while concentrating the production of consumer goods and foodstuffs in the occupied territories." Otherwise, the Germans made no attempt to rule Europe as an integral economic unit: "the main value of the occupied territories to Germany was as an area for exploitation, in the least sophisticated sense" (Milward, 1965:30, 31).

It must be said at the start, however, that from this point of view, the Generalgouvernement was not a particularly profitable acquisition. About 80 percent of Polish industry, and in some branches, 90 to 96 percent, was located in the western part of Poland, which was incorporated into the Reich (Madajczyk, 1970 v.1:510). What industry remained, particularly in the Warsaw center and the Central Industrial Region (COP), was cut off from its sources of raw materials and energy. Only 18 percent of the electric power produced in Poland before the war was produced in the GG, and coal was in equally short supply. In 1940 4 million tons of coal were used in the GG, while in 1938, in the same area, 7 million tons had been consumed (Kłosiński, 1947:94). Furthermore, although Poland was a food-exporting country before the war, the Generalgouvernement was not even self-sufficient in the production of foodstuffs (see Table IV.1).

TABLE IV.1

<small>Average Agricultural Surpluses in Poland in Export Years Before the War</small>
(In Thousands of Quintals)

Area of Poland	Wheat	Rye	Barley	Oats
Territories incorporated into the Reich	96	3,809	1,367	262
Generalgouvernement	−400	−2,022	349	180
Territories occupied by Russia	1,570	1,628	1,555	308

Source: GHSI, A 9 III 1/1; "Działalność władz okupacyjnych . . . 1.IX.1939–1.XI.1940."

Note: Another underground document, which uses slightly different estimates of the territory and population of the GG (it is very difficult to settle those major questions once and for all because of numerous shifts in the borders between occupied areas), reports that during the period 1929-1937 the annual average consumption of grain in Poland was 246.4 kg. per capita, while the yields in the area that became the GG averaged only 202.7 kg. per capita. A much more severe deficit occurred in the production of sugar beets (HIA, PGC: Box 919, File "Propaganda niemiecka w Polsce," report Konarskiego, Paris, Mar. 28, 1940; see also File "Organizacje społeczne," Uwagi wstępne do budżetu RGO, Apr. 19, 1940; Streng, 1955:12).

General directives for the economic exploitation of occupied territories were issued on October 13, 1939, by the man in charge of overall German economic mobilization, the deputy for the Four Year Plan, Field Marshal Goering. The original directive for the economic exploitation of the GG was speedily implemented by a decree issued in November 1939, under which German authorities took over all property of the former Polish state. Although, legally, two different series of decrees were issued regarding property rights—one concerned with "taking over" (*beschlagnahmt*), and the other with confiscation (*einziehung*)—there was no real difference between the two terms of seizure: changes could be made in the "taken over" property, all claims of third parties on this property were voided, and it even could be sold. To simplify things, Frank issued another decree in September 1940 stating that the property of the former Polish state was henceforth owned by the Generalgouvernement.

A naural extension of this decree was another, issued in January 1940, on the "taking over" and "confiscation" of private property. According to the new decree, private property could be taken over when such an act was justified by the "public interest."[1] District governors and organs specially designated by the governor general had the right to take over and/or confiscate. Military authorities, police, and the SS had special privileges in this area and were not subject to the "limitations" of decrees regulating expropriation.

The continuity of economic life was badly shaken by these decrees because, according to the law, the prewar financial obligations on seized property were voided, that is, the trustee did not have to pay its debts to any Polish creditor. Since the property of the Polish state had been taken over by the Generalgouvernement, all institutions or persons from whom the state or state enterprises had borrowed in the past lost their money. On the other hand, all confiscated or taken-over "legal persons" were entitled to demand payment from their Polish debtors. Although the payment of debts was facilitated because of the deprecia-

---

[1] A "trustee" (*Treuhander*) was appointed as caretaker of the property. Confiscation applied automatically to all "ownerless" property, that is, property whose owners were not in residence in the GG or property that was not properly registered with the authorities. In addition, all property owned by Jews was either taken over or confiscated. Only articles for personal use were exempted from confiscation. As an exception to these procedures, the property of the Polish Railways, Post, and Telegraph were taken over by the German Eastern Railroad and German Eastern Post. A separate system existed for expropriated agricultural property and forests, which were administered by the Department of Forests and the Liegenschaftverwaltung.

tion in real value of the Polish currency, and both agriculture and industry were able to repay quickly what they had borrowed in the past, several enterprises were hit hard by the new financial regulations, and not infrequently they gave themselves up into trusteeship in order to be relieved of their financial burdens (GSHI, A 9 III 1/1: "Działalność władz okupacyjnych . . . 1.IX.39–1.XI.40," p. 52).

The scope of the seizures is reflected in Table IV.2:

TABLE IV.2

POLISH PROPERTY TAKEN OVER BY WARTIME OCCUPIERS
(In Millions of Złotych)

Area of Poland	Value of Property Confiscated in 1939-1940	Material Losses Incurred Through September 1939
Territories incorporated into the Reich	6.631	236
Generalgouvernement	1.921	712
Territories occupied by Russia	2.176	74

Source: GSHI, A 9 III 1/1: "Działalność władz okupacyjnych . . . 1.IX.39–1.XI.40," pp. 92-93.

Note: In the first half of 1942 the Trustee Office controlled 3,296 enterprises, excluding the district of Galicia (Pospieszalski, 1958: 246). Those figures do not include seizures made by the army, nor the property formerly belonging to the Polish state and already "owned" (rather than "held in trust") by the GG. Underground documents compiled in London in 1943 indicate that at that time the Wehrmacht took over 27,863 pieces of real estate in the GG (75,674 buildings) (HL, PUC: MSW, *Wydział Społeczny*, "Sprawozdanie sytuacyjne z ziem polskich," no. 1/43, p. 178), and that in February 1943 the Liegenschaftverwaltung administered 2,600 land properties, the Waffen SS and police 47, and the Wehrmacht 42 (Pospieszalski, 1958:47). H. Streng says that there were 2,367 "large land properties" in the administration of the Liegenschaftverwaltung and that their total area was 717,000 hectares, including 595,000 hectares of arable land. In addition, it administered "10,000 smaller properties," each 50 hectares or less (Streng, 1955:27, 28).

Considering that before the war the state owned a sizable share of the nation's wealth in Poland, and that in seizing private property the Germans were choosing the largest and best units, the bulk of the productive potential of the GG fell directly into the hands of the administration and other German organizations (see Table IV.3).

TABLE IV.3

COMMERCIAL BUSINESSES IN CRACOW AT THE END OF 1941

Business	German Owners	Polish Owners
Food and groceries	69	1,829
Garments and footwear	25	340
Hardware and metals	25	127
Stationery and lumber	14	131
Drugstores	14	122
Household goods	6	39
Coal	0	68
Other	4	160
Total businesses	157	2,816
Total turnover in 1941 (in złotych)	72,069,000	156,122,000
Average turnover for one business in 1941 (in złotych)	459,000	55,000

Source: Dąbrowski, 1946:133.

OTHER FORMS OF EXPROPRIATION

The transfer of ownership alone does not reflect the full scope of appropriations by the Germans in the economic sphere. Compulsory deliveries of foodstuffs or ad hoc collections of various items (warm clothing, skiing equipment, nonferrous metals, etc.) were all cases of appropriation. This process was also disguised, for example, in the German policy of forcibly closing down "inefficient" Polish businesses that were allegedly either too small or too antiquated.[2] In effect, German economic policy amounted to the suspension of property rights.

A variety of fiscal measures were also included in the German plan. The mark was overvalued in the GG by 33 percent in its official rate of exchange with the złoty.[3] Individual bank accounts were blocked and only limited withdrawals permitted. Later, the authorities decided to change the currency in order to stop the flow of Polish bank notes from outside of the Generalgouvernement. On this occasion, according to an underground source, the population lost about 800 million złotych (GSHI, A 9 III 1/1: "Działalność władz okupacyjnych . . . 1.IX.39–1.XI.40," p. 87).

The government of the GG took over all state monopolies and introduced new ones. In addition, it levied heavy taxes and ad hoc contributions on the Polish population (Kłosiński, 1947:81-82); in 1942, in the GG alone, taxes and excise and monopoly fees totaled twice as much as they had in 1939 for the entire Polish republic (Bloch, Hoselitz, 1944:77). Finally, to measure fully the pauperization of the Polish population, we must take into account what is perhaps the most important factor: skyrocketing inflation (Skalniak, 1966:247).[4]

THE IMPOVERISHMENT OF THE POLISH POPULATION

Taking all of the German economic measures into consideration, the underground compiled an estimate of the

[2] About 10% of all Polish enterprises, usually the smaller ones, closed down as a result of this policy (Pospieszalski, 1958:254).

[3] It was the same in other occupied territories: in Croatia the mark was overvalued by 24%, in the Netherlands by 44%, and in Belgium and France by 50% (Milward, 1970:54).

[4] A comparison of the following figures gives some idea of the scope of exploitation during the occupation: Poland's estimated war losses during the hostilities were one billion złotych, while material losses during the occupation of the area within the prewar boundaries were estimated at 62,020 billion.

97

distribution of the GNP in the Generalgouvernement in 1940-1941. The figures point out the dramatic impoverishment of the population as the net income of the Poles that year fell below 40 percent of that in 1938 (see Table IV.4). Other estimates of the GNP made during the war confirm these findings.[5] According to all available data, as time went on the Germans appropriated ever larger shares of the GG's GNP.[6] As early as September 1940, the governor of

[5] In 1943, for example, Prime Minister Mikołajczyk stated in an official speech that the GNP had fallen by 50% (1938 = 100), of which 35% was taken away by the Reich and 17.5% was the cost of bribes paid in various forms to the Germans. These figures show that in 1943 the Polish share of the GNP was less than 30% of the 1938 level (GSHI, PRM 115: "Przemówienie Premiera"). According to an estimate by Dąbrowski, the 1940-1941 GNP was about 60% of 1938 level; this figure does not contradict the underground's 38% because it refers to the total GNP in that year, not the Polish share in it. The two estimates are, in fact, almost identical. Dąbrowski (1946:129) claimed that the 60% level was maintained until about 1943-1944, when it fell to about 33 to 40% of the prewar level.

[6] This does not mean that there was no revival of economic production after the initial period of looting and expropriation. Kłosiński (1947:91, 92) suggests that there were three periods of German economic policy in the GG:

1. From the beginning of the occupation until the outbreak of the German-Russian war. In this period about 40% of all enterprises were put into operation, and output reached about 30% of its 1938 level. Madajczyk (1970, v.1:576) quotes here the figure of 37%.

2. From mid-1941 until, roughly, the defeats at Stalingrad and in Africa. In this period the GG was "promoted" from *Nebenland* to *Zwischenland* of the Reich, and certain industrial tasks were assigned to it relating to the conquest of territories further east. Deliveries of raw materials from the Reich were arriving in larger quantities, and there was a noticeable buildup of the armament industry, with production in some areas exceeding that of 1938. Roughly 80% of all enterprises that existed in 1938 were functioning. The total output of industrial products did not exceed 60% of the 1938 output.

3. The last period was characterized by the closing down of numerous smaller enterprises and by shortages of raw materials

TABLE IV.4

PREWAR AND WARTIME GNP DISTRIBUTION IN THE GENERALGOUVERNEMENT
(In Millions of 1938 Złotych)

| Source | Distribution in 1938 | Distribution in 1940-1941 | | | Productive Income in 1940-1941 | Depreciation in 1940-1941 |
		To the Polish Population	To the Occupier	Total		
TOTAL	5,640	2,505	1,165	3,670	3,345	325
Agriculture	1,810	1,300	490	1,790	1,465	325
Industry	1,370	210	310	520	520	
Crafts	670	230	20	250	250	
Commerce	700	265	105	370	370	
Transport	260	95	80	175	175	
Health	140	85	10	95	95	
Domestic help	80	40	0	40	40	
Real estate	260	210	10	220	220	
Public administration	350	70	140	210	210	

Source: HL, PUC: MSW, *Wydział Społeczny*, "Sprawozdanie sytuacyjne z ziem polskich," no. 2/43, p. 17.

the Warsaw District, Fischer, wondered what people were eating in Warsaw. The majority, he said, was probably living on dry bread and ersatz coffee (Frank, 1970 v.1:245).

Impoverishment of the Polish population, particularly in the cities, proceeded at a fast pace, and by mid-1941 about 25 percent of the population of Warsaw was being helped in some way by welfare agencies. In July 1941, 111,539 portions of soup were handed out daily to the hungry of Warsaw. The caloric content of soup could at best only supplement the daily energy requirements of an adult: in July

and manpower, for which the Reich had first priority. Only about 60% of the enterprises in operation in 1938 were still functioning in December 1943.

1940 it was 381 calories; in December 1940, 460 calories; in May 1941, 259 calories; in July 1941, 153 calories; in August 1941, 164 calories (GSHI, A 9 III 1/4: "Raport sytuacyjny," July 29–Aug. 30, 1941, p. 25). Simultaneously, in the Warsaw ghetto, about 130,000 people were living on soup from "popular kitchens," which often meant no more than a prolongation of their agony (Madajczyk, 1970 v.2:228). In the city of Częstochowa, from September 1940 to March 1942, a total of 3,377,497 dinners were distributed by welfare agencies free or for a token fee, in addition to considerable amounts of money and various foodstuffs, clothing, and other badly needed articles (Rybicki, 1965:115-123). In his report of October 30, 1940, Adam Ronikier, the president of the Main Welfare Council, estimated that 2.6 to 2.9 million people in the GG, not including unemployed industrial workers, could not support themselves. Thus, one year after the occupation began, between 20 and 25 percent of the GG's population suffered severe material hardships that could not be overcome without outside help (GSHI, PRM 24: Ronikier . . .). A comparison of indexes of wages and costs of living provides a clearer picture of the kind of economic pressure that built up against the Poles.[7] Although the data quoted in Figure IV.1 were gathered in Warsaw, they describe a pattern of the two indicators that was typical for cities.

With the aid of "unofficial" income, Polish salaried employees were able nevertheless to maintain an adequate daily caloric intake: 2,500-2,800 in 1940; 2,050-2,400 in the winter of 1940-1941; 1,700-2,200 in the summer of 1941 and

[7] Although the policy of price and wage controls aimed at maintaining the prewar level of prices and wages throughout the period of the occupation, there was a small movement of both official prices and wages during that time. One source, disputed by others, says that in 1944 an average official worker's monthly pay was about 800-1,200 złotych, compared with 200-300 złotych in 1939 (Kłosiński, 1947:108). In terms of real wages, however, workers' income in 1944 was about 8% of the prewar income (Madajczyk, 1970 v.2:67).

100

FIGURE IV.1

WAGES OF CITY ADMINISTRATION EMPLOYEES AND COST OF LIVING IN
WARSAW

(Average Yearly or Monthly Figures)

(1938 = 100)

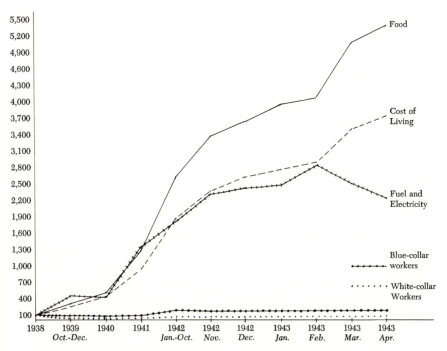

Source: HL, PUC: MSW, *Wydział Społeczny,* "Sprawozdanie sytuacyjne z ziem polskich," no. 4/43, pp. 110-113.

101

in the winter of 1941-1942; 1,700-2,100 in the summer of 1942 (Madajczyk, 1970 v.2:76). Obermedizinalrat Dr. Walbaum was therefore probably wrong when he reported to Frank in September 1941 that the majority of the Poles consumed about 600 calories per day, although neither he nor his employers could take credit for that. In his judgment, the Polish population was so enfeebled that he feared it could become easy prey to spotted fever. "The number of diseased Poles today already amounts to 40%," he concluded (United States, 1946 v.4:909). Although his findings were not literally true, they pointed up an important problem. An underground report that reached London in December 1943 describes an epidemic of tuberculosis, the sickness that goes with poverty and wretchedness. Data, which *do not* cover the Jewish population, show that the number of deaths from tuberculosis increased in 1940 to ·420 per 100,000 of the population, compared with 136 per 100,000 before the war (GSHI, Kołekcja Kota, no. 25/10: Dec. 4, 1943).

Frank was not overly concerned about this situation until 1943, when he began to lose control of it. In December 1941 he actually expressed satisfaction with this state of affairs. As long as Poles had to direct all their efforts toward providing food for themselves and their families, he said, they could not use their energy for other things; therefore, their deprivation was all to the good (Frank, 1970 v.1:415). As for the Jews, starving them to death was an expedient means of getting rid of them. When in August 1942 the Reich increased its demands for food deliveries from the GG, it was decided that 1.2 million Jews not directly employed in jobs important for Germany would no longer be provided with foodstuffs (United States, 1946 v.4:893-902).

Frank and the administration were totally cynical about providing food for the local population. When the former Polish ambassador to Berlin, Wysocki, was received by Frank in December 1941 and brought up the subject of food supplies to the Polish population, Frank replied that, according to a recent report, the situation was terrible and people were starving to death en masse in Athens. He said he would be very glad to help the Polish population, but the bottlenecks in transportation that had developed with the extension of the supply lines of the German army made it very difficult. He nonetheless made a firm declaration to Wysocki that no more foodstuffs or crops would be shipped from Poland to the Reich. At the governor's request, Secretary Bühler, who was present during the conversation, confirmed this statement (GSHI, PRM 76/II/42: Dec. 14, 1941). The conversation was completely surrealistic, to be sure.

One could hardly fail to see that the economy of the GG was not geared to providing even a bare minimum of subsistence for the Polish worker. The only goods available at official prices (that is, prices that corresponded to the level of official wages) were those distributed through the rationing system, and the supply of these goods was ridiculously low. Rationing of food did not provide even minimum nourishment. Other items that were supposed to be distributed through the rationing system were never, or rarely, delivered in the quantities promised (Frank, 1970 v.2:13, 36). Warsaw, a city with over a million people, received 272,000 pairs of shoes and 17,000 dresses in 1941, and 100,000 pairs of shoes and 5,000 dresses in 1942. To obtain any of those items, however, it was not enough to have the appropriate coupons, as there were many more coupons on the market than merchandise: one had also to pay a handsome bribe to the distributor, which, of course, made the official price completely irrelevant (Madajczyk, 1970 v.2:84).

AGRICULTURE

The economic exploitation of the countryside followed a rhythm different from that of the city. In fact, all sources agree that during the first year of the occupation material conditions of life improved markedly in the countryside:

103

peasants' indebtedness to Jewish creditors was canceled, and other debts quickly diminished in value because of the rapid inflation; taxes were no longer collected; few quotas for compulsory deliveries were imposed yet; and skyrocketing food prices, rising more rapidly than prices for nonagricultural products, brought improvement in the peasants' position relative to other social strata. So the peasants were eating better (Kersten, Szarota, 1968 v.2:53; Landau, 1962 v.1:434). They purchased much-needed machinery and even acquired luxury items that had never before been available to them, as city people began to sell whatever they could spare in order to make up the difference between their salaries and the market prices for basic articles (Landau, 1962 v.1:170; Stolarz, 1965:95).[8] With the systematization of German exploitation of the countryside, things changed, but not to the point where it would be impossible to say in retrospect that in the countryside "during the war things got generally better" (Kersten, Szarota, 1968 v.2:22). Not surprisingly, the high cost of food aroused antagonisms between the cities and the countryside that ran deep and did not lessen with time, even though people began to see clearly that they were *all* being exploited by the occupier (GSHI, PRM 46a/41: no. 3726/II/43).

People in the countryside not only started to eat better, but they also began to drink more. Alcoholism soon spread throughout the country, with silent German blessing, and quickly took over the countryside, where moonshining was always a traditional sideline. Thousands of tons of potatoes and wheat were diverted during the war into the production of "hooch" (*bimber*). In 1940, as the memoirs of a peasant tell us, in a hamlet of forty crofts there were already four

---

[8] One underground commentator attributed the economic revitalization of the countryside to the peasants' insecurity; that is, they were disposing of currency that was no longer reliable rather than enjoying a real increase of purchasing power (GSHI, Kolekcja Kota, no. 25/10: "Opracowanie: zabór niemiecki," Mar. 13, 1941). There certainly was insecurity in the countryside, but, undeniably, the peasants also had much more money to spend than before.

illicit distilleries (Kersten, Szarota, 1968 v.2:132). S. Łukas-zewicz, in his penetrating novel *Okupacja* (1958), describes how all contacts with local German authorities (and they were more frequent in the countryside than in the cities) and all social occasions were flooded in hooch.

The underground became concerned about this situation, made numerous appeals in the press to contain the spread of alcoholism, and even organized several expeditions to destroy illicit distilleries, but little could be accomplished (*Placówka*, Oct. 16, 1940; *Biuletyn Informacyjny*, Jan. 27, 1944; *Przez Walkę do Zwycięstwa*, Mar. 30, 1944). Alco-holism had never carried a social stigma in Poland; moon-shining was profitable; drinking helped people forget the horrible reality in which they were living; and, last but not least, they liked it, and so it continued.

In time, German pressure on the countryside increased. The quotas to be delivered were raised, and consequently, methods of collection became more brutal. The size of the imposed quotas shows how the situation developed.

Comparison of Tables IV.5 and IV.6 is revealing in many respects. For example, at the beginning of the occupation most of the grain quotas collected by the Germans *never left the territory of the Generalgouvernement*. Slightly more than 10 percent in 1940-1941 and slightly less than 10 per-cent in 1941-1942 was shipped to the Reich. Thus, about 90 percent of the quotas was consumed by the Germans in the GG.[9] No doubt the Polish population benefited from such a situation: certainly some of the foodstuffs were sold on the black market, and through it, reached the Polish consumer. During the first year of compulsory deliveries the Germans did not enforce the law strictly.[10] Only 38 per-

[9] The proceedings of a top-level conference with Goering, held in February 1940, reveal that until that date the GG was *supplied* with foodstuffs from the Reich (Frank, 1970 v.1:144).

[10] The incentives initially used to ensure prompt delivery of quotas were of an economic nature. The Germans distributed various at-tractive products in the countryside on condition that imposed de-

TABLE IV.5

TOTAL GRAIN QUOTAS IN THE
GENERALGOUVERNEMENT
(In Tons)

Year	Quota	
	Assigned	Collected
1940-1941	1,000,000	383,000
1941-1942	770,000	685,000
1942-1943	1,400,000	1,230,000
1943-1944	1,600,000	1,500,000
1944-1945	425,000	

Source: Madajczyk, 1970 v.2:90.

TABLE IV.6

QUOTAS OF FOOD TO BE SENT TO THE REICH FROM THE
GENERALGOUVERNEMENT
(In Tons)

Year	Potatoes	Sugar	Cattle	Fats	Grain
1940-1941	121,000	4,500	7,510	800	40,000
1941-1942	134,000	4,465	21,498	900	58,000
1942-1943	434,350	28,666	54,272	7,235	633,470
1943-1944	387,741	27,546	53,768		571,682

Source: Madajczyk, 1970 v.1:533.

cent of the quotas imposed were actually collected. Beginning in 1941-1942, however, the Germans managed to raise almost 90 percent of the imposed quotas. In 1942-1943 the

liveries were fulfilled. They started, it seems, by linking the sale of sugar in the countryside to the fulfillment of quotas of eggs (Landau, 1962 v.1:504). The results were so encouraging that two weeks later the *Warschauer Zeitung* announced the beginning of a large-scale campaign to introduce various tools, sewing machines, watches, etc., as premiums to induce peasants to deliver imposed quotas on time (Landau, 1962 v. 1:531; GSHI, Kolekcja Kota, no. 25/10: "Opracowanie: zabór niemiecki," Mar. 13, 1941).

Germans increased the size of compulsory deliveries almost twofold, maintained the almost 90 percent level of collection, and, in a new move, shipped to the Reich about 50 percent of what they squeezed out of the population. (We must keep in mind, however, that the figures for 1942-1943 include the contributions from the district of Galicia, which was added to the GG after the initial German successes in the war with Russia.)

As the war went on, the Germans began to supervise the delivery of foodstuffs very strictly. In July 1942 Frank issued an order declaring a state of emergency (as if life in the GG had until then been "normal") from August 1 to November 30, in order to "secure the collection of crops." The death penalty was set for any sabotage of the German effort. Indeed, statistics compiled by Madajczyk single out 1942 as the year of a dramatic increase in German terror in the countryside.

TABLE IV.7

Poles Killed in the Countryside

Year	No. killed in pacifications and executions	No. murdered
1940	15	699
1941	20	397
1942	122	3,207
1943	308	7,383

Source: Duraczyński, 1974:80-81.

Conditions of Work

Conditions of work in the Generalgouvernement were consistent with the basic pattern of German occupation: maximum exploitation with minimum maintenance cost. In the first place, freedom of the labor market was abolished, and the Arbeitsamte could direct workers wherever they chose.

Numerous decrees regulating labor relations were issued. In most cases they stated the obligations—rarely the rights —of employees. As of August 1943, no one could refuse to work on any assignment, including those that could be completed only after regular working hours or during a holiday; only with an employer's consent could one terminate work in any enterprise. Employers, on the other hand, were forbidden to compete for labor, nor could they offer incentives or rewards in excess of the officially permitted wage scale (Landau, 1963 v.3:162). Fringe benefits for Poles were drastically reduced. The right to a vacation was canceled; a worker could be granted a vacation only at the discretion of his employer and only for a period not to exceed six days a year (Pospieszalski, 1958:278). Social security benefits were discontinued, and discretionary supplements were instead given to those in need. Unemployment benefits were practically nonexistent, and to apply for them was the equivalent of putting oneself on the list of conscripts for labor in Germany. Sick leave payments were cut in half, and the retirement pension was unified across the board and set at 200 złotych per month, which seemed to be an increase of about 72 percent for the average worker, but actually had no real value (Madajczyk, 1970 v.2:85-86). Other similar "achievements" in the area of retirement pensions were masqueraded as "beneficial acts" of the Nazi rule in Poland.[11]

A unique form of exploitation of the Polish labor force— the Baudienst—should be mentioned here. Following its introduction in December 1940, Polish men between 18 and 25 years of age were drafted into this labor service, at first for three and later for seven months. They were subjected to military discipline and received one złoty per day plus room and board. A particularly demoralizing aspect of this

[11] Pensions were granted to officers who served in the German and Austro-Hungarian army before World War I (Landau, 1962 v.1:756), and in 1943 they were extended to the families of officers killed by the NKVD in the Katyń forests (Landau, 1963 v.3:117).

service stemmed from the fact that the subleaders of the work detachments, the *Vorarbeiters*, were chosen from among the draftees and were charged with enforcing discipline in exchange for various small privileges (HL, PUC: MSW, *Wydział Społeczny*, "Sprawozdanie sytuacyjne z ziem polskich," no. 4/43, p. 16). At its peak, the Baudienst numbered 45,000 men, and through its services the Germans received 28 million working days for practically nothing. Some of its camps—in Libań, near Cracow, and Solec, in Warsaw—were well known for the brutality with which conscripted Poles were kept in obedience. The official purpose of the Baudienst was to teach the Poles work and discipline. It certainly failed in the latter: one night at the end of July 1944, when the Germans temporarily lost control of the situation, almost all the conscripts of the Baudienst ran away. The few that stayed, Frank angrily commented, had probably overslept and would soon follow in the footsteps of the others (Frank, 1970 v.2:531).

The Black Market

With more than 80 percent of the population's needs provided by the black market (Skalniak, 1966:133), the extralegal economy grew to unheard-of dimensions. The term *black economy* describes the situation better than *black market*. Everyone did *some* business on the black market, and unless one was a really big dealer, each black market transaction (typically, though not exclusively, bringing food to the city from the countryside) could be a dangerous and time-consuming undertaking.

All legitimate businesses had to deal on the black market and maintained two bookkeeping systems. Typically, they also had two wage scales for the workers. Officially, wages, though somewhat regulated, were supposed to remain frozen at the prewar level. Nonetheless, it is reported that in 1943-1944 Polish enterprises often paid 8 to 10 złotych per hour, and in some cases highly qualified personnel were

109

receiving as much as 35 złotych per hour (Madajczyk, 1970 v. 2:67). On many jobs workers were served free, or almost free, dinners,[12] or they were allowed to work on private jobs during their working hours. In other places absenteeism was tolerated; by 1943 an average of 30 percent of all workers was absent from work. Generally speaking, it was perfectly normal for a worker to show up at his place of work for only about four days a week (Madajczyk, 1970 v.2:68), so that the rest of his time could be devoted to the black market. A joke popular at the time describes the situation fairly. Two friends who had not seen each other for a long time met in the street:

"What are you doing?"
"I am working in the city hall."
"And your wife, how is she?"
"She is working in a paper store."
"And your daughter?"
"She is working in a plant."
"How the hell do you live?"
"Thank God, my son is unemployed."

As in other aspects of life in this society, the greatest difficulties in the economic sphere stemmed from the lack of free communication, that is, prohibition of the free flow of goods and information about market conditions. Such disruption of the flow of goods meant that anyone who could get hold of large quantities of some commodity could control its market by offering prices that others could not meet. Large operators had a clear advantage over small ones, since only they could buy large enough stocks and could afford to bribe the German army to make shipments in military trucks. The easy availability of transportation often tempted Germans themselves to become involved in black

[12] Warsaw's city government spent for that purpose 1.5 million złotych in 1940-1941, 4.5 million in 1941-1942, 3.6 million in 1942-1943, and 7.1 million in 1943-1944 (Ivanka, 1964:435).

110

market operations, particularly as "official" links to the Polish illegal economy were used for huge purchases by the army. Profits on successful large-scale operations were enormous, and fortunes were made in a very short time. Even on a smaller scale, profits in black-marketeering were large enough to attract literally hundreds of thousands of people who had only small amounts of money to invest. Their position was of course much more precarious, as one confiscation could wipe them out entirely.

In the absence of a free flow of information and merchandise, there emerged a fragile and diversified price system. The same merchandise sold for such different prices within the same area that the differential could only be explained by ignorance of the current price levels on the part of inexperienced or hard-pressed sellers (Radford, 1945:191). Of course, the variation in prices induced buyers to seek the most favorable buying opportunities, and instead of trying to find a job, people were often better off looking around for a chance to make a profitable deal. Such unstable conditions favored all kinds of speculators and profiteers over serious entrepreneurs and hardworking people (Landau, 1962 v.1:37).

Bottlenecks in transportation also caused wide price differences among localities. An underground source reports that *after divergences were substantially reduced* in May 1943, they could be represented by the following figures (July 1938 = 100): Lublin, 2,600; Cracow, 3,100; Warsaw, 3,300; Stanisławów, 4,900; Lwów, 6,300 (HL, PUC: MSW, *Wydział Społeczny*, "Sprawozdanie sytuacyjne z ziem polskich," no. 2/43, p. 39).

A special role was played by the ghetto. Its economy was strictly isolated. Because of the disastrous food shortage in the ghetto, the Jews were a reservoir of unusually cheap labor when paid in food purchased on the Aryan side of the wall. Naturally, almost all of its production and export were designed to provide the means to import food. Throughout this period, work in the ghetto for Polish contractors on the other side of the wall continued at a steady pace (Trunk, 1972:82, 83).

Differences in prices attracted speculators. In the overall atmosphere of risk and insecurity, everyone undertaking an economic initiative had to become a speculator. Prudence and careful analysis of investment opportunities were no longer useful; instead, the readiness to risk one's whole fortune in a single venture—and luck—made all the difference between success and failure. The necessarily speculative character of economic life under the occupation is what Kazimierz Wyka (1959) had in mind when he deplored the demoralizing effects of German rule in Poland.

With no means of exchanging information through the normal market structure, the would-be buyer and the would-be seller had no way of finding one another. The missing link was provided by the black market middleman. Indeed, a chain of middlemen appeared, each of whom took his piece from the transaction and each of whom therefore was interested in keeping others in the chain from knowing about one another, lest they be able to deal directly and dispense with his services. As a result, only those who were adjacent links in the chain knew each other, and they were familiar with only those parts of the transaction that involved them. Prices, particularly for rarely needed goods, therefore were usually fixed at random.

The situation was a bit different in the market for items handled on a massive scale, chiefly food. With production limited, the Germans taking part of it, and expansion beyond the most basic level impossible, both supply and demand were inelastic. Yet foodstuffs were distributed as if the market situation were competitive, with thousands of individual small operators having to sell their goods quickly—and hence at competitive prices—to meet current living expenses and to finance the next business operation. On the whole, it is not surprising that there was little sense of

112

fairness in the public perception of binding rules and practices of economic activity.

But we must see the black market in a more positive light as well. Because production was tightly controlled in all areas, people had to find alternative sources of income in order to survive under the pressure of skyrocketing inflation. The primitive system of economic exchange permitted many more people than before the war to make their living as middlemen performing nonproductive services in the economy.

ALIENATION OF WORK

Suddenly, some years after Marx coined the phrase, the Poles had to cope with an acute case of alienation of work. In an admirable essay, "Unplugged Economy," the literary critic Kazimierz Wyka described its consequences with insight rarely found in the analyses of social scientists. Work —one of the major modes for socializing people into patterns of cooperation, providing a powerful link between the satisfaction of individual needs and the common effort, a major avenue for status seeking and social mobility—suddenly lost its capacity for binding the social fabric together. The product of work was appropriated by the Germans and used against the interests of the group producing it, for whom the process, then, became totally alienated, even hostile.

However, even if he ignored the question of how his work was to be used and decided to conform totally to this new imposed system of labor, the worker still could not satisfy even his most basic needs. People found themselves obliged to invest eight to ten hours every day in activities that were exhausting and, from their point of view, a waste of time. "Official" work was thus the chief obstacle to providing for their still unmet, basic needs, and it acquired a powerfully double negative connotation: it demanded long

113

hours of people and prevented them from doing useful work. It is not surprising, therefore, that work-discipline disappeared. Thus the only activity that the Poles were permitted to pursue collectively lost all of its integrating potential, and they could no longer use one of their traditional strategies of opposition to the occupier. Resistance through organic work was out of the question. No one felt that the people could be asked to abstain from politics and, instead, work conscientiously to build up the spiritual and material richness of the country in order to prepare it for the time when it would win back its independence.

In response, social initiative was channeled into all sorts of activities aimed at compensating for some of the hostile characteristics of the work system. Taking care of one's needs in these days meant absenteeism, working at a slow pace, moonlighting, and finally, stealing. These activities did not seem wrong; one was simply compensating for the ridiculous wages and expropriations, and the underground itself called for a "turtle" work pace. People with ethical doubts could consider that all the means of production had, after all, been stolen from them by the Germans, so that they were simply "expropriating the expropriators." To whom did things rightfully belong? The line between reclaiming one's own goods and stealing others' was blurred, and each act was judged individually by the actors:

> Today no property has an owner, no property deserves recognition as belonging to someone. In view of constant robberies, confiscations, stealings, and all forms of compulsory deliveries, we don't feel any longer as owners of our own property, we don't respect others' property, particularly if it belongs to the state, or to the society. Every day something new is missing from tramway cars, everything which can be carried out is taken away from offices of various institutions. Sometimes this has to be done. But it is being done to a degree far exceeding what can be justified on grounds of useful sabotage or the

necessity to provide for one's family's basic needs. . . .
We have lost the sense of property, and it is one of the
elements of our depression, of our being tired beyond
description by enslavement. It is mandatory that we acquire it anew, together with getting back our human
dignity. (*Prawda*, May 1944)

The economic system had profoundly demoralizing effects on Polish society; it was desocializing Poles from the
very basic norms of coexistence, of collective life. There was
no practical way in which a new, substitute norm could be
worked out in the place of the lost "sense of property."
From this perspective, the "unplugged" economy meant
not only that material goods were no longer produced for
the betterment of society, or that individuals no longer
could earn their living, but also that the economy was "un-
plugging" people from society, from other people. It was
forcing them into activities that required a constant breach
of the norms of coexistence, making them forget that the
pursuit of individual interest could not be dissociated from
the framework of life in common. The atomization of Polish society was an effect of the work system introduced by
the Germans.

The end of the war did not bring a prompt return to the
basic norms of coexistence. Several commentators in the
underground, particularly in the last years of the occupation, had worried about such a consequence, and not without reason. Madajczyk reports that the labor force returning from Germany was far more conscientious and better
disciplined than that which had stayed in the GG throughout the occupation. People could not easily give up the pattern of fostering their individual interests at the expense of
others, even though the situation had changed, the Germans had been defeated, and "others" could no longer be
perceived as an unequivocally hostile force.

The ultimate effect of this work system was that, without
knowing Frank's confidential statements, without really

115

being exposed to the ruthlessness of full police terror, Poles still came to realize that the system of work that was forced on them did not in the least take into consideration their needs. The unlimited goals of the German occupation were disclosed through economic exploitation, and the Poles recognized this system as a strategy to disguise the planned extermination. An important consequence of this realization has already been mentioned: conformity to official norms was not a viable choice for the Poles.

CHAPTER V

Collaboration and Cooperation

TRADITIONALLY, the subject of the interaction between Poles and Germans during the occupation has been obscured by the considerable emotional involvement of the contemporaries who reported on it. All contacts across group boundaries, particularly when the groups involved have different goals and openly hostile perceptions of each other, take place in an atmosphere of suspicion of outsiders and moral censure of the group's own members against whom the charge of treason is not infrequently raised. My purpose in this chapter is to formulate the principles on which such contacts can be established and to point out the various forms they may assume. The following discussion rests on the premise that an occupying power, in its official, institutionalized contacts with a subjugated society, will seek three kinds of "goods" necessary to rule the country, and that its official relationships with that society will therefore take a form that is related to its ability to satisfy its need for: authority; expertise; and manpower. When dealing with authority, we shall speak of collaboration; in discussing the latter two goods, we shall speak of cooperation.

Before we present hypotheses about the sociology of collaboration, it may be useful to reflect on the meaning of the concept itself. Only recently has it acquired a peculiar connotation of an uneven distribution of power, an uneven partnership in which one party operates under duress or, even worse, betrays the interests of its own group. In the past, the word *collaboration* was employed only as a synonym for cooperation, specifically in reference to collective work in artistic areas.[1]

[1] A quick perusal of encyclopedias and dictionaries reveals the following: Neither the most recent edition of *Encyclopedia Brittan-*

I think it is important to make a distinction between cooperation and collaboration with the enemy, since under the civilian occupation of Poland, which lasted several years, the surface of interaction between occupier and occupied was very broad. It is inconceivable that all reac-

---

nica nor that of *Collier's Encyclopedia* have entries labeled "Collaboration." Nor can one find the subject in the *Nouveau Larousse Universel* of 1948. The *Encyclopedia Brockhaus* has the word (1970 v.10:350), but there it refers primarily to Pétain's government in France; only in small print does it inform the reader that the word may also be used more generally. *Collaboration* is defined in the *Oxford English Dictionary* of 1961 (v.2:613) (reprint of the 1933 edition) as "To work in conjunction with another or others, to co-operate; esp. in a literary or artistic production, or the like." The definition of *collaboration* in Littré's dictionary of the French language from 1881 (v.1:664) informs us of the French superiority complex: "Participation à un travail littéraire. Si l'art dramatique français règne partout, si l'on ne représente à Saint-Petersbourg, à Madrid, à Naples, à Londres, à Vienne, que des ouvrages français, à qui le devons nous? à la collaboration qui, décuplant le nombre des productions ingénieuses et même originales, permet seule à l'imagination française de devenir, pour ainsi dire, l'imagination du monde. Terme de jurisprudence. Travaux, soins communs du mari et de la femme." Robert's dictionary of 1953 gives the first meaning of *collaboration* as a common pursuit in artistic matters and then adds, as a special meaning: "Mouvement des Français qui durant l'occupation allemande (1940-1944) désiraient travailler au redressement de la France en coopération avec l'Allemagne" (Robert, 1953:819). The *Petit Littré* of 1959 does not have a word about Germany under *collaboration* (1959:369). Finally, Bataglia, in his dictionary of the Italian language (1964 v.3:279), lists four meanings of the word *collaboration*, of which the third seems to reflect specific problems of contemporary Italian politics: "(1) Contribuire con altri, ciascuno nelle propria misura e con propri compiti, alla realizzazione di un'opera, di un'attività, di un lavoro continuativo o a termine (e per lo piú nella sfera intellettuale). (2) Partecipare, apportando il proprio contributo intellettuale, morale e pratico, alla realizzazione di un ideale patriotico, sociale, umanitario. (3) Partecipare alla maggioranza governativa. (4) Attuare un'intesa e una collaborazione con le autorità d'occupazione nemiche (per lo più con riferimento al periodo d'occupazione tedesca durante la Seconda Guerra Modiale)."

tions by the occupied group were acts of resistance, but this does not mean that they were, necessarily, acts of collaboration. For the purpose of clarity, I believe it would be useful to limit the application of the term *collaboration* to the area of politics.

Someone who acquires a business and prospers with the silent blessing of the occupiers (who would typically be in for a cut of his income) should be called a profiteer or a speculator rather than a collaborator, so long as he limits his sphere of activity to profit seeking. Nor would I designate as a collaborator a confidant of the occupier's police (whom I would instead call a renegade or something other to the point) who gives his services out of personal vengeance, for the money, or because he is blackmailed. Additionally, I would not cite as a collaborator an expert who works in an organization that performs services for the local population. Thus, employees of the city administrations or, for example, of the Bank Emisyjny would not fit into this category.

I would label as collaborators those who are prepared to grant the occupier authority, rather than merely to provide expertise or information. Accordingly, collaborators include those who would make the occupier the beneficiary of the trust vested in them by the population that had elected them to positions of authority, or those who are ready to accept posts that are traditionally vested with authority in a given community. By deliberately narrowing the meaning of the word, we should be able to distinguish among different attitudes, because everyone who lived for five years under the occupation *had* to "collaborate" in some way with the occupier.

But of course one cannot easily compartmentalize the continuum of variations of human behavior. Stanley Hoffmann, in an admirable essay on collaboration in France (Hoffmann, 1974:26-44), tried to solve the problem by introducing two concepts: collaboration (that is, with Germany), and collaborationism (that is, with the Nazis).

119

However, even this division did not seem precise enough to distinguish between the different kinds of behavior that fit into the general category of political collaboration. Hoffmann therefore subdivided collaboration into voluntary and involuntary collaboration, and collaborationism into servile and ideological collaborationism (Hoffmann, 1974:29, 30). But he showed convincingly that these attitudes constitute a continuum; that one can move imperceptibly from involuntary to voluntary *collaboration d'état*, and from there to collaborationism; that the difference between the two terms is often obscure; that collaboration and collaborationism are united in a peculiar dialectic:

> there was no clear yardstick to indicate where reason of state ended and folly began. . . . The Laval of 1943 needed a Darnand as a bloody collaborationist cover behind which he could more easily pursue the laborious rearguard action of mere involuntary *collaboration d'état*. But Darnand himself, stubborn soldier and simple mind, found in *collaboration d'état* an invitation to collaborationism. (Hoffmann, 1974:29, 31)

THE SOCIOLOGY OF COLLABORATION

Collaborationists in Europe in 1939-1945 came predominantly from within the prewar power establishments. At first glance this phenomenon is puzzling and contrary to what we might expect, since it means that collaboration was not simply engineered and implemented by local fascist movements supporting the Nazi invaders. In fact, French fascists were kept at bay by the Germans in Paris, while the Pétain government was retained in "power" at Vichy (Paxton, 1972:230-231); Czech fascists were not allowed to challenge Hacha effectively (Mastny, 1971:24, 58-60); Quisling's relationships with the Reichskommissar in Norway, Terboven, were difficult, and indeed, the Norwegian Supreme Court and the civil service, two important segments of the prewar power establishment, were able to curb Quisling's zeal successfully and set the pace of collaboration themselves (Littlejohn, 1972:44, 45). This pattern of collaboration calls for explanation, if only because it contradicts what one would think should most probably happen: namely, that the majority of collaborators should be recruited from the groups that previously had been alienated from the power establishments in the subjugated countries.

Clearly, in order to understand the phenomenon of collaboration we must first study the form of government that existed in the occupied country prior to its defeat and identify the groups and/or individuals that the occupier might possibly approach. Let us not forget that in seeking collaboration he is looking for authority, and it is only from an examination of the operation of the government that he could tell which groups command this authority. Let us examine two cases.

First, let us assume that large and/or important segments of the population in a given country perceive the government as illegitimate and imposed at the expense of groups excluded from power. Where, in the context of illegitimate government, would future addressees of offers of collaboration be found? Among the groups excluded from power?

In the first place, those groups are not all equally attractive to the occupier from the point of view of commanding authentic support in the society. It is quite probable, and perhaps even inevitable, that among the excluded groups under authoritarianism (or totalitarianism) one would find some unpopular ones, whose isolation and destruction is often presented by the rulers as precisely the need that justifies authoritarianism. Thus, not every victim of illegitimate or authoritarian government is fit to inherit power from a deposed ruler and then proceed to exercise authority.

On the other hand, a quasi- or nonlegitimate government can rule only when it performs well and/or is capable of using the apparatus of coercion effectively. When it performs poorly and its ability to coerce has to be curbed, by

121

the occupier for example, it is better for the latter to look for allies elsewhere. After the country has been conquered, its preconflict quasi- or nonlegitimate government can hardly make an acceptable offer of collaboration to the occupying power. What little loyalty it commanded in the past most certainly will not survive total military defeat.[2]

Finally, social forces and leaders that were illegitimately excluded from power under prewar authoritarianism may be approached by the occupier with an offer of collaboration. But it is very unlikely that collaborators can be found among them. These leaders apparently were not willing to compromise with local authoritarianism before a military defeat; therefore one must be skeptical about their readiness to compromise with a hostile and ipso facto authoritarian foreign invader.[3]

Let us, then, examine the case in which the prewar government in a given country enjoyed strong legitimacy. Where should the occupier search for collaborators now?

It is very unlikely that collaborators who are able to command some authority can be found outside the prewar establishment. By virtue of its legitimacy, only marginal,

---

[2] Guglielmo Ferrero, in his marvelous book *The Principles of Power*, quotes a fragment of conversation that may serve here as a good illustration: " 'Do you imagine that your master could enter Paris in this fashion after having lost such a battle as I have lost.' That was the question Francis II, entering Vienna after Austerlitz amid the acclamations of his people, put to the French ambassador" (Ferrero, 1942:109).

[3] A special case should be distinguished in this analysis: occupation of a multinational state, where the invader may be recognized as a "liberator" of a sizable national minority holding accumulated grievances against the previously ruling elite. This, however, does not apply to the Generalgouvernement. Although Poland was a multinational state before the war, the Germans were trying to find collaborators in the GG, where, after the incorporation of western parts of Poland by Germany and eastern parts by Russia, the population was unusually homogenous ethnically. Only one sizable minority—the Jews—lived in the area. Obviously, their collaboration would not interest the Germans.

unimportant groups or groups recognized by the majority as hostile remain outside of the system. It would not be worth the occupier's time to seek their support because there would be a negligible difference in the cost of keeping the country under control with or without these groups' support.

On the other hand, it should be very profitable for the occupier to obtain in some form the support of the preconflict government. To be sure, interest in collaboration would be mutual. The help of the native central administration might be so valuable to the invader that he would be willing to grant large concessions in order to secure it, offering conditions under which the former government, or some part of the government structure, could cooperate without too much embarrassment. At the same time, the defeated government might want to minimize as far as possible the adverse consequences of its defeat; as a legitimate government, it has the capacity to absorb defeat and humiliation that a nonlegitimate government lacks. Thus it could function under conditions of limited sovereignty without losing the allegiance of its people in the process. It could afford, to a certain degree, to collaborate.

We may summarize the preceding discussion as follows: it is easiest, and at the same time, most rewarding, for the occupier to find collaborators within the political establishment of a country that enjoyed legitimate government prior to military defeat and occupation. Conversely, there is no immediately suitable candidate for collaboration in a country that did not have legitimate government prior to defeat, with the exception of formerly repressed minorities with irredentist sympathies. Such minorities, however, cannot command the obedience of the majority nationality in a given territory. A highly probable development in such a case would be territorial secession and establishment of a new satellite state in the areas populated by the ethnic minority.

This discussion posits as an assumption that the occupier enjoys perfect flexibility in choosing collaborators. In reality, this rarely will be the case, particularly in modern times, when conquests are no longer motivated primarily by greed but instead are justified in terms of some ideology that precludes the possibility of strictly pragmatic calculation in the choice of allies. Ideology imposes restrictions on rationality of choice. Typically, therefore, some groups living in the conquered territory will be a priori excluded from consideration as candidates for collaboration. For example, the functionaries of the Polish "bourgeois" state were summarily rejected by the Russians in the part of Poland they occupied in 1939, or, as already mentioned, the Jews would never be considered by the Germans in the territories they occupied. Such "ideological" considerations help to explain a choice of collaborators that would not follow from the paradigm we have established.[4]

[4] Thus, after the war, the Americans' uncompromising adherence to the policy of denazification forced them to turn for help in occupied Germany to the leftovers of German Jewry (Zink, 1949), while the Soviets, having taken half of Poland and being unable to fill all positions in the administration with members of the former Polish Communist Party (which was decimated during the purges), also turned to Jews for help. They rightly suspected that the policy of "Polonization" before the war had successfully alienated all ethnic groups; only the Jews would not share the separatist hopes aroused in all the other non-Polish nationalities after the collapse of the Polish state. Indeed, Polish anti-Semitism in German-occupied territories fed for a long time on news and rumors about "Jews helping the Reds" in the Soviet-occupied zone (GSHI, PRM 5: *List do gen. Sikorskiego*, Dec. 13, 1939; PRM 12: doc. no. 880/XXIII). The Germans, for obvious reasons, could not and never wished to pretend to be the "liberators" of the only sizable minority in the GG: the Jews. Did Judenrate in Eastern Europe collaborate with the Germans? Jewish communities had a long tradition of compliance with various governments' demands for delivery of goods of all sorts. But these goods were always, as Trunk says, "replaceable goods," never life itself (Trunk, 1972:xxxi). Since the latter became an issue during the Second World War, rabbinates in Kowno and Wilno ruled in the matter, and they arrived at different conclusions. Kowno's rabbi ruled that, "If a Jewish community . . . has been condemned to physical destruction, and there are means of rescuing part of it, the

124

It follows from our paradigm that there was no suitable structural framework for collaboration in the General-gouvernement. What made it even less likely that the occupiers would sponsor a collaborationist government was that the model of occupation, based on the principle of unlimited exploitation, specifically prohibited the Germans to contemplate granting any concessions to the subjugated populace. The logic of unlimited exploitation imposed no limits on the quality of sacrifices that could be requested of the subdued population, nor did it allow for justification of any delay in fulfilling them. To the extent that collaboration means that the occupying power seeks to employ in its service those local institutions that wield authority, the institutions must be allowed—on terms specified by the occupier—to exercise

---

leaders of the community should have the courage to assume the responsibility to act and rescue what is possible" (Trunk, 1972: xxxii). In contrast, the Wilno rabbinate adhered strictly to the opinion of Maimonides, who had said: "If pagans should tell them [the Jews], 'Give us one of yours and we shall kill him, otherwise we shall kill all of you,' they all should be killed and not a single Jewish soul should be delivered" (Trunk, 1972:xxxi). To what degree could the Kowno rabbinate ruling establish a basis for collaborating with the Germans? If we ask the question that way, we may completely miss the point. In discussing the question of collaboration, it is of primary importance to note that the Judenrat was called into existence by an *administrative German ordinance*, and its function was to transmit and supervise the execution of German regulations issued to the Jewish population. A *Schnellbrief* sent by Heydrich on September 21, 1939, ordered commanders of the *Einsatzgruppen* operating in Poland to establish Councils of Jewish Elders in each Jewish community. Councils were to be "fully responsible (in the literal sense of the word) for the exact execution according to terms of all instructions released or yet to be released" (Trunk, 1972:2). Two months later Frank's decree, identical in spirit to Heydrich's letter, set guidelines for the establishment of the Judenrat. The Judenrat was de facto appointed by the Germans, sometimes from among the leaders of the Jewish community, sometimes at random (Trunk, 1972:26). The position of the Judenrat was that of a group of hostages.

that authority. Within the unlimited exploitation model, they could not have this opportunity.

Nonetheless, perhaps because the logic of their own rule in the East was never stated definitively or, probably, even understood by the Nazis themselves, they made some half-serious explorations into the possibility of sponsoring a collaborationist government in the GG. Since the presence or absence of such government was a crucial factor for the plight of the occupied countries in Europe during the Second World War, I think that we should briefly describe these attempts to find collaborationists in Poland (even though we know that they were doomed to failure), for there was a certain internal logic in them.

"SOVEREIGN" POLAND

One possible solution for the Polish problem envisaged in the early days of the occupation by the Germans was the creation of a "token Polish state," a *Reststaat*.[5] Two groups in Polish society were queried about their willingness to help in such a project.

In March 1939 the Germans had tried to get in touch with peasant leader Wincenty Witos, who at the time was in exile in Czechoslovakia after having lost his appeal in the

[5] There is an interesting discussion of this problem between two Polish historians, C. Madajczyk (1961 and 1964) and L. Herzog (1962). The point in dispute is whether Hitler seriously envisaged the creation of a token Polish state. Herzog claims that all alleged attempts by the Germans in that direction were only a part of Hitler's deception, which he played so well in diplomacy and foreign policy. The documentation that Herzog quotes in support of his point seems convincing to me, but I do not think that we should therefore dismiss the whole "project" as an irrelevant incident. It should be taken seriously, if only because Hitler's subordinates believed in it; that it was only a part of a strategy of deceit was not fully clear to those who were instrumental in carrying it through. Curiously enough, Madajczyk fails to make this point in his response to Herzog's polemical article.

Brześć trial. Witos immediately informed the Polish authorities about this incident and, partly as a result of German approaches, decided to come back to Poland, although he knew that he could be sent to prison on his return (Madajczyk, 1961:28).

When the hostilities ended in October 1939, Witos was arrested shortly after being found by the Germans, along with many other Poles who had played prominent roles in public life before the war. The Gestapo sent him to the prison at Rzeszów, where he was apparently approached again with an offer of collaboration, which he refused. He also rejected a proposal that he write an "objective" history of the peasant movement, suspecting that such a work would primarily serve as a directory to ferret out all activists of the movement who had not been arrested thus far. In spite of his refusal to cooperate, the conditions of his confinement remained, to say the least, very liberal.[6] In March 1941 he was permitted to return to his house at Wierzchosławice, where he remained until the end of the war, with the authorities periodically checking on him (Kotula, 1959: 73-80; Madajczyk, 1970 v.1:105). Although this treatment was highly unusual, we should not attribute too much significance to Witos's fate. His survival was due, in all probability, more to some lucky coincidence than to a carefully designed policy. Nonetheless, it is worth noting that he was spared from death, the usual fate of members of the Polish leadership stratum and, indeed, of several other prominent leaders of the peasant movement itself.

It seems quite apparent—and Witos's fate is also indicative in this respect—that it was among the peasantry that the Germans were initially willing to look for collaborators. The *Völkisch* ethos naturally designated the peasants as vir-

---

[6] After five months in Rzeszów, Witos was taken to a jail in Berlin for another five weeks and, upon release, committed to a sanatorium in Potsdam. Later he was sent to Zakopane, a fashionable health spa in the mountains, where he remained under the Gestapo's supervision.

tually the only social class uncontaminated with either bourgeois or revolutionary influences. Also, it was in the countryside that the German armies were received with the least hostility. German officials must have taken this attitude into consideration when they prepared the internal memorandum stating that only with the support of the peasantry would Germany be able to set up a collaborationist regime in Poland (Madajczyk, 1961:28).

Another group approached by the Germans with propositions for collaboration were prominent patricians and aristocrats with openly conservative views and a political tradition of loyalty and collaboration with the Austro-Hungarian monarchy before the First World War. Professor Stanisław Estreicher, the most prominent *Stańczyk*, was reported to have been contacted by the Germans.[7] The names of Princes Zdzisław Lubomirski and Janusz Radziwiłł and that of Count Adam Ronikier were mentioned as other candidates consulted after Estreicher's refusal (Landau, 1962 v.1:91).[8]

---

[7] The *Stańczycy* were a group of conservative Galician politicians formed after the collapse of the 1863 uprising. They opposed the patriotic-conspiratorial orientation in politics and advocated collaboration with the Austrian monarchy. From the 1870s and 80s they occupied prominent positions in Galicia. Estreicher, who came from a prominent patrician family in Cracow, was a professor of law and at one time president (*rektor*) of Jagiellonian University. He was a coeditor and one of the most important contributors to *Czas*, one of the two periodicals of the Stańczyk group (the other was *Przegląd Polski*). Professor Estreicher was arrested on November 6, 1939, together with the entire professorial body of Jagiellonian University and other Cracow institutions of higher learning. He died in Sachsenhausen concentration camp.

[8] More information on this subject may be of some historical interest. Contrary to what Landau says, no German approaches seem to have been made to Ronikier in November 1939. Ronikier would have written about them in his memoirs if they had taken place, simply because he did not fail to mention a rather vague conversation held in March 1941 with an unspecified Reich minister, whom he allegedly knew from before the war. During the conversation the

Thus the Germans approached a representative of the Polish peasant movement, the least hostile, from their point of view, of the three main political movements alienated from the Second Republic. They also appealed to conservative aristocratic elements, and were justified in doing so on two grounds: first, this class had a tradition of collaboration; second, the traditional ethos of noblesse oblige stresses the responsibility of the aristocracy for "its people" when in need and its obligation to protect them. One must take into account this attitude of the aristocracy in order to understand why Prince Janusz Radziwiłł, Counts Ronikier, Po-

---

German said something to the effect that "whoever at one time was in politics will always be prone to get back into it." Ronikier responded that his "politics today is not to get involved in politics at all." In reflecting on this exchange of bon mots, Ronikier concluded that the German would have made some kind of an offer had he not answered his opening statement in this way. His supposition was reinforced when the visitor asked Ronikier for permission to relate their conversation to Goering (Ronikier, n.d.:103-105). However, it seems almost certain that in 1944 Ronikier was approached by the Gestapo and offered a safe-conduct pass out of the country in return for serving as a go-between to help to negotiate a formula of modus vivendi between Germany and the Polish government in London. He never left, however, because he did not secure permission for the journey from the Polish underground, where he was not viewed as a serious partner (Ronikier, n.d.:351ff.; HL, PUC: MSW, *Wydział Społeczny*, "Sprawozdanie sytuacyjne z ziem polskich," no. 2/44). But if the proposition had ever been made, he was a logical choice for carrying it out as the former president of the Main Welfare Council from the time of the First World War (a position that he occupied again during World War II), in the company of Estreicher and Prince Lubomirski, a former member of the Rada Regencyjna. This last institution was a temporary, three-man administrative body set up in September 1917 by the German and Austrian emperors in Warsaw. It was supposed to exercise limited authority over the territories of the former Polish kingdom until a regent or a monarch was ready to take over. After little more than a year, in November 1918, it indeed transferred its power—to Józef Piłsudski.

129

tocki, Plater-Zyberk, and Pusłowski, Countess Tarnowska, and others (Ronikier, n.d.:26) participated in the formation and works of the Rada Główna Opiekuńcza (Main Welfare Council).[9]

[9] Three more "attempts" to create a pro-German Polish government should be mentioned here in order to complete the record. The first, initiated by a declared Germanophile, Professor Władysław Studnicki, has been very well described by Weinstein (1967). Documentation presented by him shows clearly that the Germans did not take Studnicki's proposals seriously, knowing well that he could not muster enough significant support from any strata of Polish society to make his projects worth their consideration. The second attempt was an alleged public declaration by a former Polish prime minister, Professor Leon Kozłowski, of readiness to create a pro-German government after he escaped from Russia in 1941. After his release from prison in 1941 he joined Anders's Army, in which he was given the prominent post of quartermaster general (*Szef Intendentury*). However, for reasons unknown (he may still have feared the Russians), he fled to the German side of the front. He was taken to Berlin, where several officials talked to him, and he was permitted to grant an interview, entitled "De Samara à Berlin," to the *Journal de Genève* on December 20, 1941. After this, news traveled far that he had offered to join a pro-German Polish government. The rumor was false, however. The Germans must have used his defection in their anti-Bolshevik propaganda, but the whole affair was interpreted incorrectly in Polish circles as an abortive attempt to create a "Quisling" government. Kozłowski was sentenced to death for desertion by a Polish military court, but the sentence could not be carried out, as he died in Berlin in unknown circumstances, possibly during an Allied bombing. The whole affair still awaits full clarification (HIA, PGC: Box 60; Pełczyński, 1973:210). The third and last "attempt" that I want to mention here is probably linked to the preparations of the July coup by the German army. It took place in Budapest, where Count Bem, a Hungarian citizen and a major in the Polish army, was approached by an acquaintance of his, "an eminent member of Russian emigration," who told Bem that, on instructions from the German military attaché in Budapest, he was seeking contacts with the Polish government in London or with eminent members of the local Polish émigrés, preferably with officers. The Germans wanted to know under what preliminary conditions the Poles would agree to begin talks with them. Bem responded that in order to begin negotiations, Poles would demand restitution of Poland in its 1939 frontiers.

The Sociology of Cooperation

Finding collaborationists and setting up a collaborationists' regime in an occupied country requires not only that there be candidates available for that task but, first of all, that a major political decision be made by the occupier. It it necessary for the occupier to recognize the sovereignty, however truncated, of the conquered nation and to maintain such conditions in the occupation that the population recognizes that this "sovereignty," even within its limits, is the lesser evil when compared with what could be. Otherwise, collaborationists become a liability instead of an asset. Rather than placating their people so that they will willingly give the occupier what he wants—to spare him the cost of taking it by force—they will require from the occupier protection from the wrath and contempt of their own people. In this case collaboration becomes absurd, the contrary of what was intended. But with or without collaboration, the newly acquired territory must be administered in some way. Whether or not the politicians are ready to make the major decisions, they must cope with the daily tasks of administration.

When we leave the political dimension, we move from

Two days later the Russian go-between told Bem that the German attaché had called Berlin in his presence and reported Bem's opinion to a certain "N." In response, he received instructions to get in touch, through Bem, with someone who could report to the Polish government the following offer: the German side was prepared to issue immediately a manifesto proclaiming Polish independence within 1939 frontiers; Poland would be linked in an anti-Bolshevik military alliance with Germany; Polish foreign policy would be coordinated with Berlin's, and the staffs of the armies of the two countries would be in permanent contact. "Germans consider the whole matter very urgent and request a response within three days." The incident took place at the beginning of March 1944 (GSHI, PRM 121: doc. no. L.dz. 792/II/44, "Depesza Szyfr," Mar. 5, 1944). Broszat (1965:18-19) also mentions some conversations held with Polish émigrés in Switzerland in October 1939 concerning the *Reststaat*.

problems of collaboration to problems of cooperation. The occupier, its own population mobilized for total war, simply lacks the personnel to effect and supervise the exploitation of conquered territories. He needs *manpower*, to assure the sheer physical presence of his "agents" wherever necessary, and *expertise*, as some tasks can be fulfilled only by people possessing special skills. In order to find qualified administrators, he must staff the ranks of the auxiliary administration with the local population.

The pattern of cooperation of the Polish auxiliary administration during the occupation appears to have differed according to whether the administration was required to provide expertise or manpower. This functional differentiation overlapped closely with division into urban and rural administration. In the countryside the Polish administration had little to do except to supervise the collection and delivery of the agricultural quotas set by the occupier. No special skills were needed to accomplish this assignment. On the other hand, city administrations were entrusted with the complex tasks of running large bureaucracies (the Warsaw city administration, for instance, had over 30,000 employees) and maintaining at an adequate level the numerous services indispensable to an urban population. Consequently, urban administration had to be staffed by "experts" (Kulski, 1964:139, 140; Ivanka, 1964:411, 451).

Depending on whether the auxiliary administration was retained to serve the German need for manpower or for expertise, its relationships with superordinates (the Germans) and subordinates (the local Polish population) were different. In the cities the administration was able to retain some degree of independence from the Germans, and because it provided services, it was not perceived by the local population as an unequivocally hostile transmission belt of German exploitation. In the countryside administrators did not enjoy either advantage. They were not entrusted with distribution of any kind of services to the rural Polish population but were instead charged with the supervision of

German exploitation. As no expertise was required for this activity, the personnel in the administration was perfectly exchangeable and, therefore, totally susceptible to German control.

EMPLOYMENT IN LOCAL ADMINISTRATION

Immediately after the war was lost and the Polish state officially dissolved, all former employees of the public sector found themselves without sources of income, and in many cases without qualifications for anything but administrative jobs. An underground report on the activities of the occupation authorities between September 1939 and November 1940 notes that unemployment affected government employees more severely than any other workers. Employees of the local administration were considerably better off, the report states, because only 30 to 40 percent of them were jobless (GSHI, A 9 III 1/1: "Działalność władz okupacyjnych . . . 1.IX.1939–1.XI.1940," p. 240).

Such was the situation at the beginning of the occupation. Ultimately, however, and surprisingly, considering that there was no collaborationist government, a high number of "brain workers" (as they are called in Polish statistics) found employment in the public sector. At Nuremberg, Hans Frank testified that about 280,000 Poles and Ukrainians were employed as "government officials or civil service in the public services of the GG" (IMT, v.12:12). This estimate is reasonably accurate.[10]

[10] Archives of the Staatistisches Amt for the GG reveal that in March 1944, 228,600 "brain workers" were employed in the government service. This number excludes the district of Galicia and the employees of the Ostbahn in Warsaw and Cracow (Madajczyk, 1970 v.2:25). In his almanac on the GG, published in 1942, du Prel estimates the personnel of the Ostbahn at 70,000 and of the postal service at 7,000 (1942:83, 90). In another collection of articles on the GG, written by important functionaries of the German administration in 1943, the supervisor of the railway in the GG, Gerteis, estimates that Ostbahn employs 7,000 *Reichsdeutsche*, 1,500 *Volksdeutsche*, and

In comparing the 280,000 employees in the public sector of the GG with the 385,000 before the war,[11] we must remember that not all of Poland was under Frank's administration. Only half of Poland was in German hands before June 1941; the westernmost part of the country was incorporated into the Reich, and the GG originally included only about one-third of the former Polish territory, with about 45 percent of its former population. Even after the district of Galicia was added to the GG, considerable parts of Polish eastern territories were still not under Frank's administration, but under the Ostministerium. Given these facts, and keeping in mind that not until 1944 were 280,000 people employed in the auxiliary administration,[12] we must recognize that, in spite of the dissolution of the Polish state in September 1939, the majority of those who in various

---

"über 100,000 Nichtsdeutsche" (Bühler, 1943:287). Du Prel (1942) mentions various localities in which local administration was almost entirely Polish. In Warsaw alone, more than 30,000 Poles were employed in the city administration (Kulski, 1964:163). In an interview for the German press in spring of 1944, Frank estimated the number of "non-German" employees of the GG at 260,000 (Pospieszalski, 1958:49).

[11] According to Żarnowski's figures, there were 800,000 "brain workers" in Poland in 1939. About 63,000 people classified in this category were members of various "professions." Not counting the professionals, approximately 56% of all people in the category of "brain workers" were employed in public service in 1931. If we assume the same percentage for 1939 (although possibly it was slightly higher then), we have about 385,000 "brain workers," who were not members of the professions, employed in the public sector in 1939.

[12] In April 1941, for example, the total number of Poles employed by the government of the GG was estimated by Frank at 130,000 (Pospieszalski, 1958:48). But the situation changed over time, and an underground report compiled in 1944 informs us that the number of insured "brain workers" in the GG represented about 150% of the prewar level. At the same time, employment of workers had reached only 90% of the prewar level, as measured by the number of insured in the GG (HL, PUC: MSW, *Wydział Społeczny*, "Sprawozdanie sytuacyjne z ziem polskich," no. 2/44).

capacities had served the state in central and local administration eventually found employment and were discharging public functions.

CITY ADMINISTRATION

The nation-state, its institutions and its structure, is, in Talcott Parsons's words, an "institutionalized normative culture." One of the universals of this normative culture—no matter how different its content might be from one nation-state to another—is that its citizens owe loyalty to its institutions. When a state is forcibly dissolved by some external agent, a threatening insecurity enters the lives of its citizens. They lose the concrete formulations of their normative orientation, the source of authority, and the specification of appropriate behavior in many of their interactions outside the most intimate circle of "meaningful others." Typically, the population has an additional burden to bear: a last moment appeal from the former authorities that they do not surrender to force, that they not recognize the authority of the occupier, that they continue to fight against him. How does one who wishes to follow such an appeal know what behavior is expected of him? Soldiers know that when captured they are to give personal information, serial number, and outfit, and that they do not have to answer any other questions. Later, when they arrive at a POW camp, they find clear and detailed sets of regulations that they have to follow. *But there is no comparable "defeat code" for civilians.*

Since people, naturally, want to live, preferably in peace, the dilemmas of two Weberian ethics come to the fore. Should one, for instance, accept the position of mayor in the local administration if it is offered by the occupier? Should people employed in the administration yield to pressure that they sign a statement swearing that in obedience to the occupier's administration they will conscientiously and faithfully discharge their functions and that they

135

no longer consider themselves bound by their earlier oath of loyalty to the Polish state (*Wiadomości Polskie*, Dec. 15, 1940)? Should members of the professions agree to sign such statements in order to obtain licenses to practice?

With the legitimate source of authority absent, and with a patently illegitimate authority demanding that people formally (by accepting positions offered to them) or symbolically (by signing oaths of allegiance) declare their recognition of its right to command, Poles faced with such decisions experienced dramatic conflicts. Furthermore, normlessness did not end even if one received approval from, say, the underground, and was allowed to acquiesce in initial German requests. Indeed, his new problems might be more subtle, difficult to handle, and frustrating, as they required that he, while on the job, constantly evaluate specific German requests and decide wether compliance was justified. The chief representative of the Polish underground in the country, the Government Delegate Cyryl Ratajski,[13] reported to London on March 13, 1941: "Normalization of opinion in the society: this is one of the most difficult tasks. Different social groups ask for my opinion in matters related to their professions—railmen, artists, doctors, employees of city administration, etc., and they demand that I inform them *what are the admissible limits of their cooperation with the occupier*. Through various social organizations I try to answer their queries, keeping in mind than an over-

[13] The Government Delegacy was the highest civilian office in the underground. From April 1944 its incumbent carried the title of Deputy Prime Minister of the Polish Government. The office in the GG (initially there were three separate delegacies: in the territories occupied by the Soviet Union, in the territories incorporated into the Reich, and in the GG) was successively occupied by Ratajski (Dec. 3, 1940–Sept. 15, 1942), Jan Piekałkiewicz (Sept. 5, 1942–Feb. 19, 1943), Jan Stanisław Jankowski (Mar. 1, 1943–Mar. 27, 1945), and Stefan Korboński (Apr. 1, 1945–June 29, 1945). On the negotiations that led to the creation of the office of the Delegate, and on temporary arrangements prior to the nomination of Ratajski, see Korboński (1975:40-45) and Garliński (1975:225-226).

hasty decision, which could not be complied with by the society, would harm the prestige of the office of the Delegate" (UPST, *Teka* 74/26).

Normative void was one of the most painful consequences of the dissolution of the Polish state. People did not know how to behave when they were forced to interact with the occupier; they could scarcely be expected to make decisions on their own. They sought advice frantically, looking for others who indirectly could share responsibility with them, or simply for someone who would tell them what to do. But where could they turn for consultation and advice?[14] Only during the latter part of the occupation did the underground become so firmly institutionalized that various groups and individuals had relatively easy access to its highest echelons.

It is important to note here that in these circumstances the Polish auxiliary administration in the cities was able to cope with the apparent normlessness better than many other professional groups in the society. How did this come to be so? In my opinion, it was an unanticipated consequence of the German policy of granting exemptions from labor conscription to those who worked in enterprises related to military production and in various agencies of the local government. Those persons caught in a roundup who could show an *Ausweiss* proving their employment in these organizations had (at least in the first few years) a good chance of being released instead of being sent to work in Germany or to a concentration camp. Consequently, employment in German-sponsored institutions, the source of good "identification papers" and therefore of relative security (Broszat, 1965:77), was used for cover by the underground. The employment of members of the underground in the local administration and the consequent opportunity for the heads of that administration to be in permanent consultation with civilian underground authorities (Rybicki, 1965:66-68, 104; Kulski, 1964:30-43) helped to reduce the normative ambig-

[14] See Chap. XI below for more details about this aspect of authority vacuum and ways to cope with it.

uity of that institution. It was very significant that those people who knew well priorities and requirements, stemming from their active participation in an organized collective effort to eventually regain independence, worked in agencies of the local administration. There they could engage in large-scale activities of dubious legality that depended on the knowledge and active support of relatively large numbers of employees. Both Julian Kulski and Stanisław Rybicki, the Polish mayors of Warsaw and Częstochowa, respectively, testified to the integrity and courage of their administrations.

Because certificate of employment in local government resulted in relative security, another social initiative developed that further contributed to strengthening the ability of the local government to cope with normlessness. Since the intelligentsia was threatened with extinction, Poles already serving in the city government created many new positions calling for "experts" and manual workers and tried to inflate the ranks of administration in order to provide not only income but also the valuable *Ausweiss* for members of the intelligentsia. As a consequence, local government, which had a direct and important impact on the functioning of the German occupation, was staffed with personnel unusually skilled, flexible, versatile, and ingenious. The very jobs that in normal times were performed by unimaginative clerks and bureaucrats were in wartime held by university professors, lawyers, politicians, officers, and high civil servants, who were by training and experience able to react promptly to unexpected and unusual events. This pattern of recruitment helped to reduce the normative ambiguity experienced by employees of the local administration, who were exposed to contradictory pressures of the occupier's demands on the one side, and the population's needs on the other. In addition, as people like Kulski, Ivanka, and Rybicki testified, the high quality of professional services and expertise of the administration gave it a certain degree of independence, a certain prestige and power, vis-à-vis the

Germans.[15] By realizing that power within bureaucracies rested with "experts," they anticipated by some twenty years Crozier's analysis of the bureaucratic phenomenon. Thus, curiously, it seems as if the pressures of occupation made the Polish society adjust in a manner that Mancur Olson singled out as the most economical when he argued that the most critical commodity that permits a social system subject to unusually severe strains and shortages to survive is neither food nor raw materials but "skilled and versatile people" (Olson, 1963:146).

THE AUXILIARY ADMINISTRATION IN THE COUNTRYSIDE

The reception given the invading German army in the countryside has not been a very fashionable theme in Polish historiography, which has tended by and large to picture the war period as one of heroic struggle by a united society against the "Hun invasion." Nonetheless, even in official published sources we find acknowledgment that the invader was not received in the same manner throughout the country, and that not all strata of Polish society participated in the underground struggle with equal zeal.[16] Several

[15] Kulski's personal translator throughout the war was Dr. Emil Kipa, the former Polish consul general in Hamburg. The German mayor of Warsaw, Leist, always addressed him as Herr Generalkonsul (Kulski, 1964:24). For more information on how Polish experts employed in the administration enjoyed relative "power," consult the memoirs of Ivanka and of Feliks Młynarski, the director of the Bank Emisyjny in the GG (1971:406-445).

[16] We have to understand that, after the war, interpretation of the years 1939-1945 was a problem of immediate political relevance. After the Communists took power against the will of the overwhelming majority of the population, their first task was to rewrite the history of the resistance. Thus, it received numerous self-serving interpretations by "court" historians. Not until 1956, for example, could the Home Army be mentioned without an accompanying string of adjectives like "bourgeois," "reactionary," "collaborating" (with the Germans), and "pro-fascist." A recent example of a "court historian" interpretation, which is clearly inspired by the atmosphere of the

sources specifically state that the German victory was received with joy by the peasants in certain areas and that the entering German army received a friendly greeting from the population in many ethnically Polish hamlets and villages (Stolarz, 1965:95; Kersten, Szarota, 1968 v.2:24; Kisielewski, Nowak, 1968:387-388). Of course, this warmth did not represent the predominant mood, but rather an extreme form of an attitude unique to the countryside, which stemmed from the peasants' alienation in prewar Poland. On the other hand, the occasional friendliness of the rural population was visible enough to have been reported in memoirs written several years later, against the general trend of "heroic" interpretation of the war period.

The Germans encountered few problems in their search for pliant local Polish administrators. Many farmers of German origin were willing to join the DVL (Stolarz, 1965:96; Kisielewski, Nowak, 1968:176). In addition, many *Volksdeutsche* were recruited from families who had been forcibly resettled in the GG from the western parts of Poland that were incorporated into the Reich (Szarota, Kersten, 1968: 245). These refugees usually knew German and therefore were assigned to intermediary positions as translators and auxiliaries between the German apparatus and the Polish population. After their resettlement they owned nothing but their jobs, and thus their livelihood depended on their ability to keep them. It is not difficult to understand how this dependence could have fostered servility toward the new masters. Local people frequently saw the newcomers

---

"March 1968" semiabortive coup d'état by populistic, nationalist, and anti-Semitic middle layers of the party bureaucracy, is the article by Eugeniusz Duraczyński, "La structure sociale et politique de la resistance anti-hitlerienne en Pologne 1939-1945," published in the *Revue d'histoire de la deuxième guerre mondiale* (1970). The author in several places stresses two points, neither of which is historically correct: that the Communist-sponsored resistance was the major part of all anti-German activity; and that Jews played no part in the anti-German underground.

meeting with the Germans—because they could speak to each other—which intensified their hostility toward them. In some areas this anger toward their countrymen was stronger than their hostility toward the Germans (GSHI, PRM 45c/41: "Dwa lata okupacji niemieckiej w Polsce," Aug. 1941). Finally, the Gestapo not infrequently found confidants among the local population (Kisielewski, Nowak, 1968:151, 171), and personal feuds, particularly disputes involving partitioning of inherited land, occasionally led people to denounce their kin or neighbors to the police (HI, PGC, Box 919: File "Organizacje Społeczne"; GSHI, Kolekcja Kota, no. 25/10: "Nastroje i morale społeczeństwa w GG," July-Sept. 1940).

Except when they wanted to promote ambitious new *Volksdeutsche* in the area, the Germans would usually leave the old *sołtys* (village head) in his post, and he was smart enough to become aware that many candidates were eager to take his place. Therefore, he made sure that his performance satisfied the Germans. In fact, 73 percent of the *wójts* (chief administrative officers at the *gmina* [township] level) and mayors in the GG (excluding the district of Galicia) were Polish (see Table V.1).

The Polish administration in the countryside was caught

TABLE V.1

NATIONALITY OF WÓJTS AND MAYORS IN THE GENERALGOUVERNEMENT AS OF JANUARY 5, 1944

District	German	Polish	Ukrai-nian	Belo-russian	Gorale	Un-known	Total
Galicia	6	3	346	0	0	27	382
Cracow	36	188	59	0	5	81	369
Lublin	24	120	55	3	0	43	245
Radom	59	237	2	0	0	3	301
Warsaw	19	169	1	0	0	26	215
Total	144	717	463	3	5	180	1,512

Source: Madajczyk, 1970 v.1:222.

in a very difficult situation. First, local government officials were totally visible to the Germans and fully replaceable, as no special skills were needed to run a rural hamlet. They could not disappear and hide, except in forests, leaving behind family and possessions. They were therefore totally dependent on the mercy of the local German gendarmerie and administration officials. Second, the only tasks assigned to local administrators involved exploiting the local population rather than rendering any service.[17] They were only the last tool in the German system of imposing and collecting quotas of various articles from the Poles.

The alienation of Polish officials from the local population was increased when they were granted discretion on the village level in allocating the individual share of the imposed quotas that each farmer had to deliver. Thus, although they were powerless when it came to imposition of the total quota itself, local Polish officials possessed full power to help anyone on an individual basis. However, since they could not help everyone, it was easy for the population to perceive them as refusing to help anyone. To make matters worse, they were personally charged with selecting the people who were to go to work in Germany after the administration imposed "human quotas" on rural communities. Consequently, though powerless, the sołtys wielded *visible* power on the local level. Their position subsequently became more important—and more hated—as the German-imposed quotas were increased and the material conditions and security of life in the countryside worsened.

As we can easily imagine, this deterioration was largely

[17] The Polish administration in the cities could easily be perceived by the population not only as a German auxiliary but also as a distributor of much-needed services (Ivanka, 1964:486). For example, the budget of the Polish administration of Warsaw included large sums allocated for various social services. In 1942-1943, for instance, out of its total budget of 205,251 million złotych, 13,127 million were for education, 3,447 million for "culture and art," 35,735 million for health services, and 60,796 million for welfare.

blamed on the local Polish administration. It was not un-
common for a sołtys and his cronies to form a closely knit
clique that exploited the situation for their own advantage,
using their power to set each individual's share in the quotas
to extract favors and bribes. Indeed, in numerous memoirs
it is recorded that wealthier farmers, who could bribe the
local administration, were exempted from making compulsory deliveries of foodstuffs and from being sent to Germany
to work. Frequently, the local Polish administration on the
gmina level imposed higher quotas than those actually set
by the Germans in order to make sure that the real quota
was fulfilled on time, and to leave room to make a profit by
accepting bribes in exchange for lowering the quota set for
individual villages or farmers.[18] Delegate Jankowski mentioned these facts to a visiting courier from London, indicating that he intended to begin a campaign against abuses,
as well as against other forms of demoralization among the
Polish population that could be traced to the conditions of
life under the occupation (GSHI, Kolekcja Kota, no. 25/9:
"Sprawozdanie Celta"). With their function as administrators for the Germans confined to collections from the local
population, and with delivery of services prohibited, the
Polish auxiliary administration was increasingly viewed as a
hostile force that had to be deceived and/or placated
through bribes.

In a closely knit, intimate rural society, the local administration was in an excellent position to blackmail and extort

[18] This practice is described in detail by Kisielewski and Nowak
(1968:87-89). It occurred in gmina Karczew, which was at that time
the center of illegal meat production in the Generalgouvernement.
The Polish administration, when challenged by local farmers who
discovered their fraud, argued that it needed income from the sale of
additional foodstuffs in order to have a "bribe fund" for the local
German police and administration. Indeed, in small towns, villages,
and hamlets all over the GG, German administration personnel and
gendarmerie were treated by the local Polish administration with
gourmet foods that the Poles were not supposed to have under penalty
of death (Kisielewski, Nowak, 1968:198-199).

favors because it knew precisely what resources each individual possessed. At the same time, peasants who fell into disgrace or were threatened could not simply change address and disappear in the street. So it was natural for the individual to sever his ties with the local community in order to make it more difficult for the Germans to extract information about himself and his affairs. One was now much less willing to share one's surplus with neighbors who suffered a shortage; one could no longer expect reciprocity, nor be sure that today's surplus would not be tomorrow's scarcity. The future was totally unpredictable—anyone at any moment could become the victim of a gendarme, a quota-collector, an angry neighbor making a denunciation, a bandit. Indeed, it was best, safest, to keep away from others. Mutual suspicions and mistrust developed (HL, PUC: MSW, *Wydział Społeczny*, "Sprawozdanie sytuacyjne z ziem polskich," no. 8/43, p. 130), as did relationships based on immediate reciprocity: one had to "pay" on the spot. Mutual mistrust, however, generated some relief: since everyone was evading regulations, people hesitated to denounce one another because they were themselves vulnerable to denunciation (GSHI, PRM 45c/41: "Dwa lata okupacji niemieckiej w Polsce," Aug. 1941).

I stated at the beginning of this chapter that one is likely to encounter a great variety of behavior in a society under occupation. It should be clear by now, however, that this variety is not unlimited. It is of particular interest that the regularities one may indentify in the domain of political relationships between the occupiers and the occupied seem to be determined not so much by the moral character of individual actors as by the social space in which the actors happen to be living.

CHAPTER VI

Corruption

ANALYSIS of the economy imposed by the German occupiers and of the normative ambiguities under which the Polish population lived in the Generalgouvernement leads unavoidably to identification of a social process that I have as yet named only in passing: corruption. In fact, I consider corruption to be the single most characteristic social phenomenon in a society under occupation.

It is not unusual to view corruption as an efficient mechanism assuring the fulfillment of various goals for whose attainment the institutional framework existing in a given society is inadequate. "Economic development through corruption" and "corruption as a substitute for reform" are propositions that those who study modernization must have encountered in their research. My analysis of corruption in the Generalgouvernement leads me to the formulation of an even stronger proposition, namely, that corruption acquired nomic quality in the GG and established social bonds where only coercion would otherwise have existed. It may be viewed as the only system within which exchange, transaction, and reciprocity take place. Corruption thus emerges as the principal mode of integration, in much the same way as kinship structure is regarded in a primitive society, and economic exchange, a legal system, or, finally, the state in a modern polity. Consequently, I think, the peculiar general phenomenon of a *corrupt state* can be distinguished from, merely, the corruption of state officials.

A DEFINITION OF CORRUPTION

Corruption has been studied primarily as it exists in developing and colonial nations and as a phenomenon of

145

political patronage in developed countries. In spite of this diversity of perspective, the various definitions of corruption converge at one point. Some authors define corruption as that kind of behavior in which public office is used for private gain; others, as that which results from a conflict between parochial, kinship loyalties and broader, national obligations; still another writer calls it "an extra-legal institution used by individuals or groups to gain influence over actions of the bureaucracy" (McMullen, 1961; Leff, 1964; Nye, 1967; Scott, 1972). All these definitions refer to the interaction between the *private-individual* and the *public-collective*. It appears, therefore, that corrupt behavior may occur only in a society that has both public and private forms of ownership.[1] A comprehensive definition of corruption must additionally capture the illegal character of this peculiar form of transaction involving publicly and privately owned goods. Let us then define corruption as *the behavior of people who, when deprived of goods that the public sector controls, attempt to obtain those goods illegally by conspiring with officials, and the behavior of those officials, who are temporarily acting as if they owned those goods instead of holding them in public trust.*

Since corruption involves a trade-off, each party offering something the other desires, the likelihood of its presence predictably depends on several factors, including: (a) whether the discriminating group is the only one in possession of the goods denied to other segments of society (since we are speaking of publicly controlled goods, this is essentially the question of whether people are free to leave the country, that is, escape from this particular distributor of public goods, or to change the government); (b) whether the group discriminated against retains control of *some* valuable resources (corruption always accompanies power), that is, how central, or marginal, is its position in society;

[1] Scott makes this point implicitly when he recommends that a comparative analysis of corruption in two or more nations be preceded by a comparison of the size of their public sectors (Scott, 1972:8).

(c) how severe the discrimination against the latter group is, that is, which of its needs are provided for "legally" within the system and to what extent; (d) whether the system of discrimination is enforceable; and (e) what alternatives for influencing the public sector are available to the group discriminated against, for example, the possibility of organizing legitimately into pressure groups or political parties or of resorting to violence and the overthrow of the government.

In terms of the relationship between society and government—and the five points above are dimensions of this relationship—and its bearing on the likelihood of corruption, the Generalgouvernement was uniquely suited for corruption.[2]

CORRUPTION AND SOCIAL ATOMIZATION

Alex Weingrod (1968), in his analysis of patron-client relationships, observes that corruption thrives in segmented societies where social ties hold only within small communities or between family members; where there are "gaps

[2] (ad.a) It was not possible in practice to change the government or to leave the country. (ad.b) The whole society was discriminated against, rather than only a marginal group in it. There were differences in degrees of hardships suffered, but no exemptions. The society still possessed enough material goods, produced enough foodstuffs, and had sufficient skills to be a welcome partner in trade. (ad.c) Neither the rights nor the needs of the non-German population in the GG were recognized or incorporated into the official policies of the German administration. (ad.d) The laws of discrimination were not enforceable. Finally, because of the contingencies formulated in point (e), many authors consider corruption as an alternative to revolution or reform. Scott, for instance, convincingly presents corruption as a strategy to exercise influence in the system at the "output" stage (influence on enforcers) when a group finds it impossible for some reason to have anything to say at the "input" stage (influence on lawmakers) (Scott, 1972:23-25). Indeed, any influence by Poles on lawmakers was out of the question, nor could the outcome of World War II be decided by the Polish underground.

147

between regions, between communities, and between villager and city-based officials"; "where the state is centered in the capital and the great cities, and reaches out into the countryside only to preserve order and collect revenues." In such a social context of segmentation and relative isolation a category of "mediators" emerges. Through the mediators, who act as a bridge between regions or levels, individuals are able to reach beyond the circle of their local affiliations, which otherwise would be impossible because no institutions exist that could help them to do so.

Scott indicates that in societies permeated with corruption, the segmented social structure typically contains one particularly deep cleavage.[3] It is not by chance that most analysts of corruption use data from colonial regimes for purposes of illustration: the segmented structures of such societies have a peculiarly deep cleavage between the power holders and the rest of society, and a lack of institutions to bridge this gap. Thus a social stratum of "mediators" emerges, finding a natural breeding ground in the thin layer of local people employed in subordinate and auxiliary positions in the colonial administration. Altogether, the social structure in the Generalgouvernement suits this description very well. In addition, the administrative setup in the Generalgouvernement created a favorable environment for the emergence of the same phenomenon—with Polish employees of the local administration often destined to play the roles of the mediators.

The gap pointed out by Scott between the colonizers and the colonized was a salient part of life in the GG. When a

[3] "In approaching the civil servant the peasant [in transitional nations] is not generally an informed citizen seeking a service to which he is entitled, but a subject seeking to appease a powerful man whose ways he cannot fathom. The huge gap . . . that separates civil servants and their clients . . . has at least two consequences for corruption. First, the administrator can make arbitrary decisions with impunity and can extort bribes. . . . Second, the powerless client will more frequently offer a bribe in the hope of transforming the distant bureaucrat into a friendly patron" (Scott, 1972:15).

client approached a bureaucrat in the GG, there could be complete certainty that he was not "seeking a service to which he was entitled." A Polish request to the Germans could not be made in the name of the law, that is, by invoking some generalized norm. Instead, it had to be presented as a part of a trade-off, by pointing to a particularistic aspect of the transaction. Poles had no rights; if they wanted something, they had to offer something in exchange. The Germans were not concerned with the welfare of the Polish population; the German administration did not exist to render services but to demand them.

In sociological terms, one can call the German-Polish relationship a diffuse one. That is, *any* demand by a German party of a Polish one had to be met. If he were not able to meet it, the Polish party was obligated to offer justification. For the Polish party to base his noncompliance on a general rule, a right of some sort, was unacceptable. He was justified only when he could demonstrate that he did not have resources necessary to meet the demand. At that point the diffuse relationship, based on a generalized right to demand, could be turned into transaction again: "if you want me to do this," the Polish party might say, "I will have to get that." Such a request might or might not be granted. The Polish-German relationship was, within this logic, all-excluding, or, to put it more dramatically, even the right to survive was not guaranteed to the Poles. Those who survived did so at the whim of the Germans.

A phenomenon similar to one that characterized the black market, where transactions flowed through an army of middlemen, also marked the Polish population's dealings with the German administration. The pattern of interaction with the bureaucracy was neither supported by a set of generalized norms nor institutionalized. Instead, it was an empirical system based on personal contact: all cases that applicants brought to bureaucrats were disposed of on the basis of the particular relationship between the given applicant and the given bureaucrat rather than in accordance

149

with a predictable procedure. If a certain kind of case was disposed of in a certain manner n number of times, it did not mean that the same disposition could be expected the $n + 1$ time. The disposition of cases might change drastically simply with a new appointment to a post in the bureaucracy. What counted was to know the right people rather than the right procedures. For this reason, institutions—and regularized patterns of behavior—did not develop, and therefore one could not become socialized into the proper forms of behavior for dealing with the machinery of the state.

In such a situation, again, middlemen proliferated. They offered their services as go-betweens to functionaries whom, they said, they could dispose favorably toward an applicant's case. People gladly accepted their services because they knew no other way to have their problems examined favorably and because they were glad to have others, rather than themselves, approach Germans with what was a de jure criminal dealing. When social interaction proceeds in such a pattern, the middleman need only monopolize the useful contacts and keep them secret to stay in business. Thus, all parties concerned were satisfied, even the German bureaucrat, who also felt more secure in dealing with one or only a few people instead of with many.

Multiple contacts and interaction with other people in such a society are only superficially integrating; contacts do not last long and are inherently antagonistic, as each link in the chain fears that the next link will take his share of the bribe. Because the financial standing of the applicant, rather than the merit of the case or the law, determines disposition, a particularly alienating and demoralizing experience results, which solidifies atomization of the society (HL, PUC: MSW, *Wydział Społeczny*, "Sprawozdanie sytuacyjne z ziem polskich," 2/43). In Polish society all transactions, or reciprocity, could be established only in a particularistic mode: since they did not rest on any sort of general obligation, they required a specific benefit (a bribe) to a specific German agent in order to be carried out.

Corruption and the State

Heretofore we have presented corruption as a process through which private individuals or organizations benefit, with commodities that are held in the public trust handled as if they were privately owned and exchanged for other goods, without regard for general rules, that is, law. Corruption is vastly greater and acquires a new character when not only individuals violate the public trust, but the state itself—the public agent—decides to violate its own laws and acts as a private agent on the market. This situation occurred in the occupied countries. Documentary materials describe certain operations in the West and in the Balkans that illustrate governmental corruption in great detail. While few specific quotations exist that touch on this mode of corruption in the GG, there is sufficient evidence to argue that the German administration in the Generalgouvernement operated in the same manner.

The GG administration probably had no central office similar to the Central Registration Office (Z.A.M.) set up by the military commander in Belgium and northern France in February 1942, or to the Office of the Plenipotentiary for Special Missions (U.W.A.) created by Goering's decree in June 1942 (United States, 1946 v.5:623-624), but this difference was formal and not of primary importance. It should be mentioned that the U.W.A. office had only a brief existence; it was dissolved by Goering's order on April 2, 1943 (United States, 1946 v.5:629). More important, however, it was initially created to centralize *already ongoing* operations on the black market of "various offices of the armed forces and other German organizations" that were bidding competitively for various scarce raw materials and finished goods, inflating prices and snatching merchandise away from one another (United States, 1946 v.4:330). No doubt, the procurement of sought-after goods did not come to a halt after the U.W.A. was dissolved (United States, 1946 v.4:332).

Colonel Veltjens, the man in charge of the U.W.A., perceptively stated the causes for the emergence of the black market in the occupied territories: scarcity of goods; hoarding; "escape into material values"; impossibility of enforcing price limits and the resulting "enlargement of the divergence of price between raw materials and finished products on the one hand, and between goods and wages on the other"; lack of public support for the countermeasures of the local administration; and finally, "the inefficient criminal justice of the individual state criminal authorities and the lack of discipline in the civilian population." One could not agree more, but of particular interest to us is the conclusion that Veltjens drew from his diagnosis and in which he was supported by the ranking members of the German administration:

> the black market . . . has developed inevitably from the economic situation of the market and will exist and have to be exploited in the German interest, as no way has been found to break it up completely or at least check it to the extent that the amount of goods caught through it are meaningless within the framework of the total supply. . . . as long as in the occupied territories an essential part of the goods existing or produced at all, disappears by reasons of inefficient control or various other reasons in the black market, in the interest of supplying the German war economy with the most important raw materials and finished products . . . seizure of these goods could not be avoided. (United States, 1946 v.4:329-331)[4]

[4] Indeed, the Germans organized seizures on a large scale. From February to November 1942, purchases through Z.A.M. and U.W.A. in France, Belgium, Holland, and Serbia altogether amounted to 1,107,792,818 reich marks and 64 pfennigs (United States, 1946 v.4:335). Total purchases on the black market in France throughout the war were estimated in October 1944 by the Foreign Labor Staff as follows:

This statement well fits the situation in the GG under German occupation, primarily because the Polish population reacted to the unlimited goals of German exploitation by sabotaging German seizures and by withholding, hiding,

TABLE VI.1

GERMAN PURCHASES ON THE BLACK MARKET IN FRANCE
(In Billions of Francs)

Purchaser	1940	1941	1942	1943	1944	Total
Veltjens and U.W.A.	negl.	0	23.1	8.0	0	31.1
Soldiers	negl.	5.1	15.7	19.6	4.5	44.9
Importers of Reich Credit Notes	negl.	0	5.2	13.2	0.4	18.8
Total	negl.	5.1	44.0	40.8	4.9	94.8

Source: United States, 1946 v.4:335.

Thus Veltjens's action represents about one-third of all German purchases on the black market. One would be right, of course, in pointing out that the combined industrial potential of France, Belgium, Holland, and Serbia far exceeded that of Poland, and that the conditions of occupation in the West were much more favorable to the development of the local economy. But it is also true that a large part of the money spent on the black markets of these countries was used to purchase items that could very well be found in Poland too. Of the billion marks spent on the black market in 1942: in France, 46.6 million were spent on household goods, 33 million on "food and pleasure items," 50 million on wines and alcoholic drinks, and 12 million on "sanitary necessities"; in Belgium, 5.56 million were spent on "paper and packing material," 3.39 million on food and pleasure items, and almost 17 million on "miscellaneous" items (United States, 1946 v.4:337-338). In the "Christmas Drive" ordered by Goering in late September 1942—"for the purpose of increasing the supply of the German civilian population with consumer goods during the Christmas season"—goods valued at 53.3 million RM were shipped to Germany: "toys, leather goods, paper goods, cosmetic products, wicker goods, occasional furniture, house, kitchen and garden tools, and other hardware, laundry supplies, free textiles and merchandise of different kinds" (United States, 1946, v.5:627). Clearly, all of these goods, and many other items, were available in the GG, and large stocks were diverted to the black market.

hoarding, and channeling all possible goods into the black market, where, as Colonel Veltjens noted, "at the always increasing scarcity of goods, every item finds a buyer" (United States, v.4:332).

Veltjens's analysis points up that the German administration was also able to rationalize its participation in the black market, its bribe taking, etc., which would have been unacceptable under normal circumstances, by viewing these acts as extensions of the program of exploitation that was in their national interest. Considering, in addition, that customarily accepted norms of social behavior—stigmatizing stealing, cheating, bribing, or killing—were "justifiably" breached by the population in an occupied country because of an overriding norm stipulating that such actions were intended to damage the occupying power, a curious situation results, one in which *both parties not only find it profitable to break the rules that are supposed to regulate their mutual relationships, but also are able to find norms that support such behavior.*[5]

Normative order could not be imposed on this society because one party perceived the claims of the other as fundamentally illegitimate. Poles claimed the right to survive; Germans, the right to exploit beyond any limits. *Both* claims could not be validated simultaneously, and since neither side was able to fulfill its own claim unilaterally without some degree of cooperation from the other, their

---

[5] Further delegitimation of the existing order took place because the Germans had promulgated more laws than the Poles could be expected to obey or they themselves could consistently enforce. A great deal was left to the exercise of discretion, and there was of course a way for anyone accused of breaking the law to influence the judgment: "Bribery became a system. It is not any longer a breach of law by an individual official, but a social institution. Various German regulations are formulated in such a way that several interpretations of them are conceivable. For a bribe one can induce appropriate officials to apply milder interpretation" (GSHI, A 9 III 4/21: Poland Fights, [19]).

mutual relationships were a series of hit and run confrontations, handled by transactions engineered for the moment. Such transactions set no precedent for the future and did not permit the development of stable patterns of problem solving.

CORRUPTION IN THE GENERALGOUVERNEMENT

In his report, Dr. Blaschek (1965), the visitor from the neighboring Protectorate of Bohemia and Moravia and the relentless investigator of imperfections in the administration of the GG, told of an offer to sell about two thousand gallons of gasoline to the Office of Gasoline Allocation in the GG's government. The offer, of course, came from the black market. The office refused to buy the gasoline because, in its judgment, the price was too high. "One has to ask what the Poles think of German authorities if the black market operators do not hesitate to offer their commodities for sale to the appropriate German office," Blaschek commented sourly. In another instance, the GG's government sold part of its production of alcoholic beverages at black market prices in order to improve its financial standing (Blaschek, 1965:137). More evidence of official German purchases on the black market can be found in the report of the Foreign Labor Staff. However, even this well-informed German source could not provide reliable estimates of the amount of money actually spent on the black market in the GG. A prominent Polish historian and economist, Witold Kula, reported unsuccessful attempts by the German administration to confiscate nonferrous metals and a subsequent successful deal in which the Germans bought them through the black market (Kula, 1947). In a mood of resignation Governor General Hans Frank pointed out during a meeting of GG's government on June 18, 1942, that controls imposed on industry were totally inadequate. He complained that through the black market the Poles could get all the regulated commodities that for the Germans were so hard to find. When a county prefect (*starosta powiatowy*) needed iron, he did not try to obtain it through the official allocation system, but instead sent one of his aides to town with food so that he could buy the iron on the black market. "It should be stressed," said Frank, "that in principle, all offices willing to buy regulated articles should not turn to the black market" (Frank, 1970 v.1:481). Last but not least, the army was particularly active on the black market. One way of financing the occupation was for the Bank Emisyjny in Poland to charge to the Reich Treasury all purchases made by the Wehrmacht. Before 1942, the army could draw unlimited amounts from that account, which it did without hesitation as it paid black market prices for foodstuffs and other items, until eventually Governor Frank began to worry about the extent of these purchases (Skalniak, 1966: 137). The jump in virtually all prices on the black market in the spring and summer of 1941 was apparently caused by the large-scale purchases by the Wehrmacht during the period when a 2,000,000-man army was concentrated in the GG before the outbreak of war with Soviet Russia.

I have defined corruption as a mode of interaction between the private and public sectors. When it exists, it means that the trustees of the public good do not exercise their trust faithfully, but instead offer for sale commodities over which they have only custody, not ownership, in an attempt to serve their own particular interests. Sometimes, as I have indicated, not only individual public officials, but the state itself acts as though it were a private person. The Z.A.M. and U.W.A. operated on the market by using private business firms as fronts: Roges, AWG, Wabeko, Primetex, H-Fuchs, and Patewi. However, in order to suggest that the state as such was acting as a corrupt agent, one must ask *what was the commodity that it was offering for exchange, forfeiting the conditions of its public trust*? The answer is *money.*

156

The German administration was not at all concerned with inflation in the occupied countries, as long as it could be kept out of Germany (which is why there was a financial and customs barrier between the Reich and the General-gouvernement). Its fiscal policy had but one aim, which was only a part of its general economic policy of exploitation: to intercept for the German economy and consumers as large a stock of goods as possible. In the General-gouvernement itself, the Germans would simply print more money when needed.

Corruption and the Creation of Social Bonds

It appears that in occupied Poland, particularly in the Generalgouvernement, corruption as a method of coping with a variety of otherwise unresolvable problems was supported by both the organizers of the public order and by its subjects. In spite of frequent police raids against the black market and vicious propaganda campaigns against "speculators" and "profiteers," the Germans, of course, tolerated it. They admitted that they did so, not only in discussions among themselves, but also in speaking with representatives of Polish society. During an official audience in 1942 Cardinal Sapieha and Count Ronikier asked Secretary of State Bühler how the Poles were supposed to survive on official food rations. Bühler replied that the black market operators every day brought wagons of foodstuffs into the cities, and that the German administration knew about it and deliberately tolerated it (GSHI, PRM 118: doc. no. L.dz. 304/II/43). Not only did both parties practice corruption, but, as I have shown, each also had a normative justification for its behavior. How is one to interpret this situation?

When a ruling group, having excluded an important segment of society from access to political power, tries to establish its legitimacy, it may find itself damaged by the corruption in the bureaucracy: most of the coups in states

157

that are trying to modernize are made in the name of cleaning out the corrupt elements. But if the ruling elite is not really concerned with establishing its legitimacy, as in the case of the German occupation of Poland, corruption may very well serve its purposes by moderating the effects of some of the irrationality of the state's policies, and it may provide a certain minimal degree of coalescence and interaction in the system. Bitter conflicts on the leadership level of German police, administration, and army were mitigated to a large extent by the practice of corruption by all echelons. Mutually profitable "business partnerships" between Poles and Germans were not infrequent, and there were even cases of German-Jewish cooperation (Pospieszalski, 1958:225). Arrests of local black market operators sometimes followed that of their German partners.

Those private persons who participate in corrupt exchanges with public officials acting as private persons compensate for, and avoid, some of the consequences of their inferior status. Such a situation arises whenever access to the public sector is restricted to a small part of the population. The larger the area regulated by the government and the larger and more central the group denied access to the government, the more likely it is that corruption will emerge as one of the alternative methods of compensating for the inferior status of the excluded group. But the more central the excluded group is, the more difficult it is for the system as a whole to operate. If neither reform nor revolution are possible, corruption will emerge as a dominant strategy for reducing frictions and conflicts in the system, as the dominant *strategy for pulling together all resources of the polity*.

Since the government tried neither to seek normative legitimation of its rule nor to run society's business efficiently, and since coercion alone cannot suffice to hold together a society of fifteen million people, some other integrating factor had to be found to maintain this group of people for five years. Profit seeking, mutually advantageous economic cooperation, and common interests were the chief integrating forces, along with police terror, that held the Generalgouvernement together throughout the war.[6]

[6] The Generalgouvernement was a very good example of Etzioni's dual utilitarian-coercive organization. Power in this type of social system is of a mixed coercive and utilitarian nature, while involvement is calculative-alienative. What I have termed corruption corresponds to utilitarian and calculative in Etzioni's terms (Etzioni, 1961).

CHAPTER VII

The Texture of Life

"CALAMITIES generate two opposite movements in different sections of the population," said Sorokin (1943:161), "one is a trend toward unreligiousness and demoralization; the other is a trend toward extreme religious, spiritual and moral exaltation." Before we turn to the investigation of the most structured form of the solidaristic mode of the Polish population's response to occupation—the underground—we should say more about social disorganization.

Alcoholism, the gradual loss of a sense of private and public property, corruption—all were symptoms of social disorganization in the Generalgouvernement. But above all, the society was increasingly exposed to violence. The Germans were by no means the sole perpetrators; as the occupation continued, conferences on security matters in the districts of the GG indicated that there was a tremendous rise in the number of "armed assaults," which were variously classified as "robberies" and as "politically tainted robberies." In reality, they were undoubtedly a mixture of both.[1]

Armed assaults were increasingly concentrated on Kreis (powiat) and gmina offices and were directed at the destruction of official documents used in connection with the

[1] In the district of Radom, for instance, the number of "armed assaults" before April 1942 had never exceeded 100 per month. Subsequently, the figures were: July 1942, 206; November 1942, 365; February 1943, 493; March 1943, 705; April 1943, 965 (Frank, 1970 v.2:109). The worst situation existed in the Lublin district, where for the sixteen-month period from January 1942 to May 1943 "armed assaults" numbered: 96, 61, 120, 300, 780, 1,140, 1,400, 1,400, 1,600, 1,700, 1,700, 1,700, 1,296, 1,600, 2,306, 2,320 (Frank, 1970 v.2:122).

requisitions of labor and foodstuffs for the Reich. Also, attacks were aimed increasingly at functionaries of the local administration, the wójt and the sołtys. Large numbers of Gestapo agents were liquidated during that time (Landau, 1963 v.2:318): "Those times when the killing of a policeman or a German confidant terrified people in the anticipation of German reprisals are gone forever. Armed fights take place all the time," wrote Landau (1963 v.2:188, 336) in February 1943. Krüger himself was wounded in April in a murder attempt by the underground. Significantly, no reprisals followed this action (Landau, 1963 v.2:380).

Brutal mass roundups organized by the police in January 1943, apparently without Frank's authorization (Frank, 1970 v.2:14), induced people to speculate that the Gestapo was trying to provoke a premature uprising in order to have an excuse to apply ever more cruel and bloody measures in dealing with the Polish population (Landau, 1963 v.2:90). The most influential paper of the underground, *Biuletyn Informacyjny*, ridiculed widely circulating rumors that May 3 was the alleged date for the beginning of the uprising: "The rumor is stupid and ridiculous. Never in history has any national uprising begun on an anniversary of a national holiday" (*Biuletyn Informacyjny*, Apr. 29, 1943). Another paper, *Reforma* (May 10, 1943), joined in criticizing the rumors. "There may be only one uprising, and as a result it must bring freedom," it stated wisely. But the rumors, and the need to refute them in the most authoritative sources, indicated that an unprecedented level of insecurity and fear had been reached on both sides.

German panic must have reached considerable proportions. During a government meeting in October 1943 it was suggested that a regulation be issued forbidding all civilians to keep their hands in their pockets. In any case, it was argued, "armed and uniformed Germans should be prepared to use firearms whenever a civilian, with hands in his pockets, is coming near them" (Frank, 1970 v.2:243). Adolf

161

Stahl, Frank's deputy leader of the NSDAP, spoke openly of a "psychosis of fear" that spread among Germans residing in "this country" (Frank, 1970 v.2:76). In the countryside, Germans began to lock themselves in fortified buildings at night, together with their local Polish minions (Landau, 1963 v.2:385, 399).

The breakdown of security strongly suggests the incapacity of local law enforcement agencies to guarantee peaceful order in the manner desired by the occupier. Evidently, they could not guarantee the relative safety of the population from attacks by all kinds of bandits and robbers. Actions of the German police to maintain "order" could only be construed by the population as examples of the arbitrary nature of German rule and as indications of the breakdown of law rather than of its enforcement.[2]

As the underground network strengthened, people took their complaints to the local commanders of the underground, who sometimes intervened against the bandits. On several occasions the local Polish auxiliary police (the so-called "dark-blue police") and the underground jointly staged raids against the bandits (Stolarz, 1965:130). But the plague of banditry continued to escalate until the end of the occupation. Often, armed detachments of the underground made requisitions in excess of their needs, or turned to banditry themselves (Stolarz, 1965:103, 114). "Patriotic bandits multiply at a horrendous pace in various parts of the country," wrote the *Biuletyn Informacyjny* on November 26, 1942. Several factors contributed to this apparent anarchy, among them, the easy availability of firearms, the breakdown of normative order, the displacement of large numbers of people, the radical deterioration in the material

---

[2] In an episode illustrating German arbitrariness, a special court in one village pronounced death sentences on 14 of 28 peasants arrested in connection with the murder of a German gendarme. However, only the few actually involved in the killing were named in the sentence; the rest had to draw lots to fill the quota (GSHI, Kolekcja Kota, no. 25/10: "Niemcy w Polsce," signed: Józef Podolski).

conditions of life, and the lack of effective control over many of their local units by various underground organizations.[3]

As another symptom of social disorganization, we must also consider a more narrowly defined type of behavior: the deliberate exploitation for private gain of the existing conflicting systems of norms. People sometimes used the legitimacy of conspiratorial organizations as a cover for behavior motivated by self-interest only. At other times, for their own benefit—but often to the detriment of their fellow citizens—they took advantage of the norms imposed by the Germans.

By 1940, less than a year after the capitulation, the underground press reacted to apparent misuse of the authority of the underground. Articles in *Pobudka* (Aug. 14, 1940) and *Głos Warszawy* (Sept. 1940), for example, warned

[3] In the midst of these tumultuous events, on May 31, 1943, Frank informed his associates of his decision to increase food rations for the Polish population beginning September 1. "It is possible to make draconian experiments on the population of the occupied territories," he said on this occasion, "but under the condition that the end of the war is near. Now, however, it is difficult to predict when it will end" (Frank, 1970 v.2:141). At the same time, he was able to convince Von den Bach-Żelewski, Himmler's deputy for coordinating antipartisan warfare in the East, that Krüger's and Globocnik's actions were responsible for the security breakdown. Bach-Żelewski agreed to ask for their removal on the grounds of inadequate performance, and he was apparently successful in removing them from their posts (IMT, v.12:132-133). But the suffering of the Polish population did not abate. The most terrible wave of terror and public mass executions followed a decree by Frank on October 2, 1943, *Rozporządzenie celem zwalczania zamachów na niemieckie dzieło odbudowy* (*Verordnungsblatt für das GG*, 1943, no. 82:589-590), which stated that "people of non-German origin who with the intention to hamper or make more difficult the German rebuilding effort in the GG do not comply with decrees, orders and dispositions of the authorities are punishable by death. Instigators or accessories to the deed are punishable as perpetrators. Intended action is punishable as if it had been actually carried out." A massacre followed, but order was not restored.

against the solicitation of financial contributions by a certain "military organization." The solicitors promised contributors of large sums handsome rewards in the future and threatened with reprisals those who would not support the patriotic cause. Such solicitations must have occurred repeatedly during the occupation, as similar warnings were issued by the Directorate of Civil Resistance (*Rzeczpospolita Polska,* June 21, 1943) and, a few months later, by the Directorate of Underground Resistance (*Przez Walkę do Zwycięstwa,* Nov. 20, 1943). That there must have been a massive problem is obvious from the latter's denunciation as illegal and arbitrary any solicitation of voluntary contributions, levying of contributions, and pronouncing sentences on citizens by *several* underground organizations (Polska Organ Walki Zbrojnej, Komenda Konspiracyjna, Tajny Związek Obrony Polski, ZWC, 3, Kierownik Walki Podziemnej, etc.).

Even more dramatic were the attempts by underground organizations of different political persuasions to settle scores, real or imagined, by resorting to violence, killing, and denunciation to the Gestapo. Especially well known was the liquidation of several high-ranking employees of the Bureau of Information and Propaganda of the Home Army by members of the National Armed Forces (NSZ), a radical right splinter organization. The chief of the Information Department, engineer Jerzy Makowiecki, was killed, and Professor Marceli Handelsman, an eminent historian of Jewish origin, was delivered into the hands of the Gestapo (Korboński, 1975:110; Rzepecki, 1971a:139; Rzepecki, 1971b:169). Many other people, particularly those on the left (including the non-Communist left, or just liberal-democrats like Makowiecki), were denounced to the Germans or killed (Bartoszewski, 1974:553-554; WRN, Sept. 24, 1943; Landau, 1963 v.3:145-146).

On several occasions the underground deplored and denounced the use of German institutions in quarrels between Poles. The Gestapo was receiving hundreds of anonymous denunciations (GSHI, Kolekcja Kota, no. 25/10: "Nastroje i morale społeczeństwa w GG," July-Sept. 1940; *Jutro*, Oct. 9, 1943).[4] Common motivations behind such denunciations included family quarrels about division of property and old personal feuds.

The underground was also sensitive to the less dramatic ways in which Poles used German institutions against other Poles. For instance, Polish employers were warned not to apply German-imposed salary scales for Polish employees. Parties who had lost their cases in Polish courts were sometimes known to appeal to German courts, which, according to the rules of the occupation, could review all Polish adjudications. A well-known attorney, Hofmokl-Ostrowski, allegedly used this resource to help his clients who were convicted in criminal cases (*Wolna Polska*, Jan. 28, 1942). The underground branded also as nonpatriotic behavior the practice by wives of POWs of pleading for the release of their husbands with the promise that they would "favor the present regime," or the statement by job applicants that they had previously been dismissed from a job because of pro-German opinions.

The Directorate of Civil Resistance published strong condemnations of those who blackmailed Jews in hiding, as well as political blackmailers who extorted money for their silence about someone's activities in the conspiracy. Special criticism was directed against the scores of profiteers who claimed that they could intervene on behalf of prisoners and thus obtained large sums from the desperate families of arrested people (*Biuletyn Informacyjny*, Mar. 18, 1943). In addition, the Government Delegate informed the population that the Underground Special Courts had

[4] "Anonymous and non-anonymous denunciations to the German police by renegades of Polish society multiply and seem to originate in all social strata. Everyone is being denounced—hiding military men, people thought to be active in the underground, couriers, locations of conspiratorial meetings, etc.," reported the *Biuletyn Informacyjny*, Dec. 5, 1940.

165

received instructions to judge not only political offenses, but also cases of blackmail and banditry. If found guilty, the accused could be condemned to death. "Such a decision became necessary because demoralization, resulting from prolonged war and acts committed on purpose by the occupier, is reaching deep into society. Banditry and blackmail are plaguing the population of cities and countryside. Unfortunately, banditry often appears in the disguise of work motivated by high ideals," commented the underground paper *Robotnik w Walce* (Mar. 19, 1944).

Finally, about 100,000 people living in the GG in 1943 signed the German National List (DVL), although the majority of them probably had little German blood (Pospieszalski, 1958 v.6:22). In the early summer of 1944, Emissary Celt was informed by the head of the Department of Liquidation of Consequences of War in the Substitute Administration that one of the clauses of the capitulation treaty with the Germans would demand German citizenship for all collaborators. "We estimate that there are about 850,000 to 1,000,000 of them" (GSHI, Kolekcja Kota, no. 25/9: "Sprawozdanie Celta"). (This estimate probably included all Polish territories, not only the Generalgouvernement.) Underground courts operating at that time, some of them civilian, under the auspices of the Directorate of Civil Resistance, and some of them military, issued many death sentences and an even larger number of reprimands and judgments of infamy.

Thus, the overwhelming picture is one of social disorganization and breakdown of social bonds. Constant fear for one's life, the unpredictability of German terror, and finally, anarchy (the somewhat unanticipated consequence of the all-out mobilization by the underground to resist the occupation authorities) contributed to the disintegration of social life. To a young sociologist who saw it all, it seemed indeed that in times of crisis and prolonged disasters the ranks of common, simple, decent people become precariously thin: "In borderline situations only a hair-width separates the morality of heroism and total lack of morality. There is no middle ground between cowardice and courage; between victory and fall; between meeting the requirements of brotherhood and destroying a community; between the threshold of fulfillment and the threshold of defeat" (Strzelecki, 1974:30).

THE YOUTH

A particularly destructive consequence of the authority vacuum in the Polish society during the war was the breakdown of the family. The collapse of adult authority seems to have been a phenomenon unrelated to social class; in all environments and milieus, young people were becoming emancipated at a rapid pace. First, economic difficulties often made it very unlikely that parents could continue to support their children. The period of transition to adulthood was cut short for the young, who had to assume responsibility early for meeting their own needs and very often for supporting their parents if they had lived on fixed incomes before the war or if they were unable to adapt to the new situation. It was very common for older brothers and sisters to have to look after the younger children in the family because the parents had left, disappeared, or for some other reason could no longer care for them.

Moreover, the family ceased to be an attractive frame of reference for the young because the grown-ups very often could not provide models of successful adaptation to the new social environment. The young conformed more easily to new circumstances and often enjoyed an economic level that the old could not achieve while trying to meet their traditional responsibilities. Thus young people matured quickly and became economically independent at an early age. Exposure to the same terrors of the occupation as adults also contributed to their early maturation. If he were not in school, a boy of fourteen could be sent for labor in Germany. Of course, one joined the underground at an

167

early age too, by becoming a student in an underground gymnasium, for example, or even by getting into a "hard-core" conspiracy, such as the boy scout organization called Szare Szeregi (Gray Ranks). The plight of the young at that time was particularly difficult: because they were the most valuable human material for the Germans and were therefore the primary target of German schemes, their main preoccupation was, as Landau sadly remarked, to hide, to live outside the law.

Ambiguities of "Heroic" Socialization

War, more than any other social reality, becomes the fabric for myth-creation and the subject of idealization. In Polish literature war had been represented as a period of heroism, action, and honor, in contrast with the routine, inertia, cunning, and greed that characterized peacetime life. The message was that only in time of war can one really "serve the cause," that only through military effort can major changes be effected, setting the nation's destiny on a completely new course. There was no major work in the Polish literature written after World War I that, like the books of Hašek, Barbusse, Remarque, Hemingway, or Dos Passos, revealed the ugliness, senselessness, dirt, and dehumanizing aspects of war (Janion, 1975:8). War was described to the young in Poland as a great adventure, a period of accelerated and intensified social life that provided the proper context for "action," "real faith," "will," and "strength."

This message continued to be broadcast after World War II broke out. The most influential book published by the underground, *Kamienie na Szaniec*, established that image in the face of the realities of the Second World War and the German occupation of Poland. An influential underground periodical by young poets, writers, and critics, *Sztuka i Naród*, spoke in the same tone: in a country that already is independent "the legend of a soldier gets replaced by the legend of a bureaucrat. The chaos of political changes brings disorientation and boredom, precisely because it is chaos and not struggle. . . . [Now] for the first time there is no boredom and mediocrity in our perspective of history. There is only greatness or destruction for us in the future. . . . We want the atmosphere of ruthless struggle and we are glad to listen to the happy and righteous rhythm of soldiers' steps" (Bojarski, 1942). Another leading author in this group, in an article entitled "Lyrical and Dramatic Generation," added: "the era of words has ended, the era of deeds must begin" (Trzebiński, 1942).

Although the model was well entrenched in the historical consciousness of the Poles, some participants in the underground began to reflect on it, and in the process asked a series of important questions: Does the idealistic pedagogy practiced by the underground eventually bring frustration and disappointment when it is revealed that social reality is different from ideals? Does the underground prepare the young to live in a free society? In the course of the resulting discussion, important issues were raised.

The apolitical attitude stressed by the military underground diverts the young from the most important problems that will emerge immediately after victory, wrote Lipiński in *Płomienie* in 1944 (Lipiński, 1944). Responding to an anonymous poll conducted in the autumn of 1943 by *Prawda Młodych* on the subject of youth and conspiracy, another writer remarked that Poles appeared to have forgotten that "conspiracy, as a consequence of occupation, is also abnormal and contrary to the natural order of societal life" (*Prawda Młodych*, Oct. 1943). Conspiratorial activity, he continued, becomes idealized as a goal in itself, although it should be perceived only as an instrument that, unfortunately, must be used in the circumstances of total war to regain independence.

The anonymous author was not alone in believing that too little work was being devoted by the underground to preparing its young members to become useful and responsible citizens in the future. In a review of *Kamienie na Szaniec* in the April 1944 issue of *Płomienie*, a critic reproached its author for presenting a simplistic view of the moral choices that had to be made during the occupation. This criticism must have sprung from a sense of the dramatic urgency of the problem, for the book was widely recognized as a message from the wartime generation describing its ordeals to those who would come after.

The problem was that the socialization pattern presented in the "heroic" literature about the war was very well suited to, or perhaps reflected, a peculiar characteristic of the underground as an institution. The underground could be called, in Coser's words, a "greedy institution" (Coser, 1974). It relied on voluntary compliance, and it appeared highly desirable to those who joined it; but at the same time, it exerted pressures "to separate the insider from the outsider and to erect symbolic boundaries between them" (Coser, 1974:6).[5] Furthermore, it demanded loyalty and obedience overriding any owed to other groups, people, or institutions. Thus, on the one hand, participation in the underground brought a welcome reduction in normative ambiguity, which was particularly intense during the occupation because it resulted not only from contradictory expectations emanating from various roles individuals play in society but also from demands stated by the occupier that ran against the code of conduct expected from those who valued such principles as patriotism and loyalty to fellow citizens. On the other hand, however, the obvious exclusiveness of the underground as an institution had adverse effects, especially on its young members: it was not preparing them to handle the variety of social roles that they would eventually have to fulfill in the future peacetime society.

The number of young people who belonged to conspiratorial youth organizations was estimated by Hillebrandt at

[5] See also Simmel (1964:359, 360, 370), who argues that a secret society claims the individual wholly.

between 24,000 and 25,000 (Hillebrandt, 1973:399). Even though many more "youths" participated in the adult movement, the total of these young patriots, perhaps the best of Polish youth, was still only a fraction of the young generation. And as we have seen, people were concerned that their life style and the influences to which they were exposed might be harmful to their future, that they might grow up as a new Remarquian generation.

If there was concern about the active youth, what of the majority who did not work in the underground and what of their future adjustment? These young people were especially susceptible to the breakdown of norms; their personalities were not yet fully formed, and their social education was as yet incomplete. To make matters worse, the normal processes of socialization were severely disrupted: only a fraction of the schools were operating, families had little time for their children, and the teachings of the Catholic Church did not seem to apply to people's conduct in real life. At the same time, the youth had to cope with an unstructured reality and unanticipated events; they were witness to unprecedented violence and the general suspension of morals; if they were employed, they experienced work's alienation. Clearly, the social life under the occupation was preparing them to exist, in the future, only on the margins of postwar society.

DESTRATIFICATION

Numerous sources have called attention to the polarization of the social structure in the GG into paupers and the rich. The most important fact to note in the area of social stratification is that such dimensions as status or power, which along with wealth usually determine the pattern of social strata, lost their differentiating importance in Polish society under German occupation.

In reaction to Sanacja's authoritarian rule, public opinion became increasingly hostile to any model of elitist society.

171

"The masters," "the educated," "the well brought up," "the leaders," "the old"—all were under attack. There was a widespread feeling across the whole political spectrum that Poland after the war should be a country of "the people," of "the masses." To be sure, the populist sympathies of different spokesmen were denoted by different words—"worker," "nation," "peasant," "people"—but most pronouncements had a polemic, egalitarian tone.[6] Reflecting this prevailing mood, those who later were to become the nucleus of the progressive intelligentsia, the Płomienie group, expressed hostility toward the intelligentsia itself, which was described as self-interested, not concerned with the public good, always serving those in power, unprincipled, and elitist (*Wolność*, Jan.-Feb. 1944). The collapse of the Polish state in 1939 was no longer simply blamed on Sanacja. In fact, the word *inteligent* became a pejorative. We can most clearly see this animosity toward all forms of elitism as we follow the gradually rising strength, organization, and self-consciousness of the peasant movement.[7]

[6] For a project of "people's republic," see the coalition program agreed upon by the main underground political parties, August 15, 1943.

[7] After Mikołajczyk succeeded in 1943 to the premiership upon the death of Sikorski, a considerable effort was made to show how his career and rise differed from that of the traditional leaders. An underground monthly, *Orka*, published an article in January 1944 entitled "Silhouette of our Premier." The subtitles in this article are self-explanatory and tell us a meaningful story: "from peasant's hut to premiership"; "tough school of life"; "self-made man"; "man on whose word one can rely"; "in a modest London apartment"; "pioneer of the Central European federation"; "in close contact with the home country." These subtitles already suggest a sharp contrast to the usual character and career of one in the leadership stratum. The article further elaborates the point. The premier is described as an outsider with no influential family connections, with no education (it is proudly mentioned in the article that Mikołajczyk does not even have a high school diploma), living a frugal life (although he could use an official limousine, he walks from his apartment to the office), accustomed to hard work (he takes work home in the evening and

Notwithstanding this general mood of antielitism, which can be interpreted primarily as a reaction to the conditions of life prevailing in the prewar Polish society, direct experience of life under the Germans also showed persuasively that those who occupied a high place in the traditional class structure were by no means the most successful in adapting to the new conditions. One could argue persuasively at the time that with the unfair advantages of birth and wealth eliminated, and with the same difficult conditions of life imposed on everyone, those who succeeded were "the best." In any event, it became transparent that one's prewar position on the social scale in no way foretold how one would fare under the Germans.

Intelligentsia and professionals, finding it impossible to pursue their traditional occupations and vocations, took all kinds of odd jobs to earn a living. For example, the eminent writer Zofia Nałkowska kept a small tobacco store (Nałkowska, 1974); a group of journalists organized a cooperative and restaurant; a group of actors set up a café (Szarota, 1973b); some prominent Polish sportsmen did the same, while university professors and career officers took odd jobs in the city administration. In general, there was no longer any relationship between one's social origin and education and one's present occupation and income.[8]

Finally, the Germans' contempt for the Poles limited the surface of Polish-German relationships to one of economics. Relationships and distances between people were measured

---

sleeps little), who speaks seldom but to the point, without using the big words and phraseology so dear to all who enjoy "cheap glory and applause." His word can be trusted; he works for the unity of various peoples and does not confine himself to a close circle of advisers; he has wide contacts with the outside and is not cliquish.

[8] One of the innumerable jokes circulating during the occupation illustrates this. A beggar is sitting in front of the Church of the Savior and a simple woman is offering him a bowl of soup. He says to her, "Now, Helen, go and serve dinner to Madam, who is begging in front of the Church of Three Crosses."

primarily in economic terms. Poland had no "high society" to which the Germans would aspire. There were exceptions, of course, but by and large, Polish society offered the occupier much less in the way of "social" rewards than any other Western society. A stigma was attached to the Slavs that made all of them, regardless of their previous social rank, *equally* undesirable. This, incidentally, explains why corruption in the Generalgouvernement was primarily an economic phenomenon: the Poles could offer nothing that would interest their new masters but money.

It is important to note here that the confinement of all social interaction to economic exchange signifies a dramatic weakening of a commitment to values as the regulating factors of social interaction and the disappearance of qualitative distinctions from social life. When everything is measured in terms of money, there is a price for smuggling a Jew out of the ghetto or for arranging the release of a prisoner from the Gestapo, just as for commodities people usually buy for money. The possibility of putting a price on everything, from a piece of bread to a human life, destroys moral life as we know it.[9]

The emphasis on money was evident in various aspects of Polish social life. In conditions of scarcity and inflation, the major preoccupation of people is to find ways to earn more money. It made no sense for Poles to seek positions with status or power; few were available to them in any case, except perhaps as experts (although still under the political supervision of German "commissars") in such areas as city administration or finance. Not only were such positions scarce, but they were also assigned a limited, well-defined sphere of competence, which in theory and in fact was subject to invasion even by minor German administrators and policemen. It was possible to gain power by becoming a German lackey, but owing to the indisputable hostility between the two nationalities, outright subservi-

[9] For a very intelligent analysis of this theme in the works of Tadeusz Borowski, see Werner (1971:53ff.).

ence effectively meant renouncing one's Polishness. This renunciation was accomplished formally when those who cast their lot with the Germans agreed to sign the DVL. To the extent that the old pattern of stratification crumbled under the weight of new circumstances, the effect of the whole process was to further egalitarianism.

Occupational stratification also underwent a deep transformation. Ranking jobs as "skilled," "unskilled," "professional," "clerical," etc., made little sense; under the existing conditions jobs were meaningfully divided according to whether or not they paid enough money (or left enough opportunities and time for black-marketeering) for people to survive. Strangely, unemployment was considered a blessing (on condition that one could get "good papers" that provided a "cover"), a telling fact about the revolution in occupational stratification.

Sorokin suggests that in time of war the main criterion for ranking occupations (their value in both subjective and objective terms, that is, as expressed by wages) is how "essential" or "nonessential" they are for defense and victory (Sorokin, 1945:298). Although it seems plausible, this statement may be more applicable to countries that were not under direct occupation, where one could, however superficially, measure the distance between various occupations and the enemy. In an occupied country, particularly where widespread terror was used against the civilian population, everyone was, in a sense, on the front line; everyone was in direct contact with the enemy. In these circumstances all occupations were equally "prestigious"; in other words, it mattered little what one did for a living.[10]

[10] This is not literally true. There is some ambiguity, for example, about the prestige attached to the work of smugglers who brought food into the cities illegally. On the one hand, they were accused of indecency in profiting from the inhuman conditions imposed by the occupier; on the other, they were considered the silent, unknown heros of the war (Szarota, 1973a:195-214) who, at the constant risk of death and exposed to robbery, blackmail, and extortion by Germans and Poles, were feeding starving cities.

175

Egalitarianism also affected the status of the youth. Its "liberation" from the tutelage of the older generation was only one aspect of its rising status as the gap between age groups closed. Young people's roles as leaders, particularly on the battlefield and in the underground organizations, further "equalized" different age groups. The prewar stratification of sexes was also undermined. Most women started to work, often became the heads and main providers of households while the men were gone, and fought bravely in the underground formations. Thus the inequalities of sex that in Europe had been inherent in culture and social stratification were diminishing rapidly.[11] Disaster, when its impact is sufficiently random in relation to social categories, tends to "destratify" (Barton, 1970:245). Thus, the whole process triggered a revolutionary change that set the stage for the postwar organization of societies and supranational bodies.[12] As a French historian of the period said, "whatever the outcome, it was in the underground that post-war Europe took shape" (Michel, 1972:265).

The only dimension of social stratification still effective in wartime society, the economic dimension, also demonstrated peculiar features in the Generalgouvernement. First, the middle-income group virtually disappeared. The overwhelming majority of the population lived on a bare subsistence level, while a small group of war profiteers made handsome profits and accumulated fortunes, leading to the development of a polarized social structure (HL, PUC: MSW, *Wydział Społeczny*, "Sprawozdanie sytuacyjne z

---

[11] Situations of normlessness "offer opportunities for the assertion of equality which were previously unavailable. . . . For the young as well as for the women, the revolution provides a setting for the triumph of human action over biology" (Coser, 1968:70).

[12] Sorokin (1945) mentions the war's broader consequences in regard to egalitarianism. He calls attention to the gradual disappearance of earlier differences in rank of nations, states, races, and ethnic groups, specifically the loss of supremacy of the white race.

176

ziem polskich," 8/43, p. 131).[13] Second, the wealthy group was composed largely of *nouveaux-riches*. Many prewar fortunes were confiscated, spent, or ruined, and the membership of the wealthy group constantly fluctuated. It was as easy to lose a fortune in an unlucky transaction as it was, with luck, to make one quickly. Third, wealth and worth—in its noneconomic sense—were no longer recognized as joint attributes: it was almost a citizen's duty to survive, but to live comfortably or, worse, to make a fortune invited suspicion and social censorship.

Despotic rule of terror and equality go well together, as Tocqueville predicted. Nonparticipation in power, severing of individuals' links with their traditional reference groups (be it family, social class, or professional group) through physical displacement, discontinuities in authority patterns, impoverishment, imposed changes of occupation, dissolution of the state, political parties, unions, and voluntary organizations of all sorts—all contributed to the atomization of Polish society. Added to these were the profound value crisis, the dissociation of "good" from wealth, and the loss of a sense of quality when a monetary value was placed on everything, including life. Everything in the new situation was casting the individual away from his fellow citizens, whom he no longer trusted, whom he feared, and with whom he fiercely competed in order to survive, gradually losing a sense of what are, or should be, the "rules of the game" of coexistence in society.

THE SOCIOLOGY OF COMMUNICATION

At the same time that the pressures of the occupation were producing social disorganization, many complex so-

[13] The *Biuletyn Informacyjny* (Nov. 21, 1941) observed that social stratification became simplified. Only two classes of people were left: the paupers (employed and unemployed), and those who could adjust to the new circumstances.

cial processes developed—for example, corruption and the underground state—to counter the forces of disintegration and to promote cohesion within Polish society. Here I want to draw attention to one particular phenomenon: rumors. In describing the texture of life under occupation, an analysis of rumors is necessary, if only because they were so much a part of everyday life. Furthermore, through an analysis of rumors I hope to shed light upon an important process in the preservation of social bonds.

"Normlessness," said Howard Becker (1968:76, 77), "is uncomfortable," and "it calls forth demand for norms." Consequently, in circumstances that are not routine, people demand news because they need to interpret the situation in order to decide how to cope with it. They often acquire this news in the form of rumors.[14]

It seems clear that the rumors circulating during the occupation had a cathartic function: they allowed people to interpret what was going on according to their deeply felt desires and wishes, which, through transmission into rumors, achieved a kind of reality when they were shared by large groups and thus "objectified" as "news." It would be naive, then, to be surprised that the rumors that circulated were so often out of joint with reality: "Where action is

[14] Shibutani (1966:9) appropriately defines *rumor* as "not so much the dissemination of a designated message (but) the process of forming a definition of a situation." He suggests (1966:17, 57, 164) two criteria that account for the emergence of rumors: that the demand for news exceed the supply made available through institutional channels; and that the situation in which the society is currently living be ambiguous, so that its members attempt to construct a meaningful interpretation. As Smelser (1962:81-82) also observed: "rumor and related beliefs arise when structural strain is not manageable within the existing framework of action . . . rumor and related beliefs restructure an ambiguous situation by explaining what has happened, by reporting what is happening, and by predicting what will happen." It is important to add one more condition accounting for the emergence of rumors. According to Swanson (1971:83), "Rumors are spread only in populations for which the information they are claimed to contain is believed useful for the handling of collective problems."

impossible or not seriously contemplated, accuracy of definitions is not decisive, and people may say things that please them" (Shibutani, 1966:91).[15] There was nothing strange, observes Zimand (1974), in the fact that the Jews who were being deported for extermination still did not believe that they were being led to death, in spite of all indications to the contrary. What is, after all, more improbable than a whole nation being physically exterminated? Even the Poles, who suffered less than the Jews, could not imagine enduring a prolonged German occupation.[16] After each winter, when cold and hunger added more than their usual share to the miseries inflicted by the occupiers, one would hear voices crying that the population could not take another winter like this one (Zaremba, 1957:129).

[15] "The most popular . [rumors] were those that were the least likely. . . . We are now in such conditions that it is very difficult to be critical; everything seems possible to us" (Landau, 1962 v.1:80, 633).

[16] Many rumors predicted the end of the war or some crucial events that were to bring it about shortly: "in 39-40, on the average of every six weeks, and then in 1940-41, almost every three months there was a date of an ultimatum, or bombardment, or a landing spread throughout the country. On this date Poland was supposed to be resurrected all of a sudden" (GSHI, PRM 45c/41: "Dwa lata okupacji niemieckiej w Polsce," Aug. 1941). In February 1942 the Germans were allegedly about to capitulate, and the territories they conquered about to be occupied by the armed forces of the Allies. Poland, for example, was assigned to occupy Libya (Landau, 1963 v.3:757). In August 1943 Warsaw went mad with joy, repeating a story about a German general shooting Hitler during a dispute. To make the triumph total, some rumors placed the event at Sulejówek, Piłsudski's private residence (Landau, 1963 v.3:115). Again, in late September and early October 1943 news of the forthcoming German capitulation was circulating widely, and some people were saying that they had heard of it on the German radio (Landau, 1963 v.3: 267, 277). "All this is easily understandable," wrote Landau, "in view of the lack of faith in German papers, the unavailability of other papers, and because so many people, particularly 'brain workers,' are unemployed and waiting impatiently for a change of the current situation" (Landau, 1962 v.1:76).

179

At any one moment it actually seemed much less reasonable to think of living under the Germans for another year than to envisage their losing the war in the near future. Halina Krahelska argued that the great upsurge in the popularity of astrologers, fortune tellers, chiromancers, palmists, crystal gazers, etc., during the war, together with the upsurge of belief in prophecies, forecasts, and predictions, derived from the psychological necessity of organizing the future into well-defined and, if possible, short periods so that one could *wait*. The situation was oppressive; there was nothing one could do to change it; and not very much was happening on the battlefront. Therefore, people had to structure the future in such a way that they could "hang on" to it.[17]

[17] A political emissary returning from Warsaw in 1941 reported that the population held a quasi-mystical faith in victory. This optimism was grounded, he speculated, in the conviction that the sufferings and hardships that the population had already gone through could not go unrevenged (GSHI, PRM 46a/41: "Sprawozdanie Antoniego," App. 20). The first date set for the end of the war was December 12, 1939 (this was the interpretation of the number "12," which allegedly appeared on the picture of the Virgin Mary in Częstochowa); January 6, 1940, was another (according to the prophecy of Andrew Bobola, the enslavement was to last 101 days); then a rabbi from Warsaw predicted that the war would end on January 15, 1940, etc. (Szarota, 1973a:448-449). In January 1940 the underground put out a brochure, "The fate of Poland in Tęgobórz's, Mickiewicz's and Czyński's forecasts" (Bartoszewski, 1974: 108). Later, in November 1942, the Bureau of Information and Propaganda of the Home Army distributed about 7,000 copies of a leaflet containing optimistic forecasts about Poland's future. Also, German propaganda tried to exploit the population's readiness to study and believe in prophecies. On October 18, 1942, the official paper published in Warsaw in the Polish language, *Nowy Kurier Warszawski* (*NKW*), carried an advertisement for Nostradamus's book on the fate of Europe, in which, it said, everything since 1558 had been predicted by the great clairvoyant. In it one could learn when Bolshevism would collapse and when there would be happiness and a good life for everyone in the New Europe (Bartoszewski, 1974:312, 319).

180

However, I would like to suggest a more general interpretation of rumors. In analyzing the phenomena of communication during the occupation, the crucial issue that
must be taken into consideration is not only the scarcity of
information available, but also the deliberate feeding of
false information into the system. Over a period of time, in
a system flooded with false information, the criterion for determining the reliability of information is less and less
dependent on its content. Instead, the content and the
source of information become so connected that the assessment of the reliability of content depends primarily on
where the information originates.

Which characteristic of the source is taken into account
during the occupation, when news is evaluated in terms of
where it comes from? Contrary to what one might expect,
the reliability of a piece of information is apparently not
thought to depend on whether its source has *direct access*
to actual data. In terms of direct access to data, the Germans were the most competent to inform the Polish public
on many matters of importance. But the Poles, obviously,
rejected as unreliable any information originating from German sources. Easy access to reliable data mattered less in
the eyes of the recipient of information than the supposed
intentions of the source disseminating the information.

Thus, the whole process of receiving news is based on
an evaluation of good or bad faith on the part of the source,
in other words, on an evaluation of its *loyalty*. This point
is very important. It helps to account for the wild content
of rumors circulating in Poland by making us aware that
the critical evaluation of a message, in this society, was primarily concerned with its source rather than with its content. Strange as it may seem, the Poles were least suspicious
of information generated at random. Hence their interest in
messages "written" on their palms, their desire to know what
can be seen inside a crystal ball, their avid readership of
obscure texts from the past in order to find out about the
present and future, and their ready willingness to believe

181

that a card drawn from a well-shuffled deck will give them information necessary to make the right decision in an important matter.

I think that what has surfaced in this analysis is a general sociological principle regulating life and social interaction in the GG. For we have found that what was valued in this society was not expertise, a specific characteristic, but loyalty, a diffuse characteristic. And loyalty was the underlying principle of interaction in various areas of life, not only in the process of information exchange. In fact, it was this valuation of loyalty above all else that allowed the Polish society in the GG to avoid destruction. It is true that a joint enterprise might lose efficiency when one chooses one's colleagues primarily for their trustworthiness, for their loyalty, instead of for their expertise in whatever the undertaking may be. But stress on loyalty protects society against the worst danger: annihilation.

In fact, it has been established by Simmel that confidence is "one of the most important synthetic forces within society" (Simmel, 1969:318). Its importance as a nomic factor is directly related, according to him, to the knowledge that the actor has of the situation: he "who knows completely need not trust" (Simmel, 1969:318). Such knowledge is possible, however, only when social relations are objectified, that is, when roles, rights, responsibilities, expectations, and duties are well defined. Otherwise, "in order to produce the necessary confidence [for engaging in social interaction] despite a lack of knowledge in objective matters, *a much higher degree of knowledge in personal matters is necessary*" (Simmel, 1969:319; italics added). Furthermore, actors need to supplement "purely general knowledge" with intimate knowledge of "the personal-individual area" when they engage in interactions that involve their vital interests.[18]

[18] "[T]he merchant who sells grain or oil needs to know only whether his correspondent is good for the price. But if he takes him as his associate . . . he must have thorough insight into him as a personality" (Simmel, 1964:319).

Clearly, the structural conditions of life in Polish society under the occupation were not conducive to basing mutual relationships on "purely general knowledge." Such knowledge was impossible amid the prevailing social disorganization and ambiguity. Also, parties involved in almost all relationships saw their most vital interests, often their lives, at stake, since these relationships most likely involved a breach of law that was punishable by death. Thus confidence, or loyalty, as I call it, became the most important "synthetic force" in society. The switch from "knowledge" to "loyalty," though a sacrifice of efficiency, was a defensive measure adopted by the society to prevent its own destruction.

CHAPTER VIII

Nationalities

In my discussions of the processes of social disorganization, I have not yet mentioned one specific aspect of life in Polish society that revealed in a drastic form the limits of the solidaristic response to the German occupation: the relationships among Poland's various ethnic groups. It is sad that in a work about Polish society during the war one can devote just a few lines to the story of three million Polish citizens, the Jews, who were effectively isolated and confined, wretched beyond description, in the area of the ghettos. The ghettos and the holocaust, although both happened on Polish soil, are a distinct subject because the pace of life and death of the Jews followed its own very special rhythm.

Unfortunately, it must be recorded that the Poles by and large remained neutral observers of the horrors of life in the Jewish ghettos and of the German atrocities perpetrated against the Jewish population.[1] The commander of the Home Army reported this attitude in a dispatch sent to London in September 1941: "Please accept it as a fact that the overwhelming majority of the country is anti-Semitic. . . . Anti-Semitism is widespread now. Even secret organizations remaining under the influence of the prewar activists in the Democratic Club or the Socialist Party adopt the postulate of emigration as a solution of the Jewish problem. This became as much of a truism as, for instance, the neces-

---

[1] As with all generalizations, this one is not absolutely precise. Thousands of Poles from all social strata of the Polish society heroically helped their Jewish fellow citizens, paying only too frequently with their own lives (Bartoszewski, Lewin, 1969; Iranek-Osmecki, 1971).

184

sity to eliminate Germans" (GSHI, Kolekcja Kota, no. 25/
10: doc. no. L.dz. 3763 tj.41, Nov. 23, 1941, signed: "Kalina
354. 25.IX.41"; also see PRM 45c/41: "Dwa lata okupacji
niemieckiej w Polsce," Aug. 1941).[2] Three years later, *after*
the "final solution" had already been carried out by the
Nazis, an emissary of the London government, Celt (Andrzej Chciuk), reported on his return from Poland the
Delegate's opinion that various official statements issued by
the Government in London stressing sympathy and solidarity with the Jewish cause should be toned down. "The
government exaggerates in its love for Jews," said the Delegate. Although, understandably, some of the Government
statements are determined by foreign policy requirements,
he added, the regime should restrain its pro-Jewish pronouncements because "the country does not like Jews." Undoubtedly, the two heads of the military and civilian underground networks were well informed about the prevailing
mood of the country.[3]

[2] Incidentally, the content of this dispatch is not in the recently
published edition of documents on the history of the Home Army
prepared by the Underground Poland Study Trust in London
(Pełczyński, 1973).

[3] I would hesitate to address myself to the subject of the "Jewish
problem" in more detail. Its treatment requires more than a brief
chapter in a book devoted to a different subject. However, let me
point out three phenomena that surfaced during the occupation and
figured prominently among factors rationalizing the hostility of the
Polish population toward the Jews. First, as the consequence of
German economic policies, a large group of Poles had taken over
property formerly owned by Jews. When the Polish government
issued a proclamation in 1939 declaring that all German laws and
decrees promulgated in Poland were invalid, this group favored a
definite and swift solution of the "Jewish problem" (GSHI, PRM
45c/41: "Dwa lata okupacji niemieckiej w Polsce," Aug. 1941).
Second, until at least 1941 the Polish population generally perceived
the Jews as much less the victims of political persecution than the
Poles themselves. Poles felt that although the Germans wanted to
destroy the Jews economically, they did not interfere greatly with
Jewish local administration, that Jews were not being sent for labor
in Germany, that Jews were not arrested and tortured for the purpose

185

The Ukrainian Minority

The relationship between Poles and Ukrainians should be treated more extensively here, not because it was "better" or "worse" than the Polish-Jewish relationship, but because, unlike the Jews, neither the Poles nor the Ukrainians were isolated from the rest of the world or confined to a particular territory.[4] Their many mutual contacts should not be ignored.

General instructions issued by Rosenberg (Reichminister

---

of putting down the Jewish independence movement, etc. In a sense, the Poles argued, the Jews got the better part of the deal: the Germans wanted to exterminate the Poles, or at least make them renounce their Polishness, while Jews were only to be eventually resettled (GSHI, PRM 45c/41: "Informacja: Z placówki rzymsko watykańskiej"). This misconception stemmed from the fact that the Jews were, so to speak, persecuted without discrimination. There was no agenda establishing which Jews should be hit hardest or destroyed first. All were "equal" candidates for extermination. This lack of identified, selected targets may have caused the feeling on the part of Poles that the Jews were not subjected to *political* persecution. "Looking at each other's situation," observed an anonymous author, "Poles and Jews equally have the typical human inclination to see only advantages in the situation of the other side, and only disadvantages and difficulties in what they experience themselves." They envy each other, and consequently their mutual dislike increases, he concluded (GSHI, PRM 45c/41: "Informacja: Z placówki rzymsko watykańskiej"). Finally, the third element shaping Polish attitudes toward the Jews were reports on the way Jews behaved vis-à-vis Russian as well as German occupiers. Numerous witnesses reported that the Jews were collaborating with the Russians in the eastern parts of Poland. The public picked up this news item because it confirmed stereotypes of Jewish cosmopolitanism, weak loyalty to the Polish state, and "Judeo-communism" (*żydo-komuna*). Simultaneously, the Jews were perceived as docile, meek, and servile toward the Germans.

[4] The leaders of the Ukrainian Central Committee submitted a statement to Governor General Frank in April 1941, in which they called for, among other things, the creation of an ethnically pure Ukrainian enclave from which all Poles and Jews would be resettled and into which all Ukrainians living in the GG would be brought. Frank refused to consider this request (Kubiiovych, 1975:422-423).

für die besetzen Ostgebiete) in May 1941 stated that "the Ukraine shall become an independent state in alliance with Germany" (United States, 1946 v.3:692). In fact, the Germans had established contacts with Ukrainian nationalists, the OUN, long before the war with the USSR. In spite of these contacts and Rosenberg's readiness to work with national committees, the systematic unwillingness of the German authorities to make binding decisions as far as the occupied territories were concerned, and the attitude of Erich Koch, who was appointed Reichskommissar for the Ukraine against Rosenberg's opposition, created a situation whereby no clear decision could be made concerning the future status of the Ukraine. Initially, however, the atmosphere seemed to favor the nationalists, and they were under the impression that the creation of a Ukrainian state was only a matter of time and circumstances. In this situation the radical faction of the OUN, under the leadership of Stepan Bandera, decided to force Germany's hand. On June 22, 1941, it established a Ukrainian National Committee in Cracow, and on the thirtieth of the same month, in Lwów, without previously consulting the Germans, it proclaimed the creation of the Ukrainian state. German officials present in the area failed to realize that this might be a bluff and participated in the festivities (Armstrong, 1963:79-80; Dallin, 1957:119). A few days later the new Ukrainian "government" and Bandera himself were arrested. When Hitler decided to attach the district of Galicia to the General-gouvernement, the hopes of the Ukrainian nationalists for an early solution were doomed. Nevertheless, within the framework of the German occupation, Ukrainian nationalists were able to devote more efforts, and achieve more results, than ever before in their cause of reviving Ukrainian national life.[5]

[5] According to Kubiiovych, the global assessment of the results of the committee's work in the GG during the war is positive. It managed, he maintains, "to increase Ukrainian holdings, to eradicate Polish influences, to strengthen national consciousness of the local

187

Shortly after the German victory over Poland, a Ukrainian Relief Committee was formed in Cracow under the chairmanship of a former docent of the Jagiellonian University, V. Kubiiovych. Within months the committee, renamed the Ukrainian Central Committee in April 1940 (Kubiiovych, 1975:84), was supervising directly and indirectly the development of Ukrainian national life in cultural, economic, and political domains.

Where before the war there were only 2,510 Ukrainian-language schools, of which only 457 were exclusively Ukrainian, in the 1942-1943 school year there were 4,173.[6] The main difficulty barring even more rapid development of the school system was, according to Kubiiovych, the lack of qualified personnel. About 30 percent of all teachers were university students or high school alumni, mostly activists of OUN, who did not have either experience or qualifications to teach (Kubiiovych, 1975:50, 206-207). Not only were the Ukrainians allowed to open a few high schools in the Generalgouvernement (in addition to the large number of elementary schools), but they also persuaded the Germans that some Ukrainian youths should be allowed to study at the universities in the Reich. Quite a few young

---

population . . . to recover at least a part of what we had lost in the past . . ." (1975:359).

[6] These data are given in John Armstrong's book, *Ukrainian Nationalism* (1963:52). Stephan Horak gives a slightly different estimate for the 1934-1935 school year: a total of 2,625 Ukrainian-language schools, of which 487 were exclusively Ukrainian (1961: 144). Another source cites data on the 1942-1943 school year different from those of Armstrong. A Polish underground report, *Sprawa Ukraińska* (GSHI, PRM 124: doc. no. L.dz. 1737/IV/44), quotes contemporary Ukrainian sources as stating that in March 1943 there were: 4,135 elementary schools with 621,000 pupils and 8,822 teachers; 12 high schools (*gimnazjum*) with 5,000 students and 180 teachers; 7 junior colleges training future teachers, with 1,750 students and 56 professors; 120 vocational schools with 19,000 students and 1,020 teachers; 196 agricultural schools with 63,949 students and 796 teachers; and two institutes (university-level schools) in Lwów with 2,000 students.

Ukrainians received fellowships from the German Academic Exchange Office (DAAD) for this purpose (Kubiiovych, 1975:200, 218-219).

The economic life of the Ukrainian minority was strengthened by the fast-developing cooperative movement, a traditional arena of activity for Ukrainian nationalists (Armstrong, 1963:220-221). While at the beginning of the German occupation only 161 Ukrainian cooperatives were operating in the territory of the Generalgouvernement, a year and a half later, by March 1941, their number had increased to 1,990 (Kubiiovych, 1975:146, 149). Ukrainians also largely benefited from the expropriation of Jewish businesses (Kubiiovych, 1975:326).

Simultaneously with expansion in cultural and economic domains, Ukrainian leaders were trying to enlarge the sphere of their political and administrative influence. German officials assigned in the GG to supervise Ukrainian affairs were very helpful and sympathetic to their cause (Kubiiovych, 1975:349-351). Consequently, Ukrainian efforts to have Ukrainians assigned to all administrative and judiciary posts that were not specifically reserved for Germans (in the territories where the Ukrainian population lived) brought very good results. Local administration in those areas (except for larger towns where the Polish population was concentrated), auxiliary police, labor administration (Arbeitsamte), the post and the judiciary were all taken over by Ukrainians (Kubiiovych, 1975:177-179). At the beginning of 1944 the number of Ukrainian wójts and mayors in the administration of the Generalgouvernement stood at 463. *The majority of Ukrainian local officials served in the district of Galicia*—346 of them, contrasted with 3 Polish officials (Madajczyk, 1970 v.1:222). Furthermore, Ukrainians were often entrusted with official duties in Polish villages and hamlets with a Ukrainian minority, just as the Poles sometimes were in Ukrainian villages (*Sprawa*, Dec. 24, 1942).

The Ukrainians knew how to use their advantageous new

189

appointments to strike back at the local Polish element that had dominated the administration before the war (Pel-czyński, 1973:137-145). As Kubiiovych (1975:421) asserted, "we had no reasons to suffer German oppression in solidarity with the Poles and, at this time [that is, 1941], to become disloyal toward the Germans." Indeed, the Ukrainians as a group enjoyed better conditions of life than the Poles in the Generalgouvernement (Torzecki, 1972:255).

After the outbreak of the Russo-German war, when recruitment for the SS-Galizien division began, Kubiiovych, in a symbolic gesture, enlisted first and was registered as a volunteer with the number 1 (Szcześniak, Szota, 1973:123). The activists of the Ukrainian Central Committee on many occasions proclaimed their loyalty to the Third Reich and their willingness to continue at its side "the struggle against Bolshevism" (Szcześniak, Szota, 1973:79). Ukrainian youth responded en masse to German-sponsored recruitment into military formations to fight against the Soviets on the Eastern Front. Tens of thousands of people had to be rejected because there was a surplus of candidates (Armstrong, 1963:174). All Ukrainian authorities—Kubiiovych, Szeptyckij, and even the OUN (and UPA), which was at that time already in the underground—supported the recruitment drive (Armstrong, 1963:170-173; Torzecki, 1972: 293). All of them felt that Ukrainians needed a large body of armed and trained men who could fight for independence when the right time came. A considerable percentage of soldiers in the Russian Liberation Army (ROA), which was under General Vlasov's command, was also Ukrainian. Estimates vary between 35 and 40 percent, with some units reported to be as much as 70 percent Ukrainian (Armstrong, 1963:184).

After the war with the USSR began, German propaganda was swift to inform the people of conquered territories that they had been liberated from the Bolsheviks, but it was totally incapable of explaining what the Reich would offer them. A number of German observers saw clearly that if

German goals in the East were to win the war and secure manpower, "an ideological goal must be given to the local peoples of the Eastern area. . . . Never in world history has there been such a condition whereby a large people, respectively several large peoples, gave their entire working power and their blood in military commitments without knowing what results they could achieve for themselves, their children, and their children's children" (United States, 1946 v.3:932-58; original translation).

The representative of the Ostministerium who toured the area in December 1942 and prepared the report from which the preceding quotation was taken was only one of many who voiced similar opinions. Rosenberg, for instance, deplored the treatment of many prisoners of war from the Red Army, who were left to starve to death:

> The treatment of POW's appears to be founded in great part on serious misconceptions about the people of the Soviet Union. One finds the opinion that the people become more inferior the further one goes east. If the Poles already were given harsh treatment, one argues, it should therefore be done to a much greater extent to the Ukrainians, White Ruthenians, Russians, and finally the "Asiatics." It was apparently completely ignored, in the treatment of POW's, that Germany found, in contrast to the West (France, Belgium, The Netherlands, Norway), a people who went through all the terror of Bolshevism, and who now, happy about their liberation, put themselves willingly at the disposal of Germany. A better gift could not come to Germany in this war, which requires every last man. But instead of accepting this gift, the people of the East are being treated more contemptibly and worse than the people of the West, who do not hide their enmity toward Germany. (United States, 1946 v.3:128)

This memorandum is a most revealing statement from one of the top officials whose job it was to supervise *directly*

191

the task of empire construction. It calls for no less than a revision of the racial doctrine of which he himself was one of the authors. The need to give peoples in the East "some general system of values" was recognized by Himmler as well, although his ideas on the subject had less far-reaching implications than Rosenberg's: he thought that religious sects preaching nonviolence should be cultivated among the subjugated peoples.[7]

Why did the Ukrainians collaborate so willingly, even though the Germans offered no political solution of the Ukrainian problem, and even though they failed to order the return to private ownership of the land collectivized under the Bolsheviks? A satisfactory answer to this question calls for a complex statement, I believe, but part of the answer is that the Germans unleashed Ukrainian nationalism and let it unburden itself on other nationalities living in the area.

The German occupation created a suitable framework to put into action early phases of the Ukrainian "nationalist revolution" (Torzecki, 1972:223-224). The Ukrainians gambled on the outbreak of Russo-German hostilities and a German advance into the USSR: otherwise, the Ukraine could not be territorially united. Thus, in the preparatory phase, before the outbreak of hostilities and during the early stages of the Russo-German war, Ukrainians and Germans were natural allies, as both benefited from cooperation. In the long run, however, their interests in the area were different. In the event of a German victory, the Ukraine could be established as a sovereign state only through an unlikely act of selfless renunciation by Germany of a part of the territories it had already conquered. Consequently, since Soviet victory spelled doom for Ukrainian

---

[7] Thus he was ready to spread Buddhism among all Turkic peoples (i.e., Moslems) and promote among Christian Slavs the teachings of Jehovah's Witnesses. He even went so far as to order Kaltenbrunner to ferret out Jehovah's Witnesses from the concentration camps to which they had been committed in the meantime (Dallin, 1957:616).

192

national aspirations, the Ukrainians could only hope for a simultaneous German and Russian defeat. Needless to say, however, they could do little to bring about this welcome repetition of the outcome of the First World War. They could, on the other hand, make sure that should this favorable situation recur, they would be prepared and mobilized to create, through their own actions, the fait accompli of Ukrainian sovereignty. This was the inspiration behind the "nationalist revolution" and the meaning of its preparatory phases, during which a "cleaning-up" operation was to be conducted (Torzecki, 1972:291).

At the end of 1942, large detachments of Ukrainian auxiliary police, which had discharged their duties faithfully under the Germans, were ordered by the Ukrainian underground (OUN) to abandon their posts and to join or form partisan formations.[8] Then the bloodbath began for the Polish population living in Wołyń and in Eastern Małopolska. In several instances Ukrainian nationalists carried out extermination raids with the knowledge, and sometimes the help, of local German commanders (Szcześniak, Szota, 1973:127; Pełczyński, 1976:34, 59). What started as killings of single individuals and isolated Polish families developed into the systematic extermination of entire Polish hamlets. The Polish population either fled the area or set up armed encampments—sometimes ten to twenty thousand people strong—where it defended itself against Ukrainian nationalists. Although estimates are difficult to make, Ukrainian nationalists murdered sixty to eighty thousand Poles in eastern Poland between 1941 and 1944 (Szcześniak, Szota, 1973:166-167, 170; Torzecki, 1972:328-330). The Home Army (AK) was criticized in the underground press for not adequately protecting Poles in the east. Simultane-

[8] The order to go "into the forest" was allegedly issued because German policies of reprisals against Communists (for which, among others, Ukrainian police were employed) had ceased to be discriminatory and were injuring "the patriotic Ukrainian peasantry as frequently as they did Communist sympathizers" (Armstrong, 1963:148).

193

ously, Polish partisan formations—the Home Army and the National Armed Forces (NSZ)—are known to have killed entire populations of isolated Ukrainian hamlets in reprisal for murdered Poles (Szcześniak, Szota, 1973:186; Torzecki, 1972:297).

Old scores were being settled in this way, and a policy of fait accompli was being pursued. It was argued that in the event the Germans were defeated and the weakened Russians pushed back east, the Western Allies could not refuse Ukrainian claims to independent statehood in territories that by that time would be virtually *Polenrein* (*Kraj*, Nov. 22, 1944). Such was the calculation; it did not prove correct, but it cost many lives.

There was strong opposition to this course of action within the Ukrainian community itself. Metropolitan Szeptyckij, for example, denounced it (Pełczyński, 1976:60). There were also reports of contacts between the Polish underground and the OUN headquarters as late as 1944, when the apparent similarity in the position of the Polish and Ukrainian independence movements (they both faced the prospect of fighting against German and Russian armies) led some people to think that the two parties could reach an understanding on common aims (GSHI, PRM 124: doc. no. L.9z.1737/IV/44, App. 6; Pełczyński, 1976:60, 299). But once unleashed, terrorist action could not be easily stopped, particularly with all the difficulties central leadership has in controlling its subordinates when they are in the loose structure characteristic of partisan formations.

Ukrainian nationalists made considerable progress between 1939 and 1944 toward preparing for the establishment of an independent state. They exploited opportunities made available to them by the Germans and responded shrewdly and flexibly to various German moves. They started a strong partisan movement, centralized in 1943 by the Bandera wing of the OUN, the so-called Ukrainian Partisan Army of between 40,000 and 100,000 men (Armstrong, 1963:156). About 100,000 Ukrainians served in German-sponsored armed forces. And a skeleton of a local administration received training through its employment by the Germans, while cultural and educational activity continued.

With silent German blessing, Ukrainians were pushing out or openly exterminating the Poles living in the Western Ukraine (not to mention the Jews, of course, who were the first ethnic group exterminated in that territory). They waged another campaign, not only as German auxiliaries but also on their own, as partisans, against Communist partisans and sympathizers in the local population who had revealed themselves during the Russian occupation in 1939-1941 or earlier under Soviet rule. Altogether, the Ukrainians were setting the stage for their ultimate takeover in the aftermath of the war. They were determined that after the war Poles would no longer be able to suppress Ukrainian nationalist claims by force of arms, as had happened in 1918-1920. Accordingly, they began their campaign against the Poles before the war came to an end.

Modification of Nazi Racial Theory

The Nazis, if one is to judge them according to the "ideology" they preached, believed that all fundamental problems of social organization could be solved by the clear determination of every individual's racial group and his assignment afterwards to a proper place in the polity. In practice, of course, the issue was more complex than a simple division into *Über-* and *Untermenschen*. The process of selection, resulting from the pursuit of racial policy by the Nazis, involved two complementary, and yet conflicting, tasks: it called for discovery and proper labeling of undesirables, and, simultaneously, it stipulated that *Wiedereindeutschung*, that is, "removal of every valuable trace of German blood from Polendom" (Koehl, 1957:122), be pursued with determination. This introduced a tension on the level of ideology to abandon the notion of a polar distinction into Germans and non-Germans and recognize, instead,

195

that Germanism represents a quality that may be had in larger or smaller degrees.

The same modification of the racial theory appeared necessary for practical reasons as a result of imperial expansion beyond historically German territories and the need to assure some degree of participation by the conquered populations in the regimes of occupation. Consequently, the ascriptive interpretation of the concept of race had to be abandoned little by little. If any non-Germans were to be kept alive (and some had to be), a labeling system had to be devised that would permit the ranking of the subdued population on a scale of Germanism. Therefore Germanism had to be defined in such a way that one could have more or less of it. The concept of race thus began to acquire an achievement dimension. On December 12, 1941, for example, the following advertisement was placed in the *Warschauer Zeitung*:

> A donor of Nordic blood is being sought in connection with an on-going research project. Inquiries should be made only by fellow countrymen of distinctly leadership type [Herrentypus]. Characteristic features: aggressive, fond of sports, composed and self-assured, sedate, able to think penetratingly, sagacious, tolerant, taciturn, long-headed, with blond hair, bright eyes, tall, slender, young, healthy—encountered most frequently in northwestern Germany. (Bartoszewski, 1974:242-243)

More solid evidence is also available to support this point. Significantly, the German National Lists (DVL), which served as an instrument of naturalization, as we would say today, included four different categories, and specific performance standards had to be met in order to qualify for a given classification. Thus the best *Volksdeutsche* (category one on the DVL), the "fighters," had to prove membership in National Socialist organizations prior to the war. A second-class *Volksdeutsch*, a "genuine" German, was one who before the war joined some German association other

196

than a National Socialist one. Third-class *Volksdeutsche* were Poles who permitted their German spouses to raise children in the spirit of Germanism. Finally, the fourth category included "traitors," that is, Germans who renounced their German identity. In reality, this category was residual; anyone could be included in it, and in actuality many people were put on the DVL against their will.[9]

Without much ado, through mere relabeling, people could thus be co-opted into the system and drawn into active cooperation. Paradoxically, residual categories on the DVL (in practice, both the third and fourth categories) were more important for the occupation administration than the first two categories, though from the point of view of salvaging "German blood from Polendom," the opposite should be true. It was through mass inscriptions onto the DVL (categories three and four) that the local official could demonstrate the success of his administration to his superiors and simultaneously alienate the signatories from the rest of the Polish society, which viewed the *Volksdeutsche* with understandable hostility.

In view of these and other elements of German racial policies, especially the imposed stratification of the Poles into such subgroups as *Deutschstammige* or *Leistungpole*,[10]

[9] The Polish government knew about this, and a projected decree on responsibility for wartime crimes, prepared in February 1943, proposed no legal responsibility for merely signing the DVL (GSHI, A 9 III 4/21: Feb. 8, 1943), as it was obvious that many people had done so under duress.

[10] According to a decree of the Reich Ministry of the Interior of November 14, 1940, in order to be classified as a "Pole," one actually had to prove one's Polishness by establishing that he had actively manifested his patriotism. The document specified further that no Lithuanians, Great Russians, Ukrainians, Czechs, Mazurs, Gorals, Kaszubs or Silesians could claim to be Polish (GHSI, A 9 III 1/2: "Raport sytuacyjny," Nov. 10, 1940–Feb. 1, 1941). This social phenomenon is perfectly assymetrical to a typical mechanism regulating status differentiation, where a proof of eligibility is requested, but only of those who aspire to be admitted into "higher" categories on the social scale.

197

one cannot but conclude that the modification of the Nazi ideological stance (reflected in the shift from emphasis on ascription to invocation of achievement as the primary *definiens* of race) took place in order to accommodate pragmatic requirements of day-to-day administration of the occupied territories. No sensible policy of collaboration could be articulated by spokesmen of a simultaneously revolutionary and racist doctrine of society. Thus, in order to allow for some participation of some segments of the conquered population, the Nazis proceeded to redefine its race so as to make such participation acceptable to themselves. Germanization was simultaneously designed to change the mentality of the conquerors and to modify the racial identification of the conquered. This policy captured, as it were, the moment of interplay between ideology and practice. Unmistakably, the Nazis engaged in the process of racial redefinition out of pure necessity, in order to preserve the *existence* of the polity. In this respect, it was parallel to corruption, which, as I have argued, provided a way out from the economic and political illogicalities of the German program of occupation.

CHAPTER IX

Terror and Obedience

AUTHORITY AND COERCION

In discussing corruption, I indicated that coercion alone does not suffice to make a society of fifteen million people "operate" for an extended period of time. Coercion stimulates alienative involvement, and we know of no social systems that can survive for long on coercion alone, except those that are limited in size and maintain a high staff-inmate ratio and facilities for keeping inmates in isolated, easy-to-control subgroups. I have also suggested that in the Generalgouvernement the Poles were induced to develop calculative involvement. Now I want to propose that, even when power is predominantly based on coercion, subjects may still develop a kind of normative commitment to the system: in other words, it makes sense to speak of authority based on coercion.

At first glance, it would appear that we should reject such a statement outright. After all, Weber has taught us that authority begins precisely where coercion ends. But such a proposition, although rightly identifying a fundamental distinction between two modes of securing compliance—one through fear and the other through respect—leaves unexplored a blurred area where the two concepts apply simultaneously: that of legitimate uses of coercion. Weber himself recognized the importance of this seemingly incompatible mixture by making it a cornerstone of his definition of State (Weber, 1968 v.1:56). Thus, because legitimate application of coercion is also possible, we must distinguish different modes under which coercion appears in social systems, as well as consider the total area of responsibility of power holders. Only then can we arrive at an understanding of the ambiguous relationship between subordinates and superordinates in a society founded on oppression.

I would like to draw attention first to a particular phenomenon: as occupation authorities, or a revolutionary government, take over a state, they simultaneously "acquire" license to use coercion, just as they acquire, for instance, the authority to impose and collect taxes or to fix prices for commodities under the government's monopoly (such as tobacco, matches, and liquor in Poland). It is not, to be exact, the *use* of coercion by the occupier that turns the wrath of the population against him, but rather his *abuses* of coercion.

Second, I would like to reiterate that the Germans established the death penalty in almost every paragraph of the new law for all offenses, including the most trivial (Broszat, 1965:128-143). This was equivalent to sanctioning and generalizing coercion. We must be aware of this phenomenon because it is crucial, I believe, to distinguish between those systems in which law sanctions coercion and those in which coercion, although a fact of life, occurs only as an abuse of law or as its transparent misinterpretation.[1] After all, the basic tenet of a citizen's virtue and the basic focus of socialization processes in polities founded on the authority of law is obedience to the *law in general*, embodied in the concept of formal justice, rather than to *laws with specific content*. Advocates of substantive justice are more often than not revolutionaries, subversive of the old regime.

In short, fraudulent identification of violence and legality

[1] Some will say, truthfully, that such generalization of coercion will eventually only impair the law. Although this injury most probably will take place, we should not pass over the complexity of the process leading to it. In particular, we should notice the increase in the "respectability" of coercion in the process: by being incorporated into the paragraphs of law it will unavoidably share in the law's majesty.

is possible because legitimate use of coercion is a recognized fact of life. In the process, the moral authority of the law will decline, but, reciprocally, particularly in the early period of the new rule, violence will gain respectability.[2]

A consequence of this ambiguity, it seems to me, is that an imposed regime also possesses quasi legitimacy in the perception of its forcibly rounded-up subjects, because never are *all* laws, even those enforced by an illegitimate authority, considered by the public to be abuses of justice. There are always some laws that can be called regulatory. Such laws, and the normative obligation to respect them, seem to the public to be a natural and necessary component of orderly social intercourse, no matter who is charged with their enforcement. Thus in any system the guardians are perceived *also* as executors of laws that do not necessarily violate the ordinary citizen's sense of personal dignity and justice. As a result, some degree of ambiguity is introduced into the citizen's understanding of the limits of legitimacy in the rule of his oppressors, and the necessity of recognizing which acts are outside and which within these limits makes strong demands on the subject's sense of discrimination.

The cognitive strain of having to make an independent decision about the legitimacy of each separate request of the authorities might well produce the wish to reduce that strain. Radical approaches would be, on the one hand, to reject all such requests, that is, to become a revolutionary committed to the overthrow of the regime, or, on the other, to *recognize*, for the time being, all requests as legitimate. Neither decision results from cold, rational calculation, but is the result, at least in part, of those psychological factors

[2] How could we otherwise account for publication of numerous books by high State Secret Police (ChK) officials, boasting of their exploits, in the years immediately following the October Revolution? It is from such official sources that Solzhenitsyn compiled factual documentation for his denunciation of the officially sponsored terror and mass exterminations that occurred long before Stalin came to power.

that make us either avoid or redefine situations in which we experience cognitive dissonance. Thus, whether one will become revolutionary or conformist depends on many factors, the most important, perhaps, being the "style" of oppression by the rulers. I believe the German occupation had certain characteristics that made it easier for the Poles to become revolutionaries rather than conformists, because, if I may anticipate what will be argued later in greater detail, the Germans applied coercion at random, so that conformism guaranteed no security, while rebellion at least allowed one to retain normative integrity with values such as loyalty and patriotism.

Subjects who choose the nonrevolutionary path of avoidance may find it impossible to follow all the rules, but they will try to conceal their transgressions, not only from fear of punishment, but also because they feel "ill at ease," "uncomfortable," even "guilty," whenever the guardians of the public order reproach them for illegal behavior.[3] This sense of guilt gives the authorities an advantage over the lawbreaker and explains why the lawbreaker is ready to accept punishment as something deserved. Said Zhivago in the last conversation with his childhood friends, who, like himself, were the last survivors of the Russian intelligentsia: "I found it painful to listen to you, Innokentii, when you told us how you were re-educated and became mature in jail. It was like listening to a horse describing how it broke itself in" (Pasternak, 1958:483). People, unlike horses, "break themselves in," and in that sense we may speak of authority, rather than merely rule, based on coercion. We must therefore make a distinction between systems that sanction coercion legally and those that only use it.

Authority based on coercion produces an atomized

[3] Conversely, one might add that those who have not broken the law have a false sense of security and often are more vulnerable to reprisals than active revolutionaries who carefully avoid all "accidental" contacts with repressive organs of the authorities (see Chap. XI below).

society. To be subjected to violence is a solitary experience. To be subjected to authority based on coercion does not make one a member of any community or group. The only conceivable collectivity that one can become a part of would be the group composed of other potential targets of violence, potential victims. Such a group, however, possesses no integrating bond. Quite the contrary. To the extent that the means of coercion, because of material limitations, cannot be applied simultaneously against all members of the subjugated group, there will always be a part of the group of potential victims that is not physically tormented. The temporarily privileged subgroup tries to maintain this state of affairs, even at the cost of letting others be subjected to violence. If in no other way, this is expressed in their psychological attitude: they feel compassion for those who are actually tortured, but also relief that it is not their turn. And, of course, they would like such a situation to last as long as possible.

A community of victims does not exist until individuals find some collective value for which they are willing to suffer, or until they revolt.[4] Either way, however, in the emergence of a collective value that permits the creation of a bond establishing moral life, the role of coercion exists only for contrast. The most we can say for it is that it *precedes* the creation of a moral life temporally, or logically, but does not contribute to it. In a system where authority is based on coercion there is no integrating bond to make a *collective* of the people who accidentally find themselves in it. Social atomization here is overcome only when the formula of authority is opposed, when the subjects stand up against oppression. But oppression itself cannot produce morality, that is, collective life. In fact, the German occupation was a revolution designed to produce social atomization.

[4] Revolt in itself, as Camus points out, is a recognition of such a value that establishes a community: "Je me revolte, donc nous sommes" (1951:36).

SATISFACTION AND OBEDIENCE

The phenomena we have just examined are normative ambivalences that still do not reveal what behavior to expect from people experiencing them. After normative commitments crystallize, we still have to find out about "situational facilities" (Smelser, 1971) in order to be able to predict the likelihood of compliance with demands of the authorities.

Two components, it seems to me, must be taken into consideration: the anticipated level of deprivation by one who would decide to conform to the demands of the agents of social control; and the anticipated level of deprivation in the consequence of punishment should one decide to ignore and violate the demands. Here two countervailing mechanisms are involved: the more one's obedience to the law prevents the satisfaction of one's needs, the more one is ready to break the law; however, the more laws one breaks, the more severe is the negative sanction to which one might be exposed.

Without tackling the distributive problems that result from the different quantities of strategic resources that individuals command within the system, it still makes sense for us to maintain that for each individual, given the resources he controls, there is a certain maximum level of satisfaction he can achieve within the system without violating its laws.[5] Let us call this maximum the "welfare concern" of the system. On the other hand, a given individual may not necessarily reach the maximum point because of mismanagement of resources under his control. Should any-

[5] "Satisfaction" is, of course, a subjective dimension. For the moment, however, we are not concerned with interpersonal comparisons but rather with comparing levels of satisfaction in one person's experience. What I am postulating is that satisfaction can be measured on an ordinal level for each individual. The concept of choice is grounded in the feasibility of such ordinal measurement.

one desire more satisfaction than the legally feasible maximum, he would have to break the law to acquire it. By how much? We cannot tell exactly, but we can say specifically that an individual must engage in a certain *minimum* amount of disobedience in order to obtain a given increment in satisfaction.[6]

An ideal legal system would be constructed in such a way as to make all such considerations obsolete. If the law is to function as a deterrent, there should be no inducement to break the law. Therefore, for all citizens and all wants the following relationship would apply: The penalty for the minimum disobedience necessary in order to obtain a given increment of satisfaction should bring more "negative satisfaction," in absolute terms, than the sought-after increment of satisfaction brings enjoyment. Obviously, such an analysis is based on an assumption untenable in real life: that each breach of law is detected and punished according to the letter of the law. Such a situation does not exist. In the "real world" we are dealing always with probabilities. Consequently, if "crime pays," it is not because the penalty for breaking the law brings less discomfort compared with the satisfaction one derives from committing the forbidden act,

[6] This proposition is straightforward and based on common sense. There are different levels of disobedience that, if one decided to pursue them, would yield the desired outcome, that is, provide a certain level of satisfaction. Among them, there is a particular activity for which, if an individual were caught practicing it, he would receive a lighter sentence than for anything else he could have done to accomplish the same goal. We can imagine someone seeking a lawyer's advice on how to set up a deal in such a way that, if caught, he would receive the least possible penalty. Theoretically, any breach of the law calls for a penalty that results in some level of "negative satisfaction." In terms of cost analysis, we must then take into consideration the relationship between the sought-after increment in satisfaction and the punishment that is supposed to follow every breach of the law.

but because crime often goes unpunished and the *only* product of disobedience is an increase in satisfaction.[7]

Given a certain capacity for provision of goods that might be objects of desire, a social system can maintain varying levels of "welfare concern." In the case of a country under foreign domination, the welfare concern of the system is primarily determined by the policies of the colonial power and how many goods it syphons away from the subjugated society. With varying opportunities present for legitimate satisfaction, the incentive to break the law will also vary in order to achieve satisfaction in excess of what is legally allowed.

With the increased frequency of transgressions, problems of effective law enforcement will grow in number and difficulty, so that eventually the proportion of offenders who are punished will diminish, not simply because the law enforcement agencies are inefficient, but also as a consequence of the delegitimization of the law. The proportion could not be increased simply by modernizing and improving the agencies because so many of their functions depend on citizens' initiative (Black, 1971); if law is not perceived as legitimate, no improvements in enforcement agencies will make them effective beyond a certain level. Obviously, recognition of the legitimacy of the law hinges also on whether people consider the level of welfare concern that characterizes their social system to be adequate.

The overwhelming majority of Poles in the General-

[7] A discussion of this problem can be found in an article by Norman Frohlich and Joe Oppenheimer (1974:46): "If he evades [paying taxes], he can anticipate a possible sanction. How much he will be willing to pay in taxes, then, depends upon how much he values being "excused" from the *threat* of punishment. This, in turn, depends upon both the severity of the sanction *and* his expectation that he will actually receive the threatened sanction. Thus, in general, freedom from the *threat* of the sanction will be valued less than the avoidance of the sanction *per se*, since delivery of the sanction is probabilistic."

206

gouvernement thought the welfare concern patently inadequate. They also discovered that because the Germans promulgated too many laws they could not enforce, the probability of being caught breaking the law was negligible. Moreover, the Germans, as I shall explain, were not interested in punishing the guilty but in terrorizing everyone indiscriminately, that is, they applied coercion at random.[8] In short, in this society powerful incentives existed to seek satisfaction in excess of what was legally allowed.

COLLECTIVE RESPONSIBILITY

The final theoretical point I want to discuss here is the distinction between those social orders in which collective responsibility is introduced and those in which it is not. In both, sanctions are ultimately applied to individuals. In a collective responsibility system, however, it does not matter whether the individual suffering punishment actually transgressed a norm, because it is not an individual but an entire collectivity that is being forced to behave in a certain way. The problem of collective responsibility must be introduced into our discussion because several occupation regimes in recent history have used that method to enforce compliance. Furthermore, collective responsibility is one of the oldest methods of social control and has only recently become a synonym for terror.

In the past, collective responsibility was used under patrimonial domination as a fully predictable method of inducing compliance with the ruler's authority under con-

[8] Although at times the boundaries between terror and other, "calculable forms of coercion are vague, coercive means other than terror leave the victim an opportunity to orient himself and foresee the consequences of his action; terror typically does not. . . . It is this element of arbitrariness—or, from the vantage point of the citizen, the unpredictability—in the use of terror that is its distinguishing mark" (Dallin, Breslauer, 1970:4).

ditions of scarcity of administrative apparatus (Weber, 1968 v.3:1022-1025).[9] As Reinhard Bendix observed in his exposition of Weber's thought: "The method of imposing a collective responsibility for the performance of public duties is a response to the administrative problems of a regime that does not possess a coercive apparatus extensive enough to enforce the personal liability of the political subjects" (Bendix, 1962:340). Indeed, as we know, the German apparatus of administration operated in the Generalgouvernement without adequate manpower.

As we are interested here in predicting compliance with demands enforced by the method of collective responsibility, we must distinguish between two contexts. Following one strategy, sanctions may be applied to individuals who are capable of influencing the collectivity's behavior. When a group of hostages is captured in a small town and threatened with execution unless certain regulations are obeyed, they may, through their kin, friends, and public opinion, exercise a restraining influence on all those who might disobey. We can calculate the probability of compliance as fairly high in such a situation. However, sanctions applied to individuals who are *not* capable of effective influence on the collectivity's behavior will fail to achieve their purpose. Thus, for example, when a group of hostages

[9] Only under conditions of "predictability" as to what group is threatened with sanctions for the misbehavior of a given category of individuals can collective responsibility produce self-policing by that group. In that sense, predictability is an indispensable element of effective deterrence through the principle of collective responsibility. In the past the sense of fairness associated with collective responsibility went very far indeed. An incident recounted by Marc Bloch in his *Feudal Society* provides an illustration: "In 1260, a knight, Louis Defeux, was wounded by a certain Thomas d'Ouzouer and proceeded against his assailant in court. The accused did not deny the fact but he explained that he had himself been attacked some time before by a nephew of his victim. What offence, then, had he committed? *Had he not, in conformity with the royal ordinances, waited forty days before taking his revenge—the time held to be necessary to warn one's kindred of the danger?*" (Bloch, 1961:126; italics added).

208

is taken in Warsaw, a city of 1,300,000 inhabitants, it is un-likely that informal groups, such as family or friends of the hostages, could persuade the whole population to comply with an imposed regulation.[10]

In a closely knit group, where the fate of each member is important to every other member, the threat of collective responsibility inspires the group to use its own internal mechanisms of social control and obliges a would-be law-breaker to take into consideration damages that may be inflicted upon his group if he breaks the law. But a member of a large, loosely knit group feels no such inhibition, since someone else, to whom he is indifferent, may suffer the consequences of his act. In the most extreme situation, when impossible demands are made of the group and the threat of collective responsibility is supported by the holding of real, randomly chosen hostages, the group will respond with either apathy or absolute disobedience aimed at destroying the agents of social control. Then the members can no longer make rational choices or evaluate means and ends; the only question involves probability. "I was calculating one's chances of surviving the occupation," wrote Zygmunt Zaremba (1957:134), the leader of the underground Polish Socialist Party, PPS-WRN. "The calculation was simple: there are about 30,000,000 Poles, every day the Germans take about 3,000 people, thus my chances of being taken are 1:10,000. Why worry then? And so we did not worry."[11]

[10] The latter case may have two variants. First, the hostages may be selected even before a violation occurs; this selection is made public, and it is therefore possible to predict the "cost" of noncompliance. Second, the hostages may be selected at random, after the crime is discovered. But even the preselection may be random, performed by street round-ups. Then, although the lists of hostages are published in advance—as they were in Warsaw during the worst police terror in 1943—the sanction is still de facto applied at random. Therefore, the distinction between preselected and randomly chosen victims does not seem to be crucial.

[11] Stenograms of conferences about security permit us to see also how the Germans perceived the problem. Krüger, during a meeting in

RANDOM PUNISHMENT

The preceding discussion indicates that collective responsibility does not necessarily result in the self-policing of the group exposed to it. Only when such a group is small and closely knit, or when the indigenous authorities and agents of social control are left with sufficient autonomy to engage in effective collaboration, can the occupier, through threats of collective responsibility, extort behavior that it otherwise would not be able to obtain. As it was introduced in the Generalgouvernement, however, collective responsibility (except for specific cases where families of hunted people were arrested in order to force fugitives to give themselves up) did not fit into any of these categories but instead had all the characteristics of punishment applied at random. Is there any rationality in such a strategy of social control?

If we assume that the most important goal of social control is deterrence (and although, as Durkheim has shown [1897], it may be contrary to sociological principles for a society to have no crime whatsoever, an ideal legal system is one that aims at just that), a steady application of random

---

1941 (Frank, 1970 v.1:320), revealed that intelligence data on the developments of the underground included an instruction allegedly issued by the underground authorities to all Poles employed by the Germans: "You should cooperate with the Germans in the most loyal fashion; you must show impeccable honesty and diligence; if you are asked to prove your loyalty we empower you to sign statements that you are ready to work for the Germans as they instruct you." "Obviously," responded Frank to this news, "that nothing has happened so far in a given sector of work, that Poles employed there were trustworthy—does not mean anything. To trust them would be completely unjustified" (Frank, 1970 v.1:331). Two months later the commander of the SD, Dr. Schöngarth, drew the final conclusions: "We must consider as members of the resistance movement not only those who actually belong to the organization. Sicherheitspolizei considers all the Poles as members of a resistance movement in the broader sense of the term" (Frank, 1970 v.1:366).

punishment would seem to have no rationale. As we are informed by a student of the strategy of conflict, however, "the deterrence concept requires that there be both conflict and *common interest* between the parties involved; it is inapplicable to a situation of pure and complete antagonism of interest" (Schelling, 1963:11; italics added). The essence of the concept is that both parties gain if the threat does not have to be carried out: the threatening party is at least spared the cost of punitive action, and the threatened party the negative satisfaction. However, *on this minimal level of gain both parties must have some common interest in maintaining the status quo*. Thus the concept of deterrence is applicable when the organizer of the public order intends to *prevent* the commission of certain acts. When threats are used to *force* the performance of some deeds, it is better to speak of them as *compelling*. On this subject Schelling tells us that "the threat that compels rather than deters often takes the form of administering the punishment *until* the other acts, rather than *if* he acts" (1963:196).

I hold that distinction crucial for the understanding of our case. It reveals that random punishment, or, more concretely, randomly applied coercion—terror—has a function clearly different from that of law and law enforcement. We see that *it is primarily an instrument of social change rather than of social conservation*; that it aims at the establishment of new relationships; that it attempts to forge a "new man" and introduce new principles of collective morality rather than to protect the status quo and allow for a pace of change in harmony with already existing norms and institutions.

If the organizers of public order are interested in creating a new order rather than in preserving the old, that is, if they intend to carry out a revolution, *terror is a rational strategy, not because it prevents counterrevolution, but because it promotes revolution* by compelling people to act in ways they never did before. For the promoters of the "new order" must forge the "new man." They are not interested in preventing something from happening; they must make things happen. In order to be successful, it is not enough for them to deter; they must compel.

The Germans were promoting a new order in the General-gouvernement. Their message was not, "as long as you don't frustrate the German war effort you will be left in peace," but rather, "unless you help the German war effort, you will be hurt." Clearly, the main concern of German-introduced law was not to deter but to compel. Hence the various forms of random punishment—the shooting of hostages and the rounding up of people in the streets and other public places and sending them for labor to Germany or to concentration camps.

One would expect that noncompliance with German demands carried such drastic penalties that scarcely anyone would dare to defy them. But full compliance was impossible; terror continued, and even intensified with time. The population quickly recognized the new logic of the situation: whether one tried to meet German demands or not, one was equally exposed to violence. We can better understand the strategy of compliance in such a context if we take into consideration the *rewards for conformity* rather than the *punishment for disobedience*. This reward is meager when punishment is applied at random rather than in a predictable pattern. If full compliance with the ruler's demands is impossible, and if he will not reduce them, it is rational for people to try to get rid of him, or to ignore him and go about their business as usual. It makes no sense, in the context of random punishment, to style one's life according to the possibility of being victimized, any more than it makes sense to orient all of one's everyday acts to the possibility of an accident.

CHAPTER X

The Underground as a Social Movement

THE theoretical introduction in the preceding chapter to the problem of resistance proposed that an underground movement would be composed not exclusively of heroes and patriots but primarily of ordinary people who decided to join it out of "rational" calculation of their self-interest. This point has not yet been established, but the paradigm sketched in the preceding chapter makes it possible to view the underground from this perspective *since the beginning* of our investigation into the phenomenon of resistance. Within this frame of reference we can approach our topic, I hope, more rationally.

Although "initial behavior" undertaken in response to a disaster "is likely to be highly variable" (Barton, 1970:209), to forge norms and to set up organizations to handle crises nonetheless depends largely on the form of a population's initial response. It is understandable, therefore, that the defense of Warsaw in September 1939 had a decisive impact on the establishment and the future of the Polish underground:

> The society moved to underground life without any formal leadership as recognized by the government in exile or even by political opinion in the country. Under the conditions of occupation this created the threat of complete disorganization, scattering and irresponsibility in Polish political life. The danger was averted in the initial period because of the moral leadership which emerged spontaneously during the defense of Warsaw. For Polish political life the defense of Warsaw had a crucial, almost historical, importance. It made possible,

within a period of only three weeks, the transition from old to new leadership. The defense of Warsaw, based on citizen-volunteers, drew from all political parties regardless of former feuds. It was a shortened process of emergence and evolution of political leadership. (UPST, *Teka* 15a:86)

This statement formulates well the basic theme of our investigation. We shall try to discover what processes account for the emergence of collectivity-orientation as the focus of social action in a beseiged city. Broadening somewhat the scope of Durkheim's analysis in his *Division of Labor*, we shall try to demonstrate mechanisms through which the social bond in a Gesellschaft reveals its de facto nomic quality. Consequently, and of primary importance in this book, we shall point out those processes and events that by the first month of the war had already contributed to the creation of conditions facilitating the emergence of the underground in the form that it later assumed.

On September 4, 5, and 6, 1939, the president, the cabinet, and the personnel of various ministries and government agencies abandoned the capital (Bartoszewski, 1974:26-29). The odds were against Poland on the battlefield, and the government was moving east in the hope that it would be able to organize a new line of resistance. During the night of September 6 the chief of propaganda in the headquarters of the supreme commander, Colonel Umiastowski, broadcast an appeal to all able-bodied men in Warsaw to leave the city and proceed eastward to be mobilized into the army. His appeal caused a mass exodus, panic, and disorganization—all in vain. No new line of defense was being prepared in the East; instead, a new enemy materialized. Fulfilling the secret clause of its August 1939 treaty with the Third Reich, the Soviet Union attacked Poland on September 17. In early morning hours of the following day the Polish government crossed the Rumanian frontier and subsequently was interned there. Before leaving the country the supreme commander issued orders that "Warsaw and Modlin [a fortress near Warsaw] were to be defended against the Germans as before" (Bartoszewski, 1974:45). By that time Poland had been defeated militarily, and Warsaw and a few other isolated pockets of resistance were fighting a lost battle. Why, then, did this defense, senseless from a military point of view, acquire such great symbolic importance (Bartoszewski, 1974:104; *Biuletyn Prasowy*, Sept. 30, 1940) and lay the groundwork for the formation of an anti-German conspiracy in the future?[1]

THE DEFENSE OF WARSAW

We should first note that after the state authorities left the capital and, subsequently, the country, an authority vacuum was avoided and the continuity of leadership maintained through the actions of Stefan Starzyński, the mayor of Warsaw. Starzyński had been mobilized into the army with the rank of major. Although he was issued evacuation orders by his superiors, he decided to stay on (Pawłowicz, 1961:161-162; Kulski, 1968:95; Kulski, 1964:19). Further-

---

[1] Actually, the defense of Warsaw touches an intriguing problem worth investigation in a comparative framework. This is the problem of importance, for the ultimate outcome in armed conflicts, of a successful defense of symbolic places, e.g., nations' capitals. One might argue, and find support in Clausewitz, that wars are neither lost nor won by purely military calculations or miscalculations; rather, war is a continuation of politics. Thus, for instance, Ulam argues that the German failure to capture Moscow was the major, and perhaps decisive, political victory of the Russians and the turning point in their war with Germany (Ulam, 1973:553-558). The skillful defense of Madrid, and Franco's determination not to let the Italians enter the city as victors, probably led to the Fascists' defeat at Guadalajara and to the prolongation for another year of the civil war in Spain. If the aim of war, as stated in the famous definition, is to break your opponents' will to resist, the defense of symbolic sites and sacred shrines, or the avoidance of capture by renowned leaders, can, in the long run, mean the difference between victory and defeat.

215

more, by securing his nomination to the post of Civilian Commissar from the then commanding general of Warsaw's garrison, General Czuma, Starzyński acquired the necessary authority to take over the remnants of government agencies remaining in the city.

Starzyński said he stayed in Warsaw because he felt responsible for providing the population with services that it desperately needed. But this goal could not be fulfilled easily. Although he put together all available organizational resources, he still had to appeal to the local population to perform collective tasks that ordinarily would have been done by specialized agencies of government or by the local administration.

Every apartment building in the city was organized as an antiaircraft defense unit. An organization of citizens on each block distributed food rations both during the hostilities and, later, during the occupation (Jasiński, 1965:39; Nietyksza, 1972:305-308). Starzyński also organized a substitute for the local police force that had abandoned the city.[2] Activities of organizations like the Stołeczny Komitet Pomocy Społecznej (Capital's Committee of Social Assistance) (SKSS) (Pawłowicz, 1961:160) and the Warszawski Robotniczy Komitet Pomocy Społecznej (Warsaw's Workers' Committee of Social Assistance) (Bartoszewski, 1974: 29), set up in September 1939, were designated to help the refugees coming into Warsaw and further increased the

[2] On the first day of recruitment, 1,000 volunteers for this peace-keeping force showed up; in the next few days their number increased to 5,000 (Regulski, 1965:345). The Citizens' Guard, as the new force was called, was warmly received in the city. Regulski, its commander, decided to broaden its base of participation beyond the volunteer formation and issued a regulation (dated September 7, 1939) directing tenants of all apartment buildings to create their own systems of "collective security." A watchman was to guard the gate of every apartment building, and a system of sounding alarms was agreed upon. The regulation further stipulated that in cases of emergency, theft, or robbery, all women in the block were to scream loudly through open windows (Regulski, 1965:346).

216

spirit of shared responsibility for the well-being of those people particularly hard hit by the misfortunes of the war.

Thus almost the whole population of Warsaw was drawn together to accomplish collective tasks, which, if unattended, would have resulted in greater hardships. People learned that they could be helped through collective effort, and many voluntarily joined various ad hoc organizations. In this way they grew to know each other, and during the three weeks in September when the encircled city fought the enemy, they had a chance to observe and discover who amongst them were the strongest, the most reliable, and the most capable of leadership.

Another important development was General Rómmel's creation of the Citizens' Committee on September 15. As a result, scores of prominent politicians, representing the whole spectrum of political opinion, were brought together into one deliberating advisory body (Pawłowicz, 1961:175). In addition to meeting as members of this committee, many of these prominent citizens, who until recently had carefully avoided one another's company, were gathering informally in the residence of Prince Zdzisław Lubomirski to discuss the developments of the day (Śliwiński, 1965:394). A sense of urgency brought to the attention of these former political enemies the one all-encompassing concern that made them all allies, namely, the survival of their country. In a besieged city, this feeling of common concern was translated into something more structured, an actual deliberative body.[3] Simultaneously, the practice of common deliberations of military authorities and citizens' representatives was established. The final decision to surrender Warsaw was reached during one such session. These meetings and the experience of the gallantry of the volunteer formations that

[3] The Citizens' Committees, bringing together eminent citizens and representatives of various political movements, were organized during the September campaign in various cities in Poland. Contacts that developed during their brief existence later contributed to the establishment of the underground network (Terej, 1971:119, 120, 181).

fought in Warsaw's defense strengthened, but did not entirely heal, the links of confidence between the military and civilians that had been badly undermined during the Sanacja regime.

The formation of the volunteer detachments from among the workers in Warsaw put the Polish Socialist Party (PPS), which organized the Workers' Volunteer Brigade of the Defense of Warsaw (Kenig, 1965:205; Zaremba, 1957:26-27), one step ahead of other parties in organizing an underground network.[4] In spite of the apprehension and mistrust of some influential officers of Warsaw's garrison (Zaremba, 1957:26; Kenig, 1965:207), and the reluctance to supply the workers with arms and uniforms,[5] General Czuma approved the creation of this unit, and in time it became highly regarded by the military for its gallantry and initiative (Zaremba, 1957:48; Kenig, 1965:214). In addition to the PPS-sponsored brigade, another organization of volunteers—the Battalion of the Defenders of Warsaw—was created by Starzyński. Within less than a half-hour after Starzyński broadcast the appeal to form the battalion, several thousand

[4] The response to the PPS recruitment drive was enthusiastic. People of all political persuasions were ready to join and support the undertaking. The Socialists in charge of organizing the brigade even received a letter from the head of OZON's propaganda office in Warsaw (Kenig, 1965:215; Zaremba, 1957:48) containing all of OZON's remaining funds. The spirit of the brigade was excellent. When the decision to capitulate was reached, the worker-soldiers refused to believe it and threatened to shoot the officers who told them about it. Only with the utmost difficulty was the first commander of the brigade, Captain Kenig, able to restore calm (Kenig, 1965:226-229).

[5] Kenig tells us how the brigade managed to acquire supplies of arms and uniforms on its own (Kenig, 1957:218-219). Probably on the instigation of several Bund members who had enlisted in the brigade, Kenig one day received a visit from two elderly Jews who offered to provide 6,000 uniforms in return for Kenig's word that the commission would be paid eventually. The procurement of arms was made possible through a tip from a friendly officer, who pointed out that hospitals had stockpiles of arms, probably belonging to wounded soldiers who were being treated there.

218

volunteers appeared in the designated place (Bartoszewski, 1974:38). The spirit of common fate, purpose, and effort was pervasive: people cared for one another "as if they were one big family" (Pawłowicz, 1961:171).

Starzyński's leadership was recognized by all. His daily speeches on the radio provided much-needed information and guidance to those who were donating their efforts to the common cause (Gebethner, 1961:189). The citizens of Warsaw felt great affection for him. When once his voice seemed hoarse during his daily broadcast, thousands of gifts, medications, and homemade brandies immediately were sent to city hall by concerned listeners (Ivanka, 1964: 364). It was also in Warsaw, in conversations in which Starzyński participated, that the groundwork was laid for the creation of a military underground organization that later would be called the Home Army.[6]

After the decision to capitulate to the Germans had been reached, General Michał Karaszewicz-Tokarzewski was given orders to continue to fight underground (Pełczyński, 1970:2). He immediately sketched a plan for an underground military organization that would operate with the support of the major political parties. For that purpose he called on leaders of the Polish Socialist Party, the Peasant Party, and the National Democratic Party to create jointly the Main Political Council.[7] This body, Główna Rada Polityczna (GRP), represented public opinion at the side of the underground military organization and was to be supplemented, according to Tokarzewski's plans, by a civilian commissar (Zaremba, 1957:81; Pełczyński, 1970:3-4; Duraczyński, 1966:16-17). After many discussions and interme-

---

[6] The name of this organization changed several times. Originally, it was SZP (Service for the Victory of Poland), later ZWZ (Association of Armed Struggle), and finally AK (Home Army).

[7] There is some disagreement as to whether the Democratic Party was included originally in the GRP. In any case, it was a much less significant party than the other three.

219

diary solutions, the final shape of the Polish underground turned out to resemble his original projects.

Starzyński participated in most of these discussions and for some time considered joining the underground (Szturm de Sztrem, 1965:391-392). Ultimately, however, he decided to stay in the open, accepting the Germans' offer to continue as Warsaw's mayor under German supervision. Within a short time he was arrested and shot. While still in charge of the city's government he had supplied the newly forming underground organization with blank internal passports and a sizable number of military identity cards, which were used to "legalize" officers who, because they decided not to register with the German authorities, needed military ID cards with private's rank (Szturm de Sztrem, 1965:389, 391; Lewandowska, 1973:348-349). Before the Germans entered the city Starzyński had ordered the census department to "misplace" information about several persons who, he was told, were about to begin conspiratorial work. He also helped to secure approximately 350,000 złotych (about $67,000) (Tokarzewski, 1964:23) for the initial period of the underground work. Sums of money were put in trust for several people, and Henryk Pawłowicz, one of the officials of the city administration, kept records of all deposits and trustees and in due time ordered disbursements of these funds to the underground (Kulski, 1968:105-106).[8] Army units in the process of demobiliza-

---

[8] There must have been many problems with this issue. Emissaries traveling to London reported that people with whom government money was left were afraid to disburse it because they did not know who was authorized to collect it and did not want to risk being prosecuted later. The government then passed a resolution empowering "military organizations, political parties, and social welfare organizations to claim those funds in the name of the Polish government and utilize them for social welfare and organizational purposes" (GSHI, Kolekcja Kota, no. 25/12: *Uchwała KSK*, Jan. 18, 1940). It is a rather vague denotation, but it shows that the government was willing to support *any* form of activity to help relieve the adverse consequences of German occupation.

tion donated their money for the underground (GSHI, PRM 24: M. Buka, 1940), and from General Rómmel himself, Tokarzewski apparently received 750,000 złotych (Tokarzewski, 1964:20).

Undoubtedly, many further preparations were conducted for the purpose of securing resources for future underground organizations. It is already clear, however, that the developments that took place in Warsaw during the first month of the war had a decisive influence on the underground struggle of the Poles for the next five years.[9]

What people believe a social system can be has a direct bearing on what it becomes in reality. W. I. Thomas observed that "If men define their situations as real, they are real in their consequences" (Coser, 1956:107). Whether there will be resistance to a government depends not only on the injustice it perpetrates but also on whether people believe that resistance is possible. If the police are considered to be omnipresent and omnipotent, then they *are* such in the sense that only a few desperate men will dare challenge them.

How did the Poles evaluate their chances for resistance? Before Hitler's victory in France, the Blitzkrieg in Poland had been a unique event and was a hard lesson for Poles to absorb. Their morale was low after the September campaign. Still, three things made it possible for them to maintain hope that the war would end victoriously in the near

[9] Not surprisingly, Warsaw played a predominant role in anti-German conspiracy until the destruction of the city during and after the uprising that began on August 1, 1944. In December 1943, when shootouts between the underground and the German police and the SS became an everyday occurrence, Frank angrily declared that Warsaw was the "source of all misfortunes. Should there be no Warsaw in the GG, all our difficulties would be reduced by 80%" (Frank, 1970 v.2:327-328). In May 1944 a higher SS and police leader in the GG, Koppe, suggested during a government meeting that "maybe all Germans should be evacuated from this hotbed of sedition" (Frank, 1970 v.2:459).

future.[10] First, responsibility for the defeat could be placed on a scapegoat: the prewar government of Sanacja. Second, the defense of Warsaw was a proof of the feasibility of resistance against a stronger enemy. And finally, Sikorski's government in exile emerged immediately. The question "Is resistance possible?" could be answered "yes" simply by pointing out that the defense of Warsaw had actually taken place. But the defense of the city accomplished far more than that: it created favorable circumstances for the emergence of an institutional framework for the underground. Moreover, it demonstrated to the 1.2 million inhabitants of Warsaw—about 8 percent of the population of the GG—that collective goods could be provided for most efficiently by collective effort.[11]

Although in peacetime there is apparently little sense of solidarity and common purpose felt among the members of a Gesellschaft, in times of crisis, when the usual customs of the community are radically disrupted, the extent to which members are mutually dependent is suddenly revealed. The division of labor, the differentiation of social structure into sets of narrowly specialized rules, and the standardization of procedures and products prevent people from seeing

[10] I say "near future" because the documents of this period give the impression that people did not believe that the war could last longer than a year or so: France and England were getting ready to strike the deadly blow and would, of course, be victorious. Only after France's defeat did people recognize that the war might last longer; see, for example, instructions sent from London to the Home Army commander (Pełczyński, 1970:258, 263). Paradoxically, they also regained confidence because the Polish military defeat in September 1939 no longer looked so bad in light of German successes in the West.

[11] As Olson (1968) has demonstrated, this fact is by no means obvious. Most of those who are affected by a shortage of collective goods have no incentive at all to participate in efforts to secure an adequate supply, because collective goods, once obtained, must be made available, by definition, to *all* members of the community, regardless of participation or nonparticipation in providing them.

connections between their tasks and lives and those of others. However, if only one link in this chain is broken, the whole machine experiences dramatic difficulties. Failure to perform adequately, no matter how specialized the function, affects hundreds of thousands who depend on the supply of this particular service or commodity. In performing their neatly defined, specialized functions "from here to there," in following their daily routines, people rarely remember that they are affecting the lives of others. *That members share a common lot is discovered, in a Gesellschaft, not through the benefits that accrue through cooperation, but through the hardships that result from a failure of cooperation.*

In a social environment where no one has complete control over the resources that are necessary to survive, where specialization makes people helpless to perform other than their routine tasks, and where density of population accounts for the multiplication of the adverse effects of a disaster befalling a given territory, this very same density provides a large group of individuals who may exhibit numerous and various talents for coping with emergency, and it makes obvious to all that violence, panic, and disorganization will add misery to what is already being suffered unless people cooperate with one another. People discover in time of crisis that they live in a community after all and that they must *continue* to support one another as they have been doing all along in peacetime without noticing it. Initially, panic will probably take hold of them, but it will not last long. A prolonged disaster will reveal both the virtues of cooperation and the destructive effects of behavior guided by the "everyone-for-himself" principle. Being exposed to disaster for a prolonged period will force people to adopt a "problem-solving" attitude. Panic cannot be sustained in such a situation. That is why, perhaps, we speak typically of *outbursts* of collective behavior.

As disaster affects masses of people packed into a compact area, their problem-solving strategies have to be coordinated. "If things get bad enough, average people will seek each other out in uninstitutionalized contexts throughout the entire society, and the resulting interchanges will culminate in a new sympathy and affection of man for man" (Marks, 1974:358). What occurred in Warsaw in September 1939 is an excellent example of the emergence of collectivity-orientation as the major focus of social action in a Gesellschaft facing shortages and externally produced disruptions.

We should note that whenever hardships are imposed on such a community from the outside, whenever, for instance, cities are besieged, a considerable amount of social initiative and ingenuity are devoted to collectivity-oriented pursuits. Depending on the length and severity of the hardships, such activities become more or less institutionalized. But except in short-lived disasters, voluntary organizations are not sufficient for the purpose of organizing relief and substitutes; usually a more stable organizational structure will develop and more lasting human contacts will be established. Thus, when studying resistance movements we must pay as much attention to the cities, particularly to those that were besieged during the military hostilities, as to the mountain regions or to the deep and vast forests that are geographically suited to harboring guerrilla movements.

ANALYTICAL FRAMEWORK

In light of what we already know about the German occupation of Poland, we would have to agree that the program of occupation, if implemented, would have implied a radical change of all basic components of social action for the Polish population. In the society envisaged by the Germans, Poles were forced to conform to new values, norms, roles, and patterns of individual motivation and situational facilities (Smelser, 1971). The racial doctrine underlying the philosophy of conquest provided an exclusive definition of the in-group, *Herrenvolk*, denying admission permanently to the subjugated populace. Consequently, it provided a justification for mistreatment, making it theoretically conceivable that human beings forever denied admission to the in-group "might be regarded as belonging to a different species toward whom, then, no human principles need function as guides to conduct . . ." (Abel, 1951:152). There was no guarantee in the German plans for the preservation of the lives of Poles and Jews living in the Generalgouvernement. The Germans could not come up with any political formula of occupation that offered the local population a program under which it could even consider working out a modus vivendi with the occupier. Obviously, the Germans never felt the need to legitimize their rule in the GG in the eyes of the local population. The social environment in which the Poles were forced to live did not allow for satisfaction of even *minimal* needs.

There was, in sociological parlance, "structural strain" in the social environment, and it appeared on every level of social action in the Generalgouvernement. Ambiguity developed about the "adequacy of means toward ends." More generally, strain manifested itself because "responsible performance in roles" no longer resulted in such rewards as wealth, power, prestige, esteem, or even simply security. Normative strain was present as "role strain," "role conflict," "role pressure," "role ambiguity," etc., and the difficulties in reducing it were overwhelming. Finally, the confrontation of two groups with divergent and mutually hostile value systems, and the absence of legitimacy of the new rule, created strain on the level of values (Smelser, 1971:51, 54, 59, 62). What was to be done? According to Smelser (1971:67), "The general principle for reconstituting social action is this: when strain exists attention shifts to the higher level of the components to seek resources to overcome this strain." Therefore, we should not expect that the underground, in its efforts to "reconstitute social action," would direct its actions primarily against specific German regulations or seek redress of specific grievances. To bring relief, when strain is present also on the level of norms and values, a new society must be created.

And this is indeed what had happened in Poland. A multitude of initiatives from a variety of social milieus combined to establish a framework of organizations and patterns of behavior that allowed the Poles to pursue their self-interest and try to fulfill their basic needs. Simultaneously, a broad discussion developed in the underground press, which propagated Polish patriotism, belief in human rights, and political democracy. Collective life in all its complexity emerged outside of the German-imposed and/or German-allowed institutions. German rule in Poland was not merely opposed, it was, so to speak, circumvented. This is why, ultimately, we find Smelser's prediction confirmed: a society formed itself outside of the institutional context created by the occupier. In Poland during the war we observe a formidable and prolonged phenomenon of collective behavior.

Collective action does not necessarily follow simply from the pressure of strain in a social system. What, then, accounts for the broad mobilization for collective action in the GG? Sociological literature teaches us that a variety of factors may determine the occurrence of collective behavior at a particular place and time. I shall list some of them and consider whether they were present in the General-gouvernement.

SOCIAL CONTROL

That the Germans never attempted to legitimize their rule over the Poles cannot be stressed too strongly. The German administration therefore lacked the means of exercising control that are available to a government whose power has some normative basis.[12] German propaganda

[12] I must note at the outset that I employ the concept of social control in a more restricted sense than is generally done in sociological literature that deals with socialization, internalization of norms, func-

efforts in the early months of the occupation were aimed solely at discrediting the prewar Polish government and the Polish leadership stratum in general. It was a naive strategy, but in tune with the disappointment felt by the majority of Poles, and some underground sources reported that it achieved mild success. Apparently the Germans even made some effort to identify the new rule with the legacy of Piłsudski. German authorities mounted an honor guard in front of Piłsudski's tomb in Wawel's Cathedral, and they kept his portrait on the walls of various offices, including that of the German commander of the Warsaw garrison, to whom hundreds of Polish officers not taken prisoner in September 1939 had to report (GSHI, Kolekcja Kota, no. 25/18: "Legenda Piłsudskiego w kraju").[13]

For the next few years the Germans abandoned their efforts to gain the support of the Polish population, and it was only when the Red Army began its offensive that they invented the "specter of Bolshevism." But that tactic, too, was unsuccessful. Too many atrocities had already been committed and, in fact, were being perpetrated simultaneously with gestures of goodwill. Project Berta, as it was called, proved to be a failure; the Polish population would never tolerate German protection against Red incursions.[14]

---

tioning of habits and customs, and the application of social sanctions for deviant behavior. Social control, broadly understood, can be used to designate any of these processes. However, I am concerned primarily "with the handling of open, uninstitutionalized group conflict, especially the response of the authorities . . . " (Oberschall, 1973: 246).

[13] In 1940, in a book published with the blessing of the German Office of Propaganda in Warsaw, a renegade, second-rate hack proposed that "Piłsudski was a great man and, in his time, came to terms with Hitler." Thirty pages later, he continued: "On my desk two photographs are standing—of Hitler and Piłsudski" (Brochwicz, 1940: 30, 60).

[14] In an article well-known in Warsaw and published during Pentecost 1943 in *Nowy Kurier Warszawski*, the officially published Polish-language newspaper, an author ridiculed his fellow Poles for not yet

The only "success" of German propaganda came rather late, in April 1944, when a writer of certain stature, Jan Emil Skiwski, began publication of the political bi-weekly *Przełom* (Turning Point) in Cracow. The publication turned out sixteen issues before it was discontinued in January 1945 (Bartoszewski, 1974:536; Wroński, 1974:334).

A successful model of social control for containing value-oriented movements may also be said to demand a clear definition of those governmental activities that cannot be defied without directly challenging the government's legitimacy (Smelser, 1971:364). At the very least, there should be a clear separation between the sphere of social life, where a plurality of opposing interests can be freely articulated, and the realm in which citizens must accept the verdicts of authorities or openly defy the legitimacy of their rule. The regime must not define each act of discontent as a direct challenge to its authority. There must be room for disagreement that does not threaten—according to the definition provided by the authorities—the ultimate values on

---

recognizing wherein lay their "best interests," though all other nations of continental Europe had already done so. The Poles remained adamant, however, as the following passage indicates: "France, Belgium, Holland, Denmark, Rumania, Serbia, Croatia—a long time ago broke with the past represented by their émigré circles, acquired positive orientation, and began constructive work. They declared themselves unambiguously for the alternative wherein lay the real and common future of Europe. Poland is the only European society that stopped before drawing the necessary and logical conclusions of its geographical location and from the realization that there is war. True, we are not fortunate enough to have such personalities as Pavelič of Croatia, the Serbian General Nedič, the Slovak priest Tiso, Quisling of Norway, Mussert of Holland, Degrelle of Belgium, King Christian X, or Marshall Pétain and Laval. But in our country they would be called traitors anyway . . ." (HL, PUC: MSW, "Sprawozdanie sytuacyjne z ziem polskich," no. 9/43, p. 5). The article, although inaccurately suggesting that public opinion in many European countries unanimously supported collaborationists, nevertheless was an unintended compliment to the Poles for their uncompromising attitudes on political collaboration.

which the community rests, for "if social situation is defined entirely in value-oriented terms, every protest is necessarily value-oriented" (Smelser, 1971:324) and no accommodation is possible. Obviously, the latter describes the reality of the German occupation of Poland.[15] Unable and uninterested in establishing the legitimacy of their rule, the occupiers also proved incapable of pursuing courses of action that could have provided them with an alternative to coercion as the exclusive method of social control.

STRUCTURAL CONDUCIVENESS

In the November 8, 1940, issue of *Biuletyn Informacyjny*, commemorating the independence of Poland in 1918, an editorial appeared comparing the circumstances of Polish conspiratorial military efforts during World War I and World War II. The comparison showed that the success of the contemporary liberation movement was assured: during World War II there were several million men in Poland who were both psychologically and militarily prepared to participate in an armed struggle, while in 1918 there were only some tens of thousands; after twenty years of independence a sense of national identity had been forged by the masses, and patriotism was no longer confined to a narrow group of intelligentsia; finally, in 1940, unlike the situation in 1918, a government recognized by all the Poles existed. "The score is three to nothing for today," concluded the article. We shall be looking for these and similar fea-

---

[15] Furthermore, since the subjects of the GG were not given the right to address any claims to the organizers of public order, two of the conditions formulated by Smelser as necessary prerequisites for containing value-oriented movements were not fulfilled: the authorities were neither "flexible" nor "responsive" (Smelser, 1971:364-365). By "flexibility" Smelser denotes "opening channels for peaceful agitation for normative change, and permitting a patient and thorough hearing for the aggrieved groups." "Responsiveness" means "attempting to reduce the sources of strain that initiated the value-oriented movement" (Smelser, 1971:364-365).

tures when we try to establish conditions of structural conduciveness that led to the articulation of a collective protest
movement in the Generalgouvernement.

The first element determining the forms of a group's response to a disaster situation is the group's set of beliefs
regarding prescribed forms of behavior under strain. The
question is whether normative guidelines exist for prescrib-
ing human behavior in a calamity.[16] Some students of disasters have noted that "individuals facing a new situation,
even one as dangerous as an impending disaster, tend to
react in terms of prior experiences and earlier definitions"
(Fogelman, Parenton, 1959:130).

These general sociological propositions, when applied to
an analysis of collective behavior on a macrosociological
level, and, in particular, when referring to nation-states,
are an indirect call and justification for a careful analysis
of the history of a given society and its traditions. I believe
that norms are rarely, if ever, forged outside of the context
of actual behavior. Until social groups are forced to cope
with certain kinds of environmental challenges, they will
not have a well-defined set of roles (and therefore, norms)
that establish appropriate behavior in a given situation.
From the existence of just such "widely held prior expectations in the culture of the group" one can infer strongly that
the group had to cope with a similar situation at some time
in the past. That "in the nineteenth century the Poles had
proved their ability to endure and their capability to resist" (Szczepański, 1970:20) informs us that the general
population had prior training in resistance that should not
be disregarded by students explaining patterns of resistance
to the German occupation during World War II.[17]

[16] "To start the normative mechanisms for controlling collective
behavior, it is helpful to have widely held prior expectations in the
culture of the group concerning what people are morally obliged to do
in the situation" (Barton, 1969:263).

[17] Similarly, when studying the second most effective anti-German
conspiracy in Europe, the Yugoslav movement, we should observe

Thus, we are led to the issue of "organizational prepar-
edness" and the prior training of specialized agencies and
the general population in handling disaster situations
(Barton, 1969:158-160, 195). It is assumed that the competence of performance during disasters increases when
there has been prior training of the general population,
when there are organizations with technical skills to deal
with the disaster, and when there are organizations that
have had the experience of performing under earlier disaster conditions.[18]

Investigations of the past aimed at discovering those elements of the dominant political culture that would be helpful in predicting behavior in calamities, or at locating organizational capabilities for expressing such behavior, must
be complemented by inquiries concerning the contemporary social stratification. After all, one of the classical propositions describing the conditions that facilitate the emergence of protest movements states that the mobilization of

---

that the Četnik organization had its origins in the Serbian battles of
liberation from the Turks, that it played an important role in the
nineteenth-century Balkan wars and during World War I, that it was
not dissolved during peacetime, and that, therefore, "when the Germans invaded Yugoslavia they met an organization specifically trained
and adapted for guerrilla warfare" (Roberts, 1973:20).

[18] As we are particularly interested in pointing out the pluralistic,
societal character of the underground movement, special attention
should be given to the political parties that became active during the
war. They had been harassed and persecuted by an authoritarian
government that had become increasingly repressive during the last
decade of Poland's independence. This experience, together with the
tradition of clandestine activity during the partitions, helped them,
I believe, to switch to the underground without much difficulty. It is
significant that the party with the most militant tradition from the
nineteenth century, and the one that had been the main organizer of
the center-left opposition to Sanacja—the Socialists (PPS)—was most
successful in the transition to clandestine work at the beginning of
the occupation. In short, not only was the population experienced in
living under a foreign occupier (or local authoritarianism), but organizations also were experienced in conducting struggles of liberation
(or opposition) against it.

231

effective protest is easier in a segmented society than in an integrated one. Protest movements, it is argued, develop in a segmented society because talented individuals have no opportunity for upward social mobility and cluster in the negatively privileged group. Thus, since the subordinate group in a segmented society has very few links, other than exploitative ones, with superordinates or other collectivities of the society, "the members of the collectivity are no longer available for mobilization by elites outside of their collectivity, while the members of the collectivity no longer seek out elites for the defense of their interests and for solving their problems. It is to 'inside' leadership . . . that members of the collectivity look for leadership" (Oberschall, 1973:124). Needless to say, the society of the Generalgouvernement was segmented.

Although segmentation encourages mobilization into a protest movement, whether such mobilization actually takes place depends to a large extent on the availability of leadership within the subjugated group and its readiness to build or join the movement. Furthermore, the result is dependent on the degree to which the subjugated group is organized prior to the conflict. It seems that, contrary to Kornhauser's (1959) theory of mass society, mobilization into protest movements does not proceed through the recruitment of large numbers of isolated individuals. Instead, "it occurs as a result of recruiting blocks of people who are already highly organized and participant" (Oberschall, 1973:125). Certainly, empirical findings concerning the predominant patterns of recruitment into underground organizations during World War II in Poland contradict Kornhauser's proposition. It is true that people who had no organizational affiliation before the war often became the strongest pillars of various underground organizations; nevertheless, mass recruitment in Poland was based on the penetration of entire social milieus and organizations.

To the extent that certain organizations *continued* their prewar activity, this fact is self-evident. In other cases, for example, when the National Democratic Party began to develop its armed detachments, the recruitment drive brought youths from Harcerstwo Polskie and from Młodzież Wielkiej Polski (Terej, 1971:159) into this organization. Tokarzewski's early report to Sikorski informed the supreme commander that many conspiratorial organizations had emerged spontaneously and that Tokarzewski was therefore *incorporating them* into the SZP (Pełczyński, 1970:22). Rowecki's "Organizational Order No. 1" ordering the creation of the secret military organization Związek Walki Zbrojnej (ZWZ) —the name given to the SZP before it was finally named the Home Army (AK)—emphasized that "Recruitment of new members to ZWZ is conducted individually but *in principle* through the intermediary of various social, ideological and organizational milieus existing in the country" (Pełczyński, 1970:146; italics added). A few months later, in April 1940, Rowecki reported that ZWZ had already contacted about fifty organizations and that he had begun to incorporate the more serious ones into the ZWZ and to dissolve the rest (Pełczyński, 1970:215, 216). There can be no doubt whatsoever that the organizations and social milieus with participatory traditions, rather than isolated and solitary individuals, became the building blocks of the underground movement.

However, knowing that entire social milieus and organizations were tapped into the underground should not automatically lead us to the conclusion that the leaders of those organizations also joined the underground. They were, after all, more vulnerable to repression, if only because they were better known than others; as obvious targets of German suspicion, they in fact could endanger underground organizations. Apparently, however, these and similar arguments did not matter much, for almost without exception, the Polish leadership stratum joined the movement. The intelligentsia was marked for extermination no matter what it did. People were forced to move, change addresses, and assume false identities even if they did not join the conspiracy. Indeed, as we have already seen, very little advantage was gained by nonparticipation in the anti-German conspiracy. German terror struck at random, and one had an almost equally good chance of becoming its next victim, whether or not one was in the underground. I think that it is even possible to argue that participation in conspiratorial work gave one a better chance of survival.

Membership in the underground made people more prudent and erased the false sense of security that was often fatal to those not involved in it. The conspirator was constantly alert to ensure that he did not fall into German hands (GSHI, Kolekcja Kota, no. 25/9: "Sprawozdanie Celta"). He *actively* avoided capture by the Germans, while nonconspirators were much less careful in avoiding accidental contacts with the occupiers. They often felt that should the worst come, should they be arrested, they would spend a few days in detention and later, once their innocence was established, be released. However, as there was little relationship between crime and punishment in the Generalgouvernement, this assumption was disproved time after time.

Conspirators very often had much better identification papers than nonconspirators. Their documents were up-to-date, their professions and particularly their work were marked as indispensable to the German war effort. If apprehended, they had already prepared satisfactory answers to most typical questions the police would ask. When they were caught in a round-up, someone in the network would try to get them out of prison before they could be shipped off for labor in Germany or to a concentration camp. An institution entitled to have its employees protected from labor conscription would inquire about them, their families would be given money to bribe the appropriate officials to authorize their release, and the organization itself might try to arrange for the release through its contacts.

When threatened with arrest, blackmail, or denunciation, conspirators had vast organizational resources at their disposal. The organization would help them to disappear, find them a new place to live, give them new employment, new documents, etc. In an atomized society, without institutions designed to protect the individual from the state, conspirators were privileged to be a part of an organized group that considered the protection and well-being of its own members one of its primary concerns, for in fact, only by protecting its members could it protect its own security and existence.

Aside from these considerations, the Polish intelligentsia had a long tradition of fighting for liberation even when it was not accompanied by the prospect of success. To the extent that it was *the* stratum of society upholding the sense of national identity, and to the extent that national consciousness was traditionally identified with the struggle for liberation from foreign domination, the Polish intelligentsia was ready to join the conspiracy. And indeed it did.

I have already noted that political parties restricted in their activities before the war were the major suppliers of leadership cadres for the anti-German conspiracy. Once the parties had decided to continue their political activity underground, it was more "natural" for politicians to join the conspiracy than to stay outside of it. Except for Witos, the peasant leader who was immediately arrested and subsequently closely watched by the Gestapo, it would be difficult to name one prominent politician in the Generalgouvernement during that time who did not participate in the underground.

Other groups within the intelligentsia were also active. If we take, for example, the list of members of only one organization in the vast underground network, the Bureau of Information and Propaganda of the Home Army, we find scores of names of the contemporary and future leaders of the academic community, including Professor Marceli Handelsman, Docent Ludwik Widerszal, and Doctor Ludwik Landau, all of whom were killed during the war. Others, whose careers matured only after the war, were also

235

members of this remarkable team: Władysław Bartoszewski, Aleksader Gieysztor, Stanisław Herbst, Stefan Kienie-
wicz, Witold Kula, Kazimierz Kumaniecki, Edward Lipiński, Stanisław Lorentz, Tadeusz Manteuffel, Stanisław
Płoski, Michał Walicki, and many many others who were
not only historians and economists but also lawyers, journalists, composers, actors, writers, engineers, and technicians
(Rzepecki, 1971 [no. 2]:130, 139; Rzepecki, 1971 [no. 3]:
135, 143, 158, 159). The creative intelligentsia and the
academicians were also absorbed in the underground
schools and universities and the underground press, which
was more developed in Poland than in any country of occupied Europe (Dobroszycki, 1962; Dobroszycki, 1963).

Still another milieu in the intelligentsia actively participated in the conspiracy: the so-called "non-partisan experts" (Terej, 1971:223), the higher civil servants and
bureaucrats. Most of them were concentrated in the machinery of the Substitute Administration organized by the
Government Delegate. Although appointments to the Substitute Administration had to be cleared with the leadership of the "big four" political parties, and therefore were
often made according to the political affiliation of appoint-
ees rather than because of their administrative skills, many
experts found their way into the Delegate's organization.
The first Delegate, Cyryl Ratajski, was a former Minister
of Internal Affairs; Jan Stanisław Jankowski was a former
Minister of Labor and Social Welfare, and until he became
the third Delegate, he was in charge of the Department of
Labor and Social Welfare in the Substitute Administration.
The Department of Education and Culture was headed by
Czesław Wycech, former president of the Polish Teachers'
Association (in postwar Poland he became Speaker of the
Diet); Czesław Klarner, former Treasury Minister, presided
over the Department of the Treasury; Czapski, former Vice-
Minister of Transportation, headed the Department of
Transportation; former Dean of the Bar Association Leon
Nowodworski was put in charge of the Department of Jus-

tice; another former Minister of Labor and Social Welfare, Bronisław Ziemięcki, directed the Department of Public Works and Reconstruction; the former Minister of Industry and Commerce, Antoni Olszewski, headed the Department of Liquidation of the Consequences of the War (Korboński, 1975: 49-61; GSHI, Kolekcja Kota, no. 25/9: "Sprawozdanie Celta").

The Polish leadership stratum—politicians, intellectuals, top civil servants, officers—had readily joined the conspiracy, and if there were constant complaints about the shortage of qualified people with leadership potential, it was not because the intelligentsia was reluctant to join the underground but rather because there were so many underground organizations to join. An emissary of the London government, Celt, who was on a fact-finding mission in Poland from April 4 to July 26, 1944, reported the opinion of the head of the Department of Internal Affairs in the Substitute Administration that complaints about the shortage of civil servants resulted because there were actually *four* full equipes of administration prepared independently: that of the Delegate, of Sanacja, of the radical right (the ONR), and finally, of the Communists (GSHI, Kolekcja Kota, no. 25/9: "Sprawozdanie Celta"). In short, "it is difficult to escape the conclusion that the upper and middle strata in society supplied the substantial bulk of opposition leaders in the proportions far above that of their percentage in the population at large" (Oberschall, 1973:155).[19] Finally, if we slightly modify the spirit of Tocqueville's argument from *L'Ancien Régime et la Revolution* (1856), we could say that Tocqueville's paradox—that revolutions occur not when a repressive regime becomes even more repressive but, on the contrary, when it liberalizes and begins to insti-

---

[19] Information from France, for example, supports this generalization: "It is clear that all categories of Frenchmen, both by class and profession, were represented in the resistance, the highest percentages being those of the 'executive' and the 'intelligentsia' class" (Michel, 1972:191).

tute reforms that improve the lot of the subjugated populace —offers at least a partial explanation of the emergence of the liberation movement in Poland in 1939-1944.

One might immediately object that I have been trying to convey precisely the opposite message, namely, that the realities of the German occupation were much more destructive to the Polish population than anything the Sanacja government might have done. Of course, no one would quarrel with that. However, one can argue that, in a certain sense, the lives of Poles living in the Generalgouvernement went on *as if there were no Germans present.*[20]

The random quality of the German terror, together with the impossibility of complying with German demands, left the Poles no other alternative but to *ignore* the occupier— either actively, by opposing him, or passively, by behaving as if he did not exist. Thus, the life of the Poles as a collectivity can be construed precisely as a struggle to survive in a hostile natural environment, in which external elements establish the conditions under which the collectivity must exist and determine to a large degree the shape of the institutions of collective life, although those elements are not themselves a part of the institutions. In that sense, the German occupiers and their policies established an environment in which the various forms of collective life of the Poles developed, but remained apart from the institutions that emerged.

The title of Kazimierz Wyka's collection of essays, *Życie na niby* (As if Life), grasps the essence of this split reality. Theoretically, there existed a society designed to encompass both German occupiers and Polish subjects, while actually it was the Poles who had to cope with obstacles created by the rules and realities of the occupation in much the same way as water goes around a stone placed in a river bed.

[20] Michel (1972:76) uses the term "infant opposition" to describe "the determination to behave as though the occupation did not exist." "The simplest and easiest way of opposing the occupier was to behave as if he did not exist" (Michel, 1972:195).

The German presence was in that sense a "natural" calamity rather than a part of the social system.

More can be said about the psychological dimension of the denial of the German presence in Poland. One very important mechanism was the reciprocity of contempt. Germans treated the Poles, and especially the Jews, as if they were not human beings.[21] The literature on concentration camps points out the mechanism by which the victim identifies with his oppressor. This sense of identification, however, evidently originates in a fascination with the strength and force displayed by the masters. But in a less controlled environment—in the GG at large—German contempt was not accompanied by displays of strength swiftly punishing *nearly all* acts of defiance of the occupier's authority. Thus, Poles reciprocated German contempt with contempt. In the folklore of Warsaw's streets, Germans were represented as dummies, half-idiots, and brutes. The campaign of constant ridicule conducted by the Small Sabotage—the scouting organization working in conjunction with the Directorate of Civil Resistance—stripped the occupier of all mystery and left no doubt that he was, and deserved to be, ignored and laughed at. The stupidity of the Germans and their inclination to obey blindly were a theme of jokes circulating in the country. The Germans fell victim to countless pranks and "dirty tricks." "In the countryside—where the local Germans know local people and local affairs after having been in the area for a few years—people walk around a German in the street as if he were a mad dog, they are afraid of him and not infrequently they assume the horrible smile of a slave. In Warsaw, one passes by a German as if he were a moving tree which does not deserve to be pushed away. A passer-by in Warsaw does not push a German, but

---

[21] This, incidentally, prevented the Nazis from developing a viable program of occupation: "Every durable empire has been based, in principle at least, on toleration of racial and national differences. None has endured if in addition to oppressing the subject peoples it treated them with unconcealed contempt" (Ulam, 1973:551).

he does not see him . . ." (GSHI, PRM 45c/41: "Dwa lata okupacji niemieckiej w Polsce," Aug. 1941).

Thus, paradoxically, Poles enjoyed greater freedom in the period 1939-1944 than they had had in a century. *Within* Polish society proper, no single authority could effectively curtail, limit, or repress the free articulation of all possible shades of political opinion. German terror was ruthless, but it also was directed randomly against everyone and was therefore *apolitical*. It is only natural therefore that the political geography of the underground state was so complicated. Not only did each politically conscious group feel that it was under a civic obligation to speak up when the country was in peril, but it also found that it was, in fact, *free* to speak. I think it is reasonable to assume that the multiplication of underground organizations and the proliferation of conspiratorial initiatives can be attributed in large part to the existence of political freedom in the Generalgouvernement during the war period. It is hardly conceivable that underground organizations could otherwise emerge and persist in such numbers.

In addition to the processes already enumerated, several others, less important perhaps, can be subsumed under the general category of "structural conduciveness." For example, certain characteristics of the impact (calamity) affecting a community seem to bear on the development of collective attitudes inducing people to help one another. Barton's analysis of collective stress situations indicates that sympathetic identification with victims increases with the randomness and proximity of the impact (Barton, 1971:239). It appears also that the spread of the disaster influences attitudes toward the victims: "the victims actually do more for one another than the non-victims" (Barton, 1971:248-249).

For the successful development of organized forms of self-help, of course, more is required than attitudes of sympathetic identification with the victims. Other things being equal, however, such attitudes would certainly increase the

240

chances for the emergence of organized responses to collective stress. The situation in the Generalgouvernement displayed all of these features; in fact, randomness of impact was one of the major characteristics of the occupation. Its scope was wide because it affected everyone and forced people to see numerous victims up close.

But "sympathetic identification" with victims leads, at most, to the creation of a self-help, remedial, welfare-oriented organization. It does not, in itself, stimulate the organization of a protest movement. To do this, the collectivity needs not only to sympathize with the victims but also to hold someone or some institution responsible for its plight. Hence, another point often mentioned as a precondition of a protest movement is the existence of an interpretation of the disaster that points out particular agents and "establishes" their responsibility in the eyes of the public. We shall say more on the subject when we discuss generalized beliefs, but for the moment, suffice it to say that shared objects of hostility allow for effective mobilization into protest movements and that such objects—the German occupiers—were, of course, available in the GG.

Last but not least, the availability of outside help may be of decisive importance for a collective movement to initiate mobilization (Oberschall, 1973:159) and to develop a stable structure, thereby assuring its existence, even though initial enthusiasm for the cause or commitment to a charismatic founder may in time be exhausted (Smelser, 1971:356). In the case of the underground movement in Poland, as well as of all anti-German conspiracies in the conquered countries of Europe, help from the legitimate governments or national committees, located typically in England or, as in the case of the Russian partisan movement, in the unconquered territories of Russia, was of crucial material importance. The amount of assistance sent to the Polish underground movement through the efforts of the Polish government in exile is very impressive (though small, when compared with the help extended to the French and Yugoslav undergrounds),

241

and it may serve as an indication of the scope of the conspiracy. The extent of the material resources of the underground suggests that a discussion of its budgets is necessary. Unfortunately, they cannot be reconstructed in full, but the data available allow us to see the dynamics of the growth of the movement.

FINANCES AS A FACILITATING CONDITION

How much money did the underground receive?[22] Except for the early period when certain amounts of currency in the hands of government agencies and the army were being transferred to the underground network then forming, only a very small fraction of its budget was acquired through voluntary donations from the population living in the Generalgouvernement. Of all the underground organiza-

---

[22] As most of the money transfers and budget estimates were prepared in dollars, it is necessary first to know the contemporary rates of exchange. In the summer of 1939, the official rate of exchange was $1 = 5.20 złotych. In subsequent years, the rate of exchange on the black market was highly unstable, more so than black market prices for any commodity in the regulated economy. Detailed records are not readily available, and summaries like the one in Skalniak's book (1966:149) have embarrassing gaps—no quotation from 1941, only one from 1942—not enough to allow us to see patterns of fluctuation in the rates of exchange. However, it is highly probable that such patterns did not exist. Several observers noted that international political events had a marked impact on the rates of exchange of foreign currencies: the more stable the German rule seemed to be, the less demand there was for foreign currency. Accordingly, after the initial overvaluation of the dollar (in February 1940, $1 = 200 złotych), its rate of exchange dropped to 65 złotych in August 1940, apparently reflecting the somber mood after the German victory in France. Also, a steady climb in the rate of exchange was noted as the war progressed. Occasionally, however, monthly fluctuations would upset all predictions based on such "general" rules. The rate of exchange settled around $1 = 100 złotych in 1943, but then continued to rise steadily. Such is the picture we get from Skalniak's data. Although continuing inflation also forced up the price of dollars, certainly that price did not keep pace with the rising cost of living.

tions, perhaps the most heavily subsidized by local sources was the clandestine press, but its donations are not recorded in the budget figures that I shall quote. People were very short of money at that time, and their generosity had to take other forms: they gave their time, their work, and, only too often, their lives.

As Table X.1 indicates, the available data are incomplete and, in part, inconsistent. Most important, it is not possible to establish with reasonable accuracy the total amount of money sent to the underground. Information supplied by Garliński (1971:246) about the funds delivered through the airlift from February 1941 to December 1944 (Operacja Most) shows a considerably smaller total amount than estimates we can make on the basis of partial information about budgets in particular years. Considering that budgets of the underground increased steadily from year to year, roughly by a factor of three, it is unlikely that the total amount sent to the country between 1941 and 1944 was $33 million while the budget estimate for 1943 alone was $16 million. The total amount sent to Poland was considerably higher than the sum quoted by Garliński, and since there is evidence of other supply and contact routes to Poland than the airlift, we can see how the money was delivered.[23] I would estimate the entire sum delivered to the underground to be approximately $50-60 million rather than $33 million.

How much money was it at the time? For the purpose of comparison let us look, for example, at budgets of the city administration of Warsaw for the fiscal years 1942-1943 and 1943-1944. In those years the expenditures of the city ad-

[23] It is certain that there were sources of funding other than those controlled by the government; for instance, political parties received funds independently. Considerable amounts of money were also secured through the old-fashioned method of expropriation: several bank robberies were staged by the underground. It is also very likely that in the last three years the government used several alternative routes to send money to Poland and that the assets sent through Operacja Most therefore represent only a fraction of the total government help sent to the underground.

TABLE X.1

FINANCES OF THE UNDERGROUND

Year	Civilian Underground Budget (Government Delegate)		Military Underground Budget (Home Army)		Combined Budgets
	Appropriation	Confirmed Delivery	Appropriation	Confirmed Delivery	
1940		15,000,000 zł.[a]	$204,000 12 x 62,500 RM	$121,477 13,500,000 zł.	
1941	4,000,000 zł.		$517,024		
1942	$1,600,000		$4,340,392		
1943	$5,724,000				$16,000,000
1944	$12,000,000				$47,000,000[b]

Total Amounts Delivered to the Underground

Dollars	33,059,263	
Reich Marks	19,000,000	
Złotych	40,000,000[c]	

Sources: Pełczyński, 1970:190, 321, 502; Pełczyński, 1973:78, 227; UPST, Teka 74/82; UPST, Teka 74: Od Mikołajczyka do Delegata; GSHI, A 9 III 4/20: Poczta no. XIII, Lis i Jur, Luty, 1943; UPST, Teka 78/237; HIA, PGC: Box 63, L.dz. 19870/43/Kr, Nov. 12, 1943; Garliński, 1971:246; Korboński, 1975:46.

[a] The figure of 15,000,000 zł. was reported to the budget of the Political Bureau. In 1940 the Substitute Administration was not yet set up.

[b] The amount of $47,000,000 is mentioned in a memorandum sent to the prime minister in London from the Treasury as a request for an annual budget that could not be fulfilled because it was too high.

[c] This total is reported as having been delivered through the so-called Operacja Most between February 15, 1941, and December 31, 1944.

ministration amounted to 226.6 million and 235.7 million złotych, respectively (Ivanka, 1964:486). Since the rate of exchange in 1943 was roughly $1 = 100 zł., and since the value of the dollar was even higher in 1944, the civilian underground—the Substitute Administration—had at its disposal about 600 million złotych in 1943 and twice that amount in 1944. Therefore, *in those years the civilian component of the underground state had financial resources several times larger than the administration of a city of over one million employing about 30,000 full-time people.* In addition, we may take for granted that the Home Army, as in all preceding years, continued to possess financial resources larger than those of the civilian underground.[24]

How was the money spent? A careful scrutiny of the Home Army budget in 1940 by a special commission showed that a total of 8,846,403 złotych had been spent during that year. Of this sum, 1,279,487 złotych were allocated for salaries. The pay scale was diversified according to marital status and locality; salaries in Warsaw were markedly higher than those in the provinces. The highest salary paid was $18 per month (800 zł.).

Inquiry into the distribution of budgets among various departments of the Substitute Administration reveals many interesting facts about that organization. In 1942, 30 percent of the Delegate's budget was spent for social welfare and 18 percent for education (UPST, *Teka* 74: *Od Mikołajczyka do Delegata*); in 1943, about 50 percent of the entire budget went for social welfare ($2,004,520) and education ($901,-

[24] Curiously, there is absolutely no data on the budgets of the Home Army for 1943 and 1944 in the three-volume publication of the Underground Poland Study Trust (UPST) of the most important correspondence exchanged between the commander of the Home Army and his superiors in London (Pełczyński, 1970, 1973, 1976). Financial data were of fundamental importance to those concerned at the time, just as they are to students of the period. In the documents published by the UPST there is ample information regarding Home Army budgets until 1942, and then not a single word about money.

900) (UPST, *Teka* 74: L.dz. 4802/42, Nov. 30, 1942); and finally, in 1944 also, over 50 percent of the budget—more than $6,000,000—was assigned to those two departments (UPST, *Teka* 78/237). By comparison, the third best-endowed department of the administration, the Department of Internal Affairs, which was responsible for organizing and preparing cadres of the Substitute Administration, had a budget of merely $480,000 in 1943 and $1,602,300 in 1944. Thus, almost half of the money controlled by the civilian underground was destined for purposes that, to be sure, were illegal, but that at the same time benefited many people who shied away from any work in an underground organization. In a way, the wide range of interests of the civilian branch of the underground justifies its claim that it was an "underground state": it operated as if it were a government, since no one in the population was a priori excluded from the possible (beneficial) effects of its actions.

Observers of the underground scene reveal that the Substitute Administration and the Home Army developed into bureaucratized organizations (GSHI, Kolekcja Kota, no. 25/9: "Sprawozdanie Celta"; interview with Z. Stypułkowski, London, 1972). Considering the size of their budgets and manpower, this fact should not surprise us. Indeed, both organizations had to employ full-time personnel with special skills, who, of course, had to be remunerated for their clandestine work. Professional soldiers, and also bureaucrats, were simply continuing their careers within a somewhat changed organizational framework. Some people took positions in the underground in anticipation of future promotions and benefits.[25] Thus one may point out a slight

[25] In Poland and in London there were fears that appointment to the future government would be based primarily on the evaluation of services rendered while in the underground organizations. A long publication prepared in London by Władysław Czapiński (1942) dealt with this subject: *Administrative Problem: The Question of Choice of the Upper Layers of Functionnaires of the Public Administration* (*Zagadnienie urzędnicze: organizacja doboru wyższego per-*

difference in modes of involvement in various underground organizations. "Calculative involvement" was a motivation among the leadership stratum of the Home Army, Substitute Administration, and the large political parties participating in the Underground Parliament. The same motivation was less pronounced among those who joined a variety of small conspiratorial groups. In other words, it makes sense to look at the underground as if it were composed of "professional" as well as of "voluntary" organizations.

Finally, we should mention the financing of political parties, the first and best-entrenched structures through which the nation's resistance initially took shape. Before funds from London began to flow steadily to Poland, and before the Government Delegate and his apparatus were solidly established in the underground, political parties apparently operated on rather frugal budgets and were dependent to a considerable degree on members' contributions. For example, membership fees constituted almost one-third of the budget of the Warsaw's Organization of the National Democratic Party in 1941, although in the second half of 1943 membership fees supplied only 10 percent of the funds secured by that organization (Janowski, 1972:- 179-180, 189, 199).

The principal political parties, especially those that participated in the underground Political Consultative Commit-

---

sonelu urzędniczego administracji publicznej). "We are concerned here," he wrote, "with a conception of public administration contradicting all basic principles of this service but which, nevertheless, comes back to life during, or after, every war. According to this conception public office has to be considered as a reward for services rendered during the war. This idea has roots in ancient times when princes distributed conquered lands between their warlords together with the right of jurdisdiction over them. In our times this conception returns in a slightly modified form: it is based on a claim that those who fought have a *right* to take power in their hands. In a way this is even more far reaching a claim than the one established by the old custom because now one is about to be rewarded with domination not over the defeated but over one's own people."

tee (PKP) received a quarterly appropriation from the Delegate,[26] although all of them must have had additional, independent sources of funding. The PPS-WRN was able to survive a year and a half, during which it withdrew from the PKP and was cut off from Government funds distributed by the Delegate. Meanwhile, monthly budgets of the Peasant Party in 1942 were reported to be 200,000 złotych (GSHI, A 9 III 4/1: L.dz.K.4372/42) at a time when the monthly stipend political parties were receiving from the Delegate never exceeded 50,000 złotych (UPST, *Teka* 78/119, May 21, 1943). Altogether, the financial resources of the underground were considerably larger than the sums delivered by the Government from abroad.

Considering that the masses of people who took part in clandestine activity worked often without pay, these financial resources must have provided the underground with a very solid economic base. This relative affluence was especially important in view of the corruption in the occupier's administration and the reduction of life in the General-gouvernement to a preoccupation with economic problems. As a result, the underground was the only institution in the occupied country that could solicit normative involvement —because participation in it offered symbolic reward to the Poles—and calculative involvement—because it could pay for services it needed. "The underground had at its disposal considerable financial resources, and so anyone who joined it not only took care of his worries about daily bread (on a very, very modest scale) but also maintained his place in the social, political, administrative and military hierarchy; he was working for his personal future and perhaps for medals as well" (Uziembło, 1950:18).

[26] In the third quarter of 1941 political parties received a total of 85,000 zł. (GSHI, Kolekcja Kota, no. 25/11: *Sprawozdanie finansowe*). In November and December 1942 each party received 50,000 zł. In January and February 1943 their monthly stipends were set at 60,000 zł., in March and April, at 70,000 zł.; and in May, at 150,000 zł. (UPST, *Teka* 78/119).

Generalized Beliefs

Remuneration is not all that counts. Men must have a particular interpretation of the world that surrounds them before, and while, they undertake social action. Orientation toward values and allowing intelligence rather than instinct to be the guide for action constitute the elements of social action, and also of social science. They allow for constructing an ideal type of "good society" and, presumably, for devising the best (that is, the most rational and congruent with accepted moral principles) means to achieve this ideal.[27]

The formula of the German occupation involved a direct challenge to the concept of "the good society" *shared* by all Poles. I purposely stress the word *shared* because, although different political movements disagreed passionately about their social programs, they all agreed on at least one point that was the sine qua non for the realization of all other specific points of their programs: Poland should be a sovereign country. In the German program of occupation, however, Poles were no longer allowed to determine the character of their communal life. What was being challenged was not a specific ideal of the "good society" but something much more basic: the very prerogative of making a choice. Poles were relegated to the status of slaves, and this violated the conception of the "good society" entertained by men of all political persuasions, from Polish Fascists to Socialists. Nazism brought about a revolution in German society; Nazi projects promised no less for occupied countries in the East.

In the guise of the underground state it was actually the old system (I say system, rather than establishment, because

---

[27] In functionalist sociology, the different components of social action are thought to be in a hierarchical order. Thus, a change in values at the "top" of the structure necessarily involves a radical reordering of the other components of social action. A change in the values that bind a given collectivity together constitutes a revolution rather than merely reform or a minor adjustment of the system.

249

it was not the continuation of Sanacja but of Polish state-hood) that was defending itself against an attempted revolution imposed from abroad. From this perspective, the underground was a value-oriented movement because it did not seek to find accommodation for a dissatisfied social group *within* the existing framework of institutions. As such, it was also guided by a set of value-oriented beliefs that provided an "explanation" of the existing conditions of strain, identified the sources of evil, and, finally, put forth a positive set of values.

"Value oriented beliefs," says Smelser, "arise when alternative means for reconstituting the social situation [that is, facilities, mobilization, and normative components] are perceived as unavailable" (Smelser, 1971:325). The reality of the German occupation contained the denial of all rights that would have allowed the Poles to state their grievances. In these circumstances every protest was necessarily value oriented because the "social situation was defined entirely in value-oriented terms" (Smelser, 1971:324).

The initial shock of defeat brought, as we already have learned, sobering thoughts about the quality of the pre-September leadership. German propaganda exploited the mood of discouragement engendered by these doubts (Szarota, 1972:141-142). As the occupation continued, however, the central issue shifted from the need for ascertaining who was responsible for the defeat to finding out who was responsible for the conditions of life that resulted (HL, PUC: *Raport sytuacyjny*, Nov. 10, 1940–Jan. 1, 1941) and what to do in these new circumstances. The answer to the first part of the question was easy. But simply to see in the German occupation the source of all the misfortunes besetting society did not provide a satisfactory program of action. Different social milieus were affected by the occupation in different ways; food producers, for instance, benefited materially and, in the beginning, were not subjected to terror. At first, the Germans' ultimate intentions were unknown, and the immediate outcome of the war on the continent was

250

considered to be undecided until the French army was defeated. Too many factors of fundamental importance to an interpretation of the situation were not sufficiently clear; information and discussion were necessary prerequisites for an evaluation of what was going on and what should be done about it. The main obstacle to achieving this dialogue was the German monopoly of information. Eventually that monopoly was destroyed by the underground press, which proved in time to be one of the most effective weapons in the struggle against the occupier. Every copy of an underground journal was material proof that opposition was real and active; it served as the most effective advertisement of underground organizations among those groups that had not yet been penetrated by the conspiratorial network;[28] and, last but not least, it gave its readers a sense of living through a brief moment of freedom. Since "the spread of a value-oriented movement depends on the possibility of disseminating a generalized belief" (Smelser, 1971:337), the underground press was the most important factor creating a broad base of public support for the underground.

The social function of the clandestine press, however, was not limited to furthering the cause of the underground. More important, it served chiefly to counteract the pressures of social atomization by providing information to people in various parts of the country and in several social environments about what was happening beyond the reach of their everyday experiences. It therefore contributed to breaking down the relative isolation of various groups. The press made constant efforts to draw a picture of a common fate, and therefore of a common bond, uniting Poles despite the Germans' local variation of policies and their clumsy attempts to exploit old grievances or new particularistic in-

[28] Piłsudski wrote in 1903 that, in the experience of all the conspirators he knew, whenever new cells of revolutionary organization were set up, *bibuła* (illegal publication) had always been there before. It was the "advance guard" of illegal organization (Piłsudski, 1903:239).

terests in accordance with their strategy of divide and rule. At the same time that the press was communicating the decisions of underground authorities—the Government Delegate and the Directorates of Civil and Underground Resistance—it was also publishing editorials, essays, and articles discussing problems of everyday life under the occupation. This information provided people with guidelines on how to behave in new circumstances—an invaluable help to millions who otherwise could have very well lost their sense of civic responsibility and thus contributed to fulfilling the Germans' desires to destroy the social bond that united Polish society.

Perhaps the most significant contribution of the press to the quality of underground life consisted in providing a forum for discussion of alternative political programs and related issues by different political movements and parties. This forum was extremely important in view of the fact that the very existence of the underground was an attempt to return to democratic politics. But the requirements of conspiracy, which entailed maximum secrecy about the dealing of the leaders of the underground polity and their subordinates, might have perhaps destroyed, or at least imperiled, the democratic ethos of the clandestine institutions if no visible measure of public control could be exercised over them. The underground press provided some guarantee against the isolation of the leadership of the underground, brought into the open certain conflicts, and allowed for presentation of different positions and for broad participation in all discussions. The incredible proliferation of the underground press—there were approximately 1,500 underground papers in Poland, more than anywhere else in Europe (Bartoszewski, Dobroszycki, 1968:56)—permits us to say that public opinion was, in the full sense of the term, the government's "fourth branch." Very little escaped its attention and scrutiny.

The beginnings of the underground press were very humble. Responding to a need for the kind of objective information not provided by the German-sponsored press, the majority of the first underground newspapers adopted the character of radio news bulletins (GSHI, Kolekcja Kota, no. 25/11: *Opracowanie—Prasa Polska w okresie okupacji. Stan na 1.XI.1941*; Krawczyńska, 1971:70-71). They reported predominantly international news about the war in all theaters of operation.[29]

In time, the movement gathered momentum, and, together with multiplying conspiratorial organizations, new and varied underground papers began to appear. No respectable underground organization could afford not to have a press organ. As Piłsudski, the great theoretician of political conspiracy, said half a century before, "lack of illegal publications is for a political organization . . . like

[29] Until the end of the war there was always a long section of international military and political news in the underground press. This interest in foreign developments persisted throughout the war, out of the conviction, perhaps, that military and political events taking place outside of Poland were determining the country's future, and out of the need to detach oneself from the suffocating contemporary reality. Reading it today, one cannot help but feel that precious space in those papers could have been used more effectively; clearly, an Allied bombing of some obscure oasis in Africa could not have been very important to the Polish public. But, contrary to what we would expect, it must have been significant to them. To use another example, Landau devoted one-half of each daily entry in his diary to international news, revealing the intensity of his preoccupation with these issues. Also, as in all European countries, many underground publications in Poland were addressed to German readers, mostly to Wehrmacht soldiers. Fourteen German-language underground papers were published in Poland (Dobroszycki, 1962:11). A special department— "N"—was set up in the headquarters of the Home Army (in the Bureau of Information and Propaganda) to coordinate German-language propaganda. Through its efforts, more than one million copies of various publications were issued between July 1941 and August 1944 (Grudziński, 1959:53; Rzepecki, 1971b:145-151). Its employees were able to intercept letters sent home by Wehrmacht soldiers and geared propaganda to the discrepancies they detected between the content of official German publications and soldiers' opinions and worries (Interview with T. Zawadzki-Żenczykowski, London 1972).

lack of blood: an anemia which condemns an organization to oblivion, makes it impossible for it to exercise influence on larger circles of the public, condemns it to slow death" (Piłsudski, 1903:22-23).

While in other European countries the output of the underground press increased dramatically only in the last year and a half of the occupation, in Poland it increased steadily throughout the entire war (Dobroszycki, 1962:10). Incomplete statistics compiled in 1947 show that in Warsaw there were published simultaneously 18 underground papers in 1939, 84 in 1940, 111 in 1941, 146 in 1942, 190 in 1943, and 166 in 1944 (Szarota, 1973a:374). Later, Bartoszewski (1973:387) established that a total of 650 underground papers were published in Warsaw during the war. A recent study has located 137 titles in Cracow alone (Wroński, 1974:433-440).[30]

How many millions of copies of underground publications were distributed during the war is impossible to assess. The highest circulation of a single paper was probably that of the *Biuletyn Informacyjny*, which reached 43,000 copies (Rzepecki, 1971c:164). There were approximately four hundred clandestine printing houses, about half of which were located in Warsaw. The average monthly output of the Tajne Wojskowe Zakłady Wydawnicze (Clandestine Military Printing Houses) (TWZW) was 314,000 copies of periodicals and brochures, plus an undetermined number of flyers (Bartoszewski, 1973:392). In September 1941, for instance, it put out 600,000 copies of various publications (GSHI, Kolekcja Kota, no. 25/11: *Opracowanie—Prasa Polska w okresie okupacji. Stan na. 1.XI.1941*). During its most

[30] In Cracow, a smaller city than Warsaw, conspiracy was more difficult because of the relatively large German population living there. There were 252,000 Poles and 21,000 Germans in Cracow in May 1943 (Wroński, 1974:273), while the corresponding figures for Warsaw at that time are 975,000 Poles and 28,000 Germans (Szarota, 1973a:71).

active period the monthly consumption of paper by Warsaw's Bureau of Information and Propaganda (BIP) alone was around five tons (Rzepecki, 1971c:162). Just imagine the problem of obtaining this amount of a rationed article and then transporting it in and out of most carefully hidden secret printing houses.

The variety of the underground press was also extremely impressive, closely resembling the profile of the press published in a free, peacetime society. Journals used numerous techniques and were issued by a host of different circles and organizations: political parties, other political and social groupings, military organizations, professional groups, pedagogical associations, loose coalitions of individuals, etc. The public to which they were addressed was also extremely varied: members of particular political or social organizations, soldiers, women, children and youth, certain professions, special-interest groups (alpinists, for example), Germans, prisoners of war of other nationalities, readers interested in literary and satirical periodicals (Bartoszewski, Dobroszycki, 1968:56-57; Bartoszewski, 1973:390). In Warsaw alone there were sixteen literary and eight satirical underground periodicals (Bartoszewski, 1961:81-103). Reading the underground press, one cannot escape the conclusion that clandestine life permeated the entire society.

The press was an incredibly powerful instrument for disseminating ideas and information. It was also an effective "offensive weapon." Its sheer presence broke the spell of invincibility of the German occupier. After its readership reached wide proportions it accustomed everyone to illegality, legitimized the underground, and consistently undermined the authority of the occupier. It somehow found its way everywhere, even into the tiniest villages: a Home Army courier on his way abroad stopped in a mountaineer's hut before crossing the frontier. There, on Sunday, he found an issue of *Biuletyn Informacyjny* published in Warsaw the previous Thursday (Rzepecki, 1971 [no. 4]:153).

255

The two striking features of the Polish underground press of this period—its volume and variety—permit us to state conclusively that ideas circulating in the liberation movement were disseminated throughout the entire population. One might wonder at the broad range of subjects covered by clandestine papers, since many were not related to the pressing issue of the fight for independence. The same concern for social needs, above military and political ones, apparently was true of other aspects of the civilian underground, especially as 50 percent of its financial assets went for education and welfare. One possible explanation of this situation, and one that will be further developed in the following chapter, is to realize that the underground acted primarily as a Polish *state* and only secondly as an anti-German conspiracy. Its whole structure was, first of all, designed to provide an institutional framework for the collective life of the Poles. The conspiracy could not (and it was aware of this fact) decisively sabotage, attack, or expel the Germans from the country, but it could frustrate their efforts in a more subtle and, under the circumstances, more effective way, that is, by preventing the atomization of Polish society. In that sense the underground was directed primarily *toward* the Polish population and only secondarily *against* the Germans. It was essentially a norm-creating institution for those who joined it and also for those who remained outside of its network. This function was tremendously important at a time when the major effort of the occupiers was to destroy solidarity in the subjugated society, to destroy group life in even the most intimate circles by making friend betray friend and by exchanging people taken as hostages for lives of their close relatives.

The most significant experience of those who joined the underground was that they were a group, a team, a community, that they were preserving and recreating solidarity. "One concern towered above everything else: to maintain the internal bond of the conquered nation, to preserve its personality and its active participation in the developing drama" (Zaremba, 1957:99). In this environment the traditional opposition between the individual and the collectivity made little sense: one could find oneself, ultimately, when affirming solidarity with others, under torture until death (Strzelecki, 1974:13-16, 52-53). For the entire society the "organization of the underground state became one of the factors regulating, at least to some degree, the anarchy of collective life. By creating temporary norms adapted to the conditions of life under the occupation, *by sanctioning some, and condemning other, forms of existence of a mass of people in a state of lawlessness, it was rescuing the principle of the law itself*" (Zaremba, 1957:145; italics added).

What, then, was the message of the underground that permits us to describe its principal role as we have, and that allowed it to grow and strengthen despite German victories, terror, and its own incessant quarrels? Was it the call to fight for independence? I think not. What it publicized instead was the conviction that only by opposing the Nazi conquest could people rescue *values*, that the very existence of civilization was at stake, that the confrontation was between barbarism and humanity. In Poland, people of all political persuasions realized very early that no cultural or moral order, no conception of justice or freedom was compatible with the Hitlerian social order about to be imposed in the occupied territories. The fight, therefore, was justice, freedom, culture, and morality versus their opposites. The phraseology used to express this idea differed according to the political orientation of the writer. Some spoke about the fight of "Culture against Barbarism" (*Polska*, Apr. 29, 1943), others, about the "defense of democracy" (*Biuletyn Informacyjny*, Nov. 26, 1942); in still another publication the ongoing confrontation was explained in terms of opposition between totalitarianism and democracy (*Z Pola Walki*, 1943:5, 38). "No truth, during the entire history of mankind, was as self-evident to everyone as that the present war, fought against the arsonists of the world, was waged, in the first place, in defense of the foundations of civilization, in defense of the elementary rights of men" (Z *Pola Walki*, 1943: *Manifesto to the Peoples of the World*, p. 24).

One who lived through these events captured the meaning of reality around him with unique clarity: "Evil was being perpetrated around us. And no change of perspective, no historical relativism, no sociology could make it appear different. . . . The world that they wanted to create was proclaiming an end to values. . . . We felt that we increased the gravity of the crime they perpetrated against us, if our life was devoted to values, if because of us, because of what we did, there was more beauty or love in the world. We felt deeply responsible for making their crime as great as possible, and we could do so if, by killing us, they were killing something more important than ourselves—namely, that which we would have created had we not perished by their hand. We felt that if we were not a source of values, we justified what they were doing, we diminished the dignity of life, we almost acknowledged that they were right" (Strzelecki, 1974:11, 17, 41).

CHAPTER XI

The Underground as a Polity

As I indicated earlier, the primary problem facing Polish society after the capitulation and dissolution of the Polish state in September 1939 was the need to resolve the authority vacuum. If Polish society were to survive under the occupation, lost authority had to be replaced. Reconstruction of authority proceeded through a multitude of social processes and initiatives. An unbelievable number of conspiratorial groups proliferated in occupied Poland (Pużak, 1977: 22), and no matter what their avowed purpose, all introduced their members into new frameworks of collective life and the experience of the common bond and authority that accompanies it. Individuals not affiliated with any groups consulted with friends or neighbors or sought advice from well-known and respected personalities whenever they had to make decisions that involved some form of recognition of the German occupiers.[1] Frequently, to seek advice

[1] At the beginning of the occupation, the group of "others" to whom one turned for advice was large and varied. In some cases it was the informal circle of friends and neighbors, as, for example, in the Węgrów county, where former policemen and clerks in the local administration consulted with many people about whether they should return to their work (Stolarz, 1965:97). When Stanisław Rybicki learned accidentally from a German secretary in the town hall that he was going to be nominated the next day for the position of mayor of Częstochowa, he did not know whether he should accept the nomination. That same evening he hurriedly invited two important citizens of his town to visit him (a former senator and director of the male gymnasium in town, and a former socialist deputy to the Diet) and asked for their advice (Rybicki, 1965:49). When in May 1940 the Germans refused to confirm Prince Janusz Radziwiłł as the chairman of the Main Welfare Council, Count Adam Ronikier was offered the job. Ronikier did not know what to do in this situation.

was only a preliminary step to the creation of the more permanent bond of an underground organization.

The processes of coalescence that developed at the "bottom" of society would have mattered little and, in time, would have probably withered away had they not—and this was an extremely important coincidence—proceeded simultaneously with the initiatives to build a leadership structure that originated among the politicians of opposition parties and in the officer corps (Pużak, 1977:19). When the two developments converged, when the two courses of initiative met, they provided what each needed and what neither could acquire easily on its own: leadership on the one hand, and manpower on the other.

But at that moment another aspect of the authority vacuum surfaced. When social atomization no longer appeared to be an imminent danger, it suddenly became ap-

---

Finally, he and the board, which had just resigned in protest against the refusal to confirm Radziwiłł, decided to resolve the dilemma by submitting to arbitration by a higher authority: Prince Metropolitan Sapieha. And Sapieha decided that Ronikier should take the job (Ronikier, n.d.:50-51). Similarly, the president and vice-president of the Bank Emisyjny in Poland consulted with Sapieha and other economic and "citizen" circles before accepting their nominations from the Germans (Młynarski, 1971:419). The mayor of Warsaw, Kulski, in doubt over whether he should tolerate the arbitrary anti-Polish actions of the German supervisor of city utility and transportation companies or resign, obtained an appointment with the Government Delegate and asked for his opinion. After the conversation Kulski continued on the job with explicit authorization from the head of the underground. Later, he says, his consultations with subsequent Government Delegates were frequent and almost systematic (Kulski, 1964:25, 30, 33). Ambiguities concerning what to do appear over and over, involving all areas of behavior. As the situations were often new, no norms existed to regulate them. Similarly, for a long time there was no accepted authority immediately available to consult and obey. Everyday life ceased to be routine; people constantly had to make fateful decisions. On the one hand, this gave unprecedented existential dimensions to people's lives; but on the other hand, it added a burden that not many were prepared to accept lightly. So they looked to their peers for support.

parent that the organizations emerging from this process of group formation did not know how to relate to one another. They lacked the experience of peaceful coexistence and a strong structural framework within which they could recognize the presence of others and collaborate.

The variety of emerging underground organizations indicated that the whole spectrum of political pluralism of the Second Republic (1918-1939) was in the process of articulation. Only the institutions of a democratic state could accommodate it. But there was no state; nor was there a great deal of mutual trust among those engaging in underground politics. The fantastic eruption of conspiratorial activity in the early period of the occupation made it unlikely that the explosion would subside by itself or that it could be contained from within. If the German occupation were not to end soon (and originally everyone believed that it would), the conspiracy was in dire need of an institutional framework within which all groups could peacefully work. It had to fill the authority vacuum that materialized *because* of the emergence of underground organizations; in a word, it had to build a polity. And that is indeed what happened during the occupation. Slowly, an "illegal Polish state" (Frank, 1970 v.1:395) emerged.

The difficulties of centralization, of creating a strong, unified source of authority, were overwhelming. They originated partly in mistrust carried over from prewar years and partly from the special conditions under which the conspiracy had to grow. The lost war and sober reflection upon the quality of the Sanacja government produced, as we already know, a general crisis of authority that could not be easily overcome. Furthermore, the conditions of life under the occupation were not conducive to the emergence of a strong man with charismatic qualities and a staff of followers who could "spread the word" and construct a mass movement. The Generalgouvernement was not a stage for prophets; rather, it demanded low profile and low visibility in organizational work. In fact, the conditions under which

261

the underground conspiracy operated imposed decentralization.

INITIAL PROBLEMS OF THE UNDERGROUND

During the first months of the occupation, the leadership of the prewar political and military organizations was frantically active. Army officers who had not been sent to POW camps were establishing networks of communication and building skeletons of future command structures. In September 1939, in Cracow, at least two major organizations were created by the military (Wroński, 1974:15, 22, 25), and when General Tokarzewski, commander of the SZP (the future Home Army), visited Cracow in mid-October, he was already able to incorporate into the SZP several smaller conspiratorial military organizations (Wroński, 1974:32). Many more serious military and paramilitary organizations were emerging simultaneously. Rowecki, Tokarzewski's deputy, sent a telegram to London listing some of them: Wolność, Wyzwolenie, Grunwald, Gryf, Związek Polskich Kawalerzystów, Brochwicz, Lubicz, Bicze, Kierzkowski, Kowalówka, Epler (Pełczyński, 1970:38).

Politicians were equally zealous conspirators. The Socialists, who had officially dissolved their party in order to protect from repression all members who were easily identifiable by the Germans, found a new name for their underground organization: Wolność, Równość, Niepodległość (Freedom, Equality, Independence) (WRN). They had already organized during the defense of Warsaw and were among the first to cede their party militia detachments to the SZP. Tokarzewski (1964:29) recalled that command structures had to be hastily prepared in late October 1939 in the Warsaw and capital districts in order to take over the detachments "delivered" to him by the Socialists. The leadership of the National Democratic Party met in Warsaw on October 13 (Terej, 1971:121) and made final decisions about the probable development of their underground activities. The Peasant Party convoked its first organizational meeting on a national level somewhat later, in February 1940 (Buczek, 1970:11), but it had already started its full-scale conspiratorial work on the regional level; in Cracow, for example, the conspiratorial leadership of the under-ground Peasant Party established itself on December 5, 1939 (Buczek, 1970:14; Wroński, 1974:61), and, of course, Maciej Rataj in Warsaw was active even earlier.

The major political parties were not the only ones who participated actively in the conspiracy. For example, the ONR-Falanga, the political party of the radical right, set up a conspiratorial organization under the name Pobudka (Tryc, Tarnogrodzki, 1966:261-262). The so-called Biuro Poli-tyczne and the Centralny Komitet Organizacji Niepodleg-łościowych (Central Committee of Organizations for Inde-pendence) (CKON) began operations in Warsaw in October 1939 and were the main rallying points at that early date for a wide variety of underground organizations that did not merge with the Home Army or the four major political parties (Tryc, Tarnogrodzki, 1966:250-252; Dołęga-Modrzewski, 1959:13-14).

Of course, organizations other than military and political ones were actively involved as well in those early stages of underground activity. The leadership of Warsaw's scouting organization, Związek Harcerstwa Polskiego, also decided in late September to continue its activities as a conspiratorial organization (Bartoszewski, 1974:58). In fact, several polit-ical and nonpolitical organizations did not so much *start* in those early months of the occupation as they decided to *continue* their work under new conditions (Marciniak, 1962:298).

Many more organizations were established during late 1939 and early 1940—so many that the commanders of the SZP worriedly reported to London in December 1939 and January 1940 on the mushrooming of military, paramilitary, and political conspiratorial groups (Pełczyński, 1970:22, 38). "Conspiratorial networks are being set up now not only

263

by serious politicians and public figures, but they emerge spontaneously, so that one may justifiably fear a danger of Gestapo provocation" (Pełczyński, 1970:63), read a report dispatched from Warsaw in early January 1940. A month later another report added: "As a result of the initiative of various individuals and social groups numerous organizations have emerged which, often, reach quite deep into the society. . . . In this situation we cannot simply dissolve them, because they will ignore us and further develop in a chaotic manner" (Pełczyński, 1970:98).

WHY THE UNDERGROUND EMERGED EARLY IN POLAND

There are several reasons, I believe, for the emergence of so many underground organizations in Poland in the first months after the capitulation. The brief duration of the September hostilities resulted in relatively little damage to life and property and thus left the country defeated, but not exhausted, and still in command of its considerable resources. The only institution literally destroyed as a consequence of the German victory was the central government. All the rest, including the outlawed political, professional, and voluntary associations, remained. One could say, therefore, that the infrastructure of the society, although somewhat depleted, was still standing; only the source of authority was lacking. But the absence of government in Poland was uniquely nonincapacitating. Because the Sanacja regime had lacked legitimacy in the eyes of considerable segments of the populace during the last ten years of its rule, its disappearance did not impair the possibility of organized action. In fact, Sanacja's demise had the opposite effect on those political centers that had been suppressed or limited in their opportunities to conduct public and political activity before the war. The blame for the lost war was placed squarely on the Sanacja regime. It was felt that the "leaders" had failed and that their subsequent absence was no hindrance in continuing the struggle. It was of fundamental importance to the emergence of the underground Polish state that potential leadership existed among the politicians of those parties that had been kept from power by Sanacja in the thirties. These parties were sufficiently entrenched in the political tradition of Polish society to be able to resume the burdens and responsibilities of continuing the fight against the foreign invader. They had a large membership and considerable resources and organizational skills at their disposal, and as a result of having been forced into semiclandestine activity under Sanacja's rule, they had already developed the necessary skills for organizing conspiratorial activities against the occupier.

Also, from the time that France and England entered the war against Germany, no one believed in the possibility of a German victory or in the eventuality of a prolonged war. The news that a government in exile had been created in France, with General Władysław Sikorski at its head, and that the new government showed vigorous initiative in promoting the military underground in the occupied country also added incentive to the military activity in Poland.

Finally, the German request for everyone to return quietly to his job created problems for many people whose professions and responsibilities were of such a nature that they were forced to consider whether they could continue in their prewar capacities without becoming unwilling instruments of German exploitation. Experiencing grave doubts about the morality of the behavior expected of them, people looked for legitimate sources of authority to direct them in this ambiguous situation. When they could not find these authorities, they "constructed" them by joining together in conspiratorial organizations that could at least relieve them of the responsibility of making individual decisions vis-à-vis German demands.

The new government in exile was obviously aware of the necessity of giving guidance to the population living under the occupation. Indeed, the first decree of the Committee of Ministers for Home Country Affairs (Komitet Ministrów dla Spraw Kraju) articulated plans for establishing a network of delegates (men of confidence) in all areas in the occupied country, and it stated explicitly that the population should continue to work in all branches of local administration, cooperate with the occupier in welfare actions and, in fact, abstain only from undertaking responsibilities of a direct political nature (Pełczyński, 1970:5-9). But this solution was only temporary. Very broad directives coming from abroad were patently inadequate for relieving the normative ambiguity of a population living under occupation. What was needed was a source of authority, one unequivocally recognized as such, that would be familiar with all contemporary developments in the occupied country and that could immediately communicate its directives. This ideal was never achieved because the conditions of life and political activity during the occupation, as well as during the twenty years immediately preceding the war, produced a plurality of interests and opinions that made effective centralization difficult. Nonetheless, the story of the underground state can be written almost exclusively in terms of the efforts made by a number of organizations to limit the excessive fragmentation and plurality of the underground.

A reasonable success was achieved by setting up the elaborate apparatus of the Substitute Administration under the Delegate of the London Government. Major political parties finally agreed on a common program for the future reconstruction of Poland and, from January 1944 on, met regularly as the so-called Council of National Unity (Korboński, 1975:103-105) (a name presumably reflecting their final agreement on the fundamentals of the future policies). Finally, the Home Army unified almost all armed detachments operating in the conspiracy, with the exception of a splinter from the radical right (NSZ) and the Communists. However, it took almost five years of intricate maneuvering and endless talks and consultations to achieve this unity.

DECENTRALIZATION OF THE UNDERGROUND

A typical cell of an underground organization consisted of a small group of three or five members (Pużak, 1977:18). In theory, contacts with the outside were maintained by only one person from such a group. Thus, if a member of the group were arrested, his confederates could be located and helped to change their whereabouts for a while, so that no one else would be caught. Because of its relative isolation, each cell, or for that matter, each local organization, became heavily dependent on its own resources. Personal relationships among members mattered more than official appointments and rank. Even an organization with so clearly stated a purpose as the Home Army, where we should least expect to find centralization a problem, since it was engaged in professional military preparations, displayed these features. "A loss, or a change in position of command carries a loss in organizational contacts and a partial depletion of cells in a given area. Each new commander must win his area anew, must establish personal contacts and win authority" (Pełczyński, 1973:243), wrote Rowecki in May 1942, that is, at a time when the Home Army was already well established.

An inevitable outcome of the enforced autonomy of each local organization was the notion that people in faraway centers did not really know local conditions and therefore could not make good judgments as to what course of action should be pursued in each area. This "lack of understanding" was recognized as a fundamental condition of conspiratorial life, and it had ramifications on many levels; it was believed, for example, that London did not understand what was going on in Poland, that Warsaw was ignorant about the realities of life in the countryside, etc. This attitude characterized the local network of every underground organization vis-à-vis its superiors in the organizational hierarchy. Of course, such feelings did not facilitate unification.

The necessity to be largely self-sufficient also generated a selection process whereby command of local networks was given to those who had more imagination and independence than would have been required in equivalent positions under normal conditions. Under the new circumstances more leadership qualities were required of subordinates if the organization was to thrive. But such a positive selection of the active and the resourceful to positions of authority in local cells, although necessary to promote the strength or even the survival of the organization under conditions of limited opportunities for control by the center, introduced another strong decentralizing factor into the makeup of underground organizations. It was not atypical for local leaders to rise to positions of spectacular prominence, if not virtual independence, in their regions. For example, Adam Rysie-wicz, a young student, allegedly controlled the Cracow Committee of the Socialist Party (Uziembło, 1950:16), and Tadeusz Maciński directed the Warsaw Organization of the National Democratic Party (Terej, 1971:338-340; Janowski, 1972). The requirements of conspiracy thus introduced into underground organizations a potential for irredentist tension that could not be checked effectively by the center.

In addition to the problems that were common to all clandestine organizations, there were others, peculiar to political parties, that also fostered internal divisions. Because the occupation brought political liberalization, and because former opposition parties were no longer under pressure to maintain even a superficial organizational unity within their own movements in view of the threat of *political* annihilation by a hostile establishment, there were no more obstacles to the open articulation of diverging political opinions and platforms. As late as March 1944, on the occasion of the creation of the so-called Centralizacja, an umbrella organization for about twenty-five underground political organizations of the left, an article in *Głos Wolny* (March 15, 1944) spoke about the extreme proliferation of party names. The author argued that he was completely lost in the plurality of underground organizations, for which there did not seem to be any justification. From names alone one could not tell the differences between the Democratic Party, the Party of Polish Democrats, the Party of Polish Democracy, and the Polish Democratic Party.

Similar "centralizations" (and therefore a similar spurious plurality of organizations) existed in the center and on the right of the political spectrum as well. In January 1943 the Peasant Party reported to Mikołajczyk that the Delegate was directing an umbrella organization, S.O.S., consisting of forty-seven different groups (GSHI, Kolekcja Kota, no. 25/11: *Trójkąt dla Stema*, Jan. 2, 1943). The remnants of Sanacja had no less than three such centers at this time: the OPW (Camp of Fighting Poland), KON (Committee of Organizations for Independence), and the left of Sanacja, Poland Fights (UPST, *Teka* 78/21). Finally, the radical right found its unifier in the person of Bolesław Piasecki and his Konfederacja Narodu (Confederation of the Nation). The existence of all these umbrella organizations testifies to the incredible plurality of the political organizations outside of the "big four" political parties. Moreover, the parties themselves were deeply eroded by internal divisions that were intensified by the peculiar atmosphere of the time.

The political left and the right of the former "loyal opposition" were more shaken by internal discord than the parties of the center; ideological differences perhaps matter more at the extremes. Echoing prewar political divisions, the National Democratic Party (SN) immediately split on the adoption of how exclusive (vis-à-vis other parties) an approach to take concerning the seizure of power after the war. Already in October 1939 sympathizers of the former Kowalski-Giertych faction, who favored a more radical totalitarian solution, split from the National Democratic Party and founded a separate organization under the name of the National People's Military Organization (NLOW) (Terej,

269

1971:140ff.). Later they were reintegrated into the SN, but another split occurred in 1942 after the leadership's decision to yield to government pressure and place the party's National Military Organization (NOW) under the command of the Home Army. On that occasion the dissenters established contacts with the National Radical Camp (ONR) and together founded the National Armed Forces (NSZ) (Terej, 1971:272-275).

The Socialist Party also eventually split on ideological grounds, although its initial division can be attributed to less concrete factors, such as the personal animosity between Kazimierz Pużak and Zygmunt Żuławski (Zaremba, 1957:115), the difference between Pużak and Stanisław Dubois in their styles of operating underground, and, finally, accidental factors that regulated, for better or for worse, the course of so many events and lives during the war. At any rate, when in May 1940 the PPS-WRN leadership, that is, Zygmunt Zaremba and Pużak, organized a national conference of delegates to choose and approve the wartime leadership of the movement, Dubois, Norbert Barlicki, and Adam Próchnik,[2] to name only the most prominent among the absent politicians who at that time could be reached in the GG, were not invited to attend (GSHI, PRM 76/I/42: L.dz.K. 1579/42/tj.). Roughly a year later, in August 1941, groups of Socialist conspirators met and founded a second clandestine organization under the name Polish Socialists (PS). As they drifted toward the left, the ideological gap between themselves and the PPS-WRN widened. Finally, some of the activists of the PS joined with the Communists shortly before the Red Army liberated Poland.

The Peasant Party managed to avoid major splits on ideological grounds and enjoyed a steady growth in numbers

[2] Żuławski, who was present at the meeting, had a violent exchange with Pużak and threatened to throw him out of the party. Pużak ignored Żuławski's threat, left the meeting, and did not see Żuławski again until March 1945 (Pużak, 1977:20).

and influence during the occupation, partly because it had no well-articulated ideology.[3] It was in the process of elaborating a doctrine of agrarianism but had not yet completed it. The best summary of its achievements in this field, although not intended as such, can be found in an article published in *Biuletyn Informacyjny* on May 4, 1944: "Poland has been a country of peasants; Poland must become in the future a country of satisfied peasants."

In terms of political strategy, the SL oscillated between the idea of staging a coup d'état in alliance with the PPS-WRN and becoming a pillar of the establishment sponsored by Sikorski's government after the Socialists withdrew from the Political Consultative Committee.[4] Late in 1942 the

[3] In the archives of the Sikorski Institute there is a very interesting twenty-one-page memorandum on the *lack* of a program in the Peasant Party and a proposal for the main line of its development. What is even more interesting is that it was submitted on April 25, 1944 (GSHI, A 9 III 4/24 *Pogląd na sytuację polityczną w kraju i wnioski. Ocena osobista W.B.I. zastępcy*).

[4] Strong circumstantial evidence suggests that late in 1940 and early in 1941 the PPS-WRN tried to forge an alliance with the SL and withdraw from the PKP. Both parties had apparently already prepared a common program (Zaremba, 1957:165-168; Pużak, 1977:30), and only at the last moment did the SL break the agreement. The program was later published by the PPS as the so-called Program of People's Poland. Portions of two dispatches that I found in the archives of the Sikorski Institute bear on the subject, which was never completely clarified by those involved: "The Bazylians [PPS-WRN] approached us with a proposition to renew our talks broken off last year . . . [what they are proposing] indicates that they *give up* their former position advocating the creation of a new, so-called revolutionary, government during the turning-point" (GSHI, A 9 III 4/1: L.dz.K. 2046/42, *Depesza Trójkąta*, Feb. 12, 1942; italics added). (The term *przełom*, "turning point," designated the period that would immediately follow the expulsion of Germans from Poland.) And another dispatch, prepared by Mikołajczyk for transmission to Poland: "Your agreeing with the PPS to a common candidate [for the position of Delegate] has provoked criticism here, particularly after Ciołkosz showed a copy of your agreement with the PPS in which the third paragraph entails severance of relations with

271

SL came to the conclusion that it was the strongest group numerically and that no political arrangements in independent Poland could be worked out without giving it a considerable share of power. Accordingly, it calmly watched its partners in the underground and made sure that none grew too strong (GSHI, A 9 III 4/1: L.dz.K. 4912/42, *Depesza od Trójkąta*, Dec. 6, 1942; UPST, *Kancelaria Oddz*, VI: *Duży Raport Karskiego*). Still, there were clashes among the leadership: on personal grounds, for example, between Józef Niećko and Stefan Korboński; and involving the more serious issue of the legitimacy of the wartime leadership, between Kazimierz Bagiński (on his return from Russia) and the already existing triumvirate of Niećko, Józef Grudziński, and Stanisław Osiecki.

This last dispute can be seen as parallel to the refusal of various socialist groupings to recognize the leadership of Zaremba and Pużak after the May 1940 conference. In both cases, recognized procedures for leadership selection could not be implemented during the war, and because only a part of the prewar leadership was available to continue at the head of the movement, the mandate to do so was shaky and could be challenged on formal grounds. In the case of the Peasant Party, the Central Leadership of the Peasant Movement (CKRL) was simply nominated by Maciej Rataj, the most respected person in the movement after Witos. But what might be accepted as an emergency measure in late 1939 or early 1940 could very well be challenged two years later, particularly as Rataj's personal authority was no longer available (he was executed by the Germans) to back the arrangement (Buczek, 1970:53ff.). Notwithstanding these conflicts and others that occurred because the orientation of rank and file members was more radical than that of the leadership, the Peasant Party was never afflicted by

---

the Sikorski government and the creation of a new edition of the Lublin government" (GSHI, A 9 III 4/1; *Szkic depeszy do Trójkąta*, July 1, 1941).

as much factionalism as existed in the PPS and SN. As the war progressed, the movement gathered strength and momentum.

Finally, Sanacja's abdication of power was a prerequisite for obtaining the emergent Polish underground's recognition of the government in exile and was necessary for maintaining the formal continuity of Polish statehood.[5] Nevertheless, Sanacja's disappearance added a destabilizing element to the overall situation. In the first place, to set up a new government in time of a military rout cannot be a smooth process (Kukiel, 1970). To establish links of mutual understanding and confidence, or simply to exchange information about rapidly changing developments, probably could not have been done in a reasonably short time by such a new government and the new political structures emerging in the occupied country. Consequently, the initial period of the underground's emergence was complicated by the discontinuity caused by the transfer of power to the new government. It was not a question of merely changing appearances and introducing new faces; neither Sikorski nor people like Stanisław Kot (SL) and Jan Stańczyk (PPS) could ever have obtained the premiership or ministerial assignments under Sanacja. Discontinuity was even more pervasive because the new team did not prepare itself for succession (it had not anticipated that it might take over so soon), nor was it a logically chosen and carefully assembled group. In fact, the new government was an accidental product of unexpected circumstances, both in terms of its sudden rise to power and in terms of its composition. The

[5] Had the Sanacja government escaped to England, and had it been in a position to continue as a government in exile, it seems more than likely that the majority of emerging underground organizations in Poland would have refused to recognize its authority and would have probably declared that its mandate, which was questionable after the rigged elections of 1930 and 1935, was voided by its failure to provide leadership in September and by the public outcry against it after the campaign in Poland was over.

273

premise on which it was founded can best be expressed in negatives: it was necessary, under the circumstances, that the new regime dissociate itself politically from Sanacja, and that in the process it should not alienate the military, which, after all, had powerful links to the deposed regime.

Sikorski was an excellent choice to lead in such a delicate situation. He, together with General Kazimierz Sosnkowski, a very prestigious former close companion of Piłsudski who had maintained low political visibility during the Sanacja regime, and a group of politicians from the large parties of the former opposition, constituted a government as strong as it was possible to form in exile. In addition, they satisfied a wide spectrum of public opinion and the military. Apparently the news of the new government's formation was received with relief and satisfaction in the country (Zaremba, 1958:100). Sikorski was the providential man in this situation. Perhaps it was because of the need for a symbol of unity, for a code word that would simultaneously denote resistance and hope for future victory, that he acquired a charismatic quality for the population in Poland. It did not matter who else was in the government in London, nor that the government was often ridiculed and reproached for intraparty squabbles and for its inability to read the mood of the country (exemplified, for example, by its irritating radio broadcasts to Poland). Sikorski was looked upon as a hero and savior and as a guarantee that a strong and just authority would bring order to the disorganized political life of the country after the war (GSHI, PRM 24: "Sprawozdanie z kraju," Mar. 3, 1940; PRM 46a/41: doc. no. 962/II/41, Nov. 15, 1940; PRM 45c/1941: doc. no. L.dz.802/II. 1941, Feb. 3, 1941; PRM 46a/41: "Sprawozdanie Antoniego," Apr. 1941; *Polska Ludowa*, Sept. 1943).

However, the processes of creating authority both within the country and in exile at first developed independently of one another, and the efforts to reach an understanding between the two were not immediately successful. When he left the country Sikorski had asked his friend

Ryszard Świętochowski to await messages from him and to act in the future, if necessary, as his political proxy. But when he spoke with Świętochowski, Sikorski probably did not anticipate becoming premier so quickly. Nonetheless, after Sikorski assumed new responsibilities and established contacts with Świętochowski, the latter considered himself empowered to represent the government, rather than Sikorski personally. With several other politicians of the Front Morges,[6] he established the so-called Biuro Polityczne (Political Bureau) (BP), and, having obtained funds from abroad, he financed a variety of underground groups through CKON, under which they were loosely federated (Korboński, 1975:46-48; Dołęga-Modrzewski, 1959:13-14). Thus, simultaneously with the creation of the SZP and the PKP, there was another project developing that was also supported by the government (15,000,000 złotych was sent to the BP until mid-1940) and that was hostile to the PKP. Świętochowski argued that larger parties tried to monopolize the representation of society and disregarded the multitude of smaller political underground organizations. The BP was also hostile to the SZP, which, as later became clear, was suspected of harboring pro-Sanacja, and therefore anti-Sikorski, sentiments (Korboński, 1975:46-48; GSHI, Kolekcja Kota, no. 25/12: Vogel, Sept. 20, 1940; GSHI, PRM 46a/41: "Sprawozdanie Antoniego," App. 10, "List Pana Wolskiego do Delegata Rządu," Oct. 3, 1940).

Although it soon became apparent that the combination of SZP and PKP was the strongest of all underground organizations, the most serious, and the one enjoying the widest public support, a considerable amount of mistrust, particularly toward the military organization SZP, was nurtured in the government. It did not help to restore Sikorski's

[6] The Front Morges was an anti-Sanacja alliance of politicians founded in 1936 by General Sikorski and Ignacy Paderewski. Under its inspiration a fraction of the Christian Democratic Party joined with the National Workers' Party to form the Labor Party (Stronnictwo Pracy) in 1937.

275

confidence in the loyalty of his comrades-in-arms that one of the first organizational reports sent by Tokarzewski from Warsaw, and addressed to the "Supreme Commander," was delivered (apparently by mistake) to Marshal Rydz-Śmigły (Karaszewicz-Tokarzewski, 1964:28-29).[7] In any case, throughout the first year and a half, suspicion of the SZP's pro-Sanacja sympathies was very much in Sikorski's mind, particularly as one of his closest collaborators, Professor Stanisław Kot, persisted in feeding his mistrust. Thus, from the beginning, the government itself seems to have lacked orientation and self-confidence in its contacts with the conspiracy in Poland. Indeed, there is some evidence—and it was interpreted as such by contemporaries—that the government purposely tried to impede the formation of a strong, centralized, and unified structure in the underground (GSHI, PRM 46a/41: "Sprawozdanie Antoniego").

If this is true, the government's task was facilitated by the emergence in the first months of the occupation of almost all the chief participants in the underground. The initial variety of the movement is striking in comparison with the slow and gradual development of underground networks in other European countries. Only the Substitute Administration, that is, the machine of the Government's Delegacy, was founded later. By the winter of 1939-1940 three centers, or arenas, of underground activity were already formed: the military organization (SZP); the main political parties (SL, PPS, and SN, later joined by the SP), with their Consultative Committee, and a multitude of small, independent political and military groups, who at that time were gravitating toward the BP and CKON. A

[7] The marshal apparently forwarded it immediately to Sikorski. Evidently, this mistake was the reason for the prompt removal of Karaszewicz-Tokarzewski from his command in Warsaw and for his transfer to Lwów, where he was supposed to organize an anti-Russian conspiracy. But there he was arrested on the spot and regained his freedom only after the Sikorski-Stalin pact. In a subsequent conversation with Sikorski he learned about the mistake of the messenger.

1940 report sent from Warsaw informed London that the underground movement contained three main currents: organizations of "pre-May" (1926) Poland, that is, PPS, SL, SN, and SP; organizations established by activists of "post-May" Poland, that is, the military (ZWZ); and organizations founded by young people who mistrusted all (and old) politicians (GSHI, PRM 24: "Całka: odpis raportu," Nov. 5, 1940). Characteristically, three years later, in February 1943, Sikorski gave an almost identical list of the four principal components of the underground life in the country: the Political Consultative Committee; the Delegate's bureaucracy; the military organization; and the loose political organizations sympathetic to the government (Duraczyński, 1966:245). The transformation of the PKP in January 1944 into the Council of National Unity (Rada Jedności Narodowej) (RJN), which seated representatives of parties and groups other than the major four (Korboński, 1975:103-105), was, in the first place, a political countermove in response to the organization of a Communist-sponsored Country's National Council (KRN) on New Year's Eve; it was also an expression of the solidarity of patriotic public opinion united in its opposition to the by then real danger of a Communist takeover.[8] Beyond this, it was not,

[8] A translation of a proclamation issued by political organizations in the country in January 1944 reads:

To the Polish Nation:

In view of coming events that will be decisive for the ending of the war and that require from Poland enormous and coordinated efforts, elements hostile to the republic have undertaken action which aims at weakening the unity of the Polish nation.

Under the name of the PPR (the Polish Workers' Party), foreign Communist agents carry on their actions in our territories, aiming at the most vital interests of Poland.

Following directives from an outside, non-Polish, command post, disguising their real purposes and those of their principals, they hypocritically abuse patriotic and national watchwords. The Communist Polish Workers' Party and its branch, like the allegedly "Polish" People's Army [Polska Armia Ludowa] declare their readi-

I believe, a sign of final political unification of the underground.

To speak of this plurality of conspiratorial forces, however, is not, according to my understanding of what the underground was, to point out its weaknesses. The requirements of conspiracy, which demanded that activities be pursued in small, tightly knit groups, added to prewar mistrust and fragmentation of political movements, which pro-

---

ness to give the eastern territories of the republic to Russia and denounce the Polish Government and Polish Army, abroad and in the country, which are vested with the nation's confidence.

In their efforts to weaken and destroy national strength in the decisive period of the war, Communist agencies call into existence the KRN (Country's National Council) and the supreme command of the People's Army (AL) and plan the setting up of a Temporary Government.

Notwithstanding the negligible strength and importance represented by the above, fictitious and designed to win recognition abroad, institutions, actions of the PPR must be decisively and unequivocally condemned as treason to the Polish nation and the Polish state.

Only the government of the Republic and its Delegate in the country, plus the Supreme Commander and the Commander of the Home Army designated by him can legitimately issue orders in the last stage of the struggle against the occupier—struggle, which since the very first days has been engaged in with full devotion by the entire nation.

The nation decides in political matters, never a foreign-sponsored agency.

[Signed:] Stronnictwo Ludowe wraz z baonami chłopskimi; Centralne Kierownictwo Ruchu Mas Pracujących "Wolność, Równość, Niepodległość"; Stronnictwo Narodowe; Stronnictwo Pracy; Bojowa Organizacja "Wschód"; Front Odbudowy Pol; Gwardia Ludowa; Komitet Pracy Społeczno-Politycznej "Pobudka"; Konwent Organizacji Niepodległościowych; Konwent Jedności Narodu; Obóz Polski Walczącej; "Ojczyzna"; Organizacja Polski Niepodległej; Polski Związek Wolności; "Racławice"; Stronnictwo Demokratyczne; Stronnictwo Polskich Demokratów; Stronnictwo Zrywu Narodu; Syndykalistyczna Organizacja "Wolność"; Unia; Zjednoczenie Robotników Polskich; Związek Odrodzenia Narodu; Związek Odrodzenia Rzplitej.

278

duced, in turn, fragmentation of the underground. But it is essential to observe that this fragmentation reflected the "true" nature of the underground movement. It is possible, I believe, to substantiate this statement in two ways: first, organizational fragmentation was a logical consequence of the pursuit of the collective goal to which the underground was devoted; and second, the immediate benefit that people obtained from their participation in the underground—a relatively stable normative orientation—was applied to regulate their interaction in such a variety of social pursuits that it could not be fitted into a few neatly defined organizational structures. To put it another way, the underground was a substitute for the entire society rather than for its military or political organizations only. Its foundation was a *citizen* rather than a soldier or a politician. Therefore the underground was a much more complex reality than one which could be encapsulated into organizations appropriate to the institutionalizing of political and/or military establishments.

THE LOGIC OF COLLECTIVE ACTION

As the title of this section suggests, we shall borrow here from Mancur Olson's (1965) analysis. His argumentation reveals the underlying logic of action in the pursuit of collective goods. In Olson's terminology, liberation from the German occupation, and thus regaining independence, was a collective good par excellence.[9] Olson's analysis of the logic underlying action in the pursuit of collective goods is predicated on the observation that, while it may be in the common interest of all group members to obtain a given collective good, precisely because it is a *collective*

[9] "A common, collective or public good is here defined as any good such that if any person X_i in a group $X_1, \ldots X_i, \ldots, X_n$ consumes it, it cannot feasibly be withheld from the others in that group" (Olson, 1965:14).

good, none of the members, as an individual agent, will be motivated to make any contribution for that purpose:

> The individual member of the typical large organization is in a position analogous to that of the firm in a perfectly competitive market, or the taxpayer in the state: his own efforts will not have a noticeable effect on the situation of his organization, and he can enjoy any improvements brought about by others whether or not he has worked in support of his organization. (Olson, 1965:16)

Why should anyone be willing to risk his life in the struggle for independence if, in view of the mass scale of the movement, it was more than likely that his individual contribution would not make any noticeable difference to the outcome of the struggle, and if, once independence was won by others, he could not be excluded from benefits brought about by its achievement? Olson helps us to raise important theoretical questions that reach into the heart of our discussion.

In Olson's approach there are two ways out of the dilemma raised by the theoretical impossibility of large-scale voluntary organizations pursuing collective goods and the empirical evidence that such organizations do exist. One solution of this obvious contradiction is to discover that, because these types of organizations are unable to make membership compulsory, they "must also provide some noncollective goods in order to give potential members an incentive to join" (Olson, 1965:16). The other is to demonstrate that the logic of collective action is different in small groups and that within the large-scale voluntary organizations the real framework of social action is a small group. Both lines of argumentation apply well in the case of the Polish underground.

I have already noted some of the benefits accruing to a participant in the underground: psychological comfort derived from acquiring a sense of guidance in the morally disturbing social environment of an occupied country; the sense of belonging, and a positive bond with a group at a time when isolation from other people and suspicion of their hostility was a prevalent experience; the support of a group of people who were prepared to do everything in their power to help one another in danger, if for no other reason than the imperative calling for the preservation of the organization; access to the considerable material resources at the disposal of the underground, and thus the ability to acquire good documents, to find a place to live, and to get a job through organizational contacts; training in the skills needed to avoid the random dangers of the occupier's security measures; and, finally, the chance to accumulate credentials that could be used later, after independence was won. All these palpable benefits were available to people who joined the underground network, a conspiracy aimed at providing, ultimately, a collective good to all the Poles: independence. Truly, an answer demonstrating the benefits to be gained is more convincing than an appeal exclusively to the tradition of romantic politics in Poland and the assumption that there were always people in this country ready to engage in suicide missions, particularly when independence was at stake. When reflecting on the anti-German underground in Poland during the Second World War, we should understand this tradition of dramatic and active patriotism, but it is equally, or even more, important for us to see that individuals joined the conspiracy for reasons of self-interest, although this motive perhaps was not a conscious one in the majority of cases. However, we are still only halfway through the initial dilemma. We may understand now why so many people joined the underground, but we still do not understand why it took the shape it did. Olson's theory, again, helps to shed some light on this issue.

That the underground was a "mass movement" is revealed by a single statistic; in 1943 the membership of the Home Army was estimated at 350,000 people. Notwithstanding the size of the underground, we have learned already that the actual framework of social action for each

281

of its participants was very often one of the small organizations, or at least a relatively small group of cellmates or members of the local network. This fact is of utmost significance: one of Olson's fundamental findings indicates that in small organizations the logic of pursuing the collective good is different from that in large organizations. *In a small group situation individual members find incentives to help actively in efforts to establish the collective good.*[10]

[10] Following Olson, we may formulate three propositions explaining why individual members in small groups willingly share the burden of seeking the collective good. (1) Because each member's contribution is noticeable in a small group, he will continue to provide it as long as he is interested in maintaining a certain level of supply of the collective good. Also, since withdrawal of his active participation significantly increases the burdens of others, he will suffer the social pressures of the group, which demand that all members participate actively. (2) Each member's contribution may be not only visible but also *indispensable* for continued provision of the collective good. In other words, should a member cease to be an active agent, his cell in the organization may have to be dissolved. Thus, one's unwillingness to share in the costs may not only lower the level of supply of the collective good but could conceivably cut the supply completely. The outcome would be dramatic, and it would most likely be of greater benefit to the reluctant individual to continue his role in securing the collective good rather than merely to try to preserve his own resources. (Neither of these two contingencies applies within the context of a larger group, where the particular contribution of any single individual makes no real difference in securing the collective good.) (3) "In smaller groups marked by considerable degrees of inequality—that is, in groups of members of unequal 'size' or extent of interest in the collective good—there is the greatest likelihood that a collective good will be provided; for the greater the interest in the collective good of any single member, the greater the likelihood that the member will get such a significant proportion of the total benefit from the collective good that he will gain from seeing that the good is provided, even if he has to pay all of the cost himself" (Olson, 1965:34). This last proposition agrees with our earlier observation that local leaders of underground organizations very often rose to positions of considerable prominence. They were, indeed, the members with "the greatest interest in the collective good." Thousands of individuals, for reasons as varied as human personality or accidents of life, displayed particular ingenuity, zeal, and devotion in their con-

Thus, the fragmentation of the underground should not be interpreted as a sign of its weakness but rather of its strength; it is within the framework of a small group that collective goods are most effectively pursued by organizations that cannot use coercion to secure their members' active participation. But to rest our case with this finding would be to stop short of full comprehension. Explaining the formal property of an institution in light of a set of formal principles is only a preliminary step. We want to be able to name the phenomenon under study, not just list the properties that describe its functioning. Only then will our analysis be heuristically complete.

THE FINAL INTERPRETATION

What was the underground? I have already suggested what I consider the answer to be: the underground was not primarily an anti-German conspiracy but rather a substitute for Polish society in all its functional diversity and plurality of organizational forms. Its budgets make clear its scope: they included expenditures not only for "defense" (a rational course of action for an anti-German conspiracy) but also for the maintenance of the apparatus of administration, for education, for welfare, and for cultural activity. Precisely because of this comprehensiveness, it makes sense to speak of an "underground state." Nevertheless, before drawing final conclusions, let us examine alternative ways of looking at the underground.

The underground could not single-handedly defeat the occupier. Therefore its only viable "military conception" was to prepare for a showdown in the final stages of the

---

spiratorial activity. If it is true that there was no single charismatic leader in the underground, it is also true that there were thousands of quasi-charismatic subleaders who enjoyed the trust and devotion of their colleagues and subordinates in the underground cells. Their presence was a crucial factor: on the personal level, they sustained the fragmented underground throughout the entire occupation.

war and to acquire the capability of giving a coup de grâce to the occupier when the Allied armies were actually winning the war. Indeed, this goal was, in broad outline, the rationale for the organizational work of the Home Army; practically, this objective required selecting the target for attack in the finale of the war, distributing assignments to territorial commands, and then training the personnel. Most clandestine activity consisted in recruiting, obtaining the necessary material resources, and, finally, training for the successful accomplishment of tasks assigned in the framework of the plan Tempest (*Burza*), the code word for the final uprising. But to hope for a reasonable chance of success in this final showdown, the underground in the meantime had to help the population live through the occupation. It had to act in response to the everyday measures of the occupier, lest the moral and physical exhaustion of occupation leave too few people capable of bearing arms at the moment of liberation. Thus, a strictly military orientation could be only a part, though undoubtedly a very important part, of its program.

One might wonder then why, until the suitable moment came for the final uprising, could the underground not be an organization devoted primarily to sabotage and destruction? Again, the answer is that it was such, but only up to a point. The underground in Poland was not a mass-scale guerrilla movement, first, because geography did not allow it to be, and second, because people do not just go "into the forest"—they must be driven there by desperation. When the Germans used bloody repressions for the purpose of collecting compulsory deliveries, many people of course fled their homes, and partisan detachments increased in number and strength. However, this development was not necessarily welcome from the point of view of the overall strategy of the underground. Loose partisan formations could not always be controlled and often turned to robbery and banditry. They might also, and often did, jeopardize one of the main goals of the patriotic underground: to preserve and to save from destruction the population of the nation. A tragic dilemma of the underground was a consequence of its ruthless enemy having in hand, at all times, millions of hostages. Indeed, every murder of a Pole—not necessarily even a member of the underground—was a blow against the conspiracy, a partial frustration of its goals. For if it aimed at winning back independence, there had to be people left to enjoy it. Thus the execution of innocent Poles in reprisal for some action of the underground was not only an additional burden on the consciences of the underground leaders who ordered the action, but was also an *actual material blow* against the conspiracy. *The collective responsibility introduced by the Germans was, in a terrifying way, a logical countermeasure to the collective good being pursued by the underground.*

Two conceptions of underground warfare seem to have been held by the conspiratorial movements in Europe: the Communists, when they finally joined the underground, called for immediate action; on the other hand, the national liberation movements, the patriotic conspiracies, adopted the position of "wait and see" (Michel, 1972:207-210). On the surface, this difference was merely tactical, but it was grounded in deeper motives. As long as the goal of the underground was to disrupt German communication lines with the East and to relieve some of the pressure on the Red Army, immediate action and sabotage was the logical course of action. But when winning back independence, and thereby preserving the population of the nation, was the goal, sabotage could be used only as a carefully planned, professional, and selectively targeted strategy. Otherwise, the human costs would be prohibitive.

Understandably, the Home Army and the civilian underground viewed the problem in this way. The Home Army had special detachments assigned to the task of "current struggle" (*walka bieżąca*), assembled originally in the Związek Odwetu (Association of Revenge) (ZO) and later in the Kedyw (Kierownictwo Dywersji; Leadership of

285

Sabotage), while the civilian underground was actively fighting the Germans through its Directorate of Civil Resistance (Kierownictwo Walki Cywilnej) and later the Directorate of Underground Resistance (Kierownictwo Walki Podziemnej), which was already a joint civilian and military enterprise (Korboński, 1968; Korboński, 1975). Thus sabotage was a part of the underground, but conducted by a well-defined group of professionals and by no means limited to blowing up railroad tracks. Often it was aimed at a spiritual revival of the terrorized population. For example, slips of paper with the notorious sign, "Nur für Deutsche," were glued to lampposts in Warsaw; one letter was changed in a slogan devised by German propaganda, "Deutschland siegt an allen Fronten," so that signs read "Deutschland liegt an allen Fronten"; and the name of a high SS leader that figured on posters proclaiming a mass execution in reprisal for killing the German confidant Igo Sym was changed from Moder to Mörder. These pranks were all dangerous and, of course, "forbidden" games, but the underground never even approached the scale of sabotage of which it was certainly capable, partly because full-scale sabotage of the entire imposed "new order," rather than of a narrowly specialized organization, would bring anarchy, which could only be self-defeating for the underground's purposes.

Instead of sabotage, the underground called for resistance and *boycott*.[11] This strategy was much more comprehensive, demanding the mobilization of the entire population for the observance of rules of conduct covering even trivial, superficial behavior. Decalogues of citizens' obligations, published in numerous underground sources, insisted, among other things, on such trifles as not going to the movies,

[11] Dołęga-Modrzewski (1959:45-48) reveals that in 1940 Rowecki prepared a General Instruction that was supposed to establish the principles of orientation for all strata of Polish society and facilitate their consolidation behind the patriotic underground. It put forward three principles: preservation of Polish lives; boycott; and collective demonstrations.

limiting traditional hospitality, ignoring German parades, concerts, and all forms of symbolic activities conducted in public places, and pretending not to understand German (*Biuletyn Informacyjny*, May 10, 1940; *Kodeks Polaka, Biblioteka Szańca*, 1940).

A successful countermeasure to total exploitation requires total resistance, that is, the application of a formula of resistance that will upset the calculations of the occupier. Total exploitation is possible when an individual is successfully isolated from all his attachments to others, when no commitments or obligations of any sort distract him from the full expenditure of his resources, mental and physical, in the service of the exploiter. A collection of robots with no desires, no tastes, and no attachments is an ideal group to exploit. Thus, the main thrust of the underground, as I have been suggesting, was to work against social atomization. Insofar as it was successful in accomplishing this task, it was also successful in frustrating German plans.

We can see this struggle against social atomization and normlessness in the underground's continuing search for a recognized authority. Its purpose was nothing so immediate as centralizing the resistance network or coordinating preparations for the uprising, but was chiefly aimed at reducing anarchy and providing authoritative direction in a great many areas of social life. The need for leadership lay behind the urgency felt about appointing a Government Delegate in the Generalgouvernement, an office ultimately given to Ratajski. Colonel Skorobohaty-Jakubowski, who had been sent from London to Warsaw to get the political parties and the ZWZ to agree on a candidate for that position, wrote back that the people needed an authority who could issue instructions for the "conduct of everyday struggle of passive resistance against the occupier" (GSHI, PRM 24: *Skorobohaty: raport sytuacyjny z Warszawy*). In March 1940 Rowecki also stressed the urgency of the situation and requested an immediate solution of the same problem. According to him, as long as there was no authority empowered by the Polish Government to issue directives to the society, instructing how it should react to the daily multiplying German decrees, the situation was dangerous, particularly since various incompetent sources were usurping that prerogative. People like Ronikier and Radziwiłł, and organizations such as the Warsaw welfare committee (SKSS), were approached by many with questions and gave instructions on how to behave in a variety of situations. This practice was dangerous, Rowecki warned, and should be stopped (Pełczyński, 1970:184). Ratajski's dispatch (quoted in Chap. V above), which he sent to London shortly after he began to exercise his functions, made this point explicit: one of his most difficult tasks was to answer queries by a number of social groups about the admissible limits of their cooperation with the occupier (UPST, *Teka* 74/26). Clearly, the scope of the undertaking from the beginning was not to set up an organization of saboteurs or guerrilla detachments but to coordinate resistance in the entire society. What am I to do? was a question that any Pole was likely to ask of himself sooner or later, and the Delegate was supposed to be prepared to answer him.

The mode of activity of political parties in the underground provides a further example of this strategy. Evidently, they were never distracted from the main purpose and justification of a political party—to take over the power in a state. All acted as though winning independence was a foregone conclusion. Did they suspend ideological warfare among themselves in view of the threat posed to them all? Not in the least. The National Democratic Party refused in November 1940 to sign jointly with other parties of the Political Consultative Committee a document stating that the purpose of the current struggle of liberation was to rebuild an independent and democratic Poland. It could not stomach the word *democracy* (GSHI, PRM 46a/41: *Sprawozdanie z trzech tygodni pobytu w kraju*, Nov. 1940). In March 1944 the National Democratic Party, for similar reasons, withdrew its signature from the program of unity

288

agreed upon by the parties on March 15 (GSHI, Kolekcja Kota, no. 25/9: "Sprawozdanie Celta"). In another "coup" the *Warszawski Głos Narodowy* in February of that year—almost five years after the war began—published an article entitled, significantly, "Great France or Small France," in which it praised the France of Pétain and ridiculed that of de Gaulle (Terej, 1971:248). Was it paving the way for collaboration? Not at all. The National Democratic Party was unequivocally committed to the resistance, and it paid more dearly than any other political party for that stand in the number of its prominent members who were captured and killed by the Germans (Terej, 1971:187, 297). Thus the explanation of its stand lies somewhere else. Obviously, the National Democratic Party and the other political parties did not want to part with their ideological commitments. The anti-German conspiracy was just one part of their normal activity; they were always careful to maintain a distinct identity, and they aimed eventually at winning political power in an independent Poland.

The early attacks of politicians against the ZWZ reveal a power struggle that is more relevant to the problem of succession to power in an independent Poland than to an anti-German conspiracy. It is doubtful that these attacks resulted solely from a reluctance to let Sanacja regain a foothold in the underground state. An unbiased reader would find no evidence of such a danger in the initial instructions from Sosnkowski, which speak openly of the political bankruptcy of Sanacja's system (Pełczyński, 1970: 191), or in the findings of the emissary Antoni (Iranek-Osmecki) in his report to the government in early 1941, or in the well-documented and wisely argued position of Rowecki, whose dispatches were presented in turn by Sosnkowski to Sikorski.[12] Membership in underground organiza-

[12] See particularly GSHI, PRM 25: *Pismo generała Sosnkowskiego do generała Sikorskiego w sprawie działalności politycznej ZWZ w kraju*, L.dz. 383/A tjn, Sept. 3, 1940 (not included in Pełczyński's volume), and later, in November 1940, an exchange of memoranda be-

tions was, after all, voluntary, and few would willingly join a Sanacja-sponsored organization. When we examine the case made against the ZWZ based on the alleged danger of a Sanacja takeover, we must conclude that the issue was raised as a most convenient pretext to strike at that military organization. The real danger of a takeover was completely out of proportion to the violence of the attacks against the ZWZ.

Again, this episode is more understandable when it is regarded as a part of a contest for power in the future. The political parties were justifiably worried about their political future because of the rapid growth in strength of the ZWZ, the weak legitimacy of democratic politics in Poland, and the widespread belief that what Poland needed was a strong and just man to rule over it. By attacking the ZWZ, the other parties were simply fighting their strongest opponent. With the exception of PPS-WRN, they all mistrusted the Home Army until the end and were reluctant to subsume party militias under its command. When they finally did so, they insisted upon keeping political control over those units that were incorporated into the AK with their lower command structures intact (GSHI, A 9 III 4/1: *Depesza Mikołajczyka do Kierownictwa Trójkąta*, Dec. 23, 1942). Even then the parties tried, under new names, to preserve the skeletons of some paramilitary organizations subject to their exclusive disposition, namely, the Obozowe Drużyny Bojowe (ODB) of the National Democratic Party (Terej, 1971:415-416) and the Ludowa Straż Bezpieczeń-

---

tween Sikorski (Pełczyński, 1970:324-325) and Sosnkowski (Pełczyński, 1970:328-332); the full text of this important document is also in GSHI, PRM 25. In this dramatic climax of the campaign of accusations against the ZWZ—in which apparently Kot's arguments convinced Sikorski—the prime minister and supreme commander instructed Sosnkowski to change the wording of the oath of ZWZ soldiers, substituting "they swear obedience to orders of the Supreme Commander and the Polish Government" for the previous text, according to which members were asked to swear obedience to "the authorities of the Association" (the name of the ZWZ is Association for Armed Struggle).

stwa (LSB) of the Peasant Party (Buczek, 1970:162ff.). The political parties wanted to preserve their identity and strength organizationally as well as ideologically.

Does all this interparty squabbling indicate irresponsibility on the part of the underground? Does it mean that at a time when it should have concentrated all its resources on fighting the Germans, it was wasting them on internal disputes? I do not think an unequivocal condemnation is warranted. With the Sanacja government outsted from power, the issue of political succession in an independent Poland was suddenly opened. Political battles among underground parties concerned the foundation of the political system to come, which had to be prepared beforehand to prevent anarchy following liberation. The underground rightly saw this as one of its major responsibilities. It is therefore more appropriate to speak of the plurality rather than of the fragmentation of the underground. Plurality was its natural characteristic, as it is of all free societies or political systems.

The most sweeping result of the occupation was the democratization of Polish society: differences of class, status, and power among Poles disappeared under the weight of German terror. This period also saw the mobilization of large masses of people into politics and the rapid growth of patriotic consciousness and national identification (GSHI, Kolekcja Kota, no. 25/9: "Sprawozdanie Celta"). And finally, it was a time when the democratic political establishment re-emerged from obscurity and established itself more firmly than ever before. In the words of a French historian:

> Clandestine resistance represented nothing less than the Polish nation in existence as a national entity as in prewar days. But it was something else as well—an emergent democracy; in occupied Poland political parties were more powerful, more emancipated and more active than in independent Poland which had been a dictatorship. Polish resistance, therefore, had cohesion and strength unparalleled in Europe. (Michel, 1972:299)

291

CHAPTER XII

Final Remarks

> It seems to me that the tragic vision, when it remains true to its "type," excludes any other deliverance than "sympathy," than tragic "pity"—that is to say, an important emotion of participation in the misfortunes of the hero, a sort of weeping with him and purifying the tears by the beauty of Song.
>
> RICOEUR, *The Symbolism of Evil*

THERE is no theory of tragedy says Paul Ricoeur (1969) in his investigations into the symbolism of evil. A theory of tragedy cannot be formulated explicitly because it is impossible for theology to contain a concept of a "wicked God": it would result in the self-destruction of religious consciousness. Still, a sense of the tragic and experience of the tragic are man's constant companions in this world. How do we become acquainted with the tragic if it is literally impossible to *know* it? We can do so, the philosopher answers, but only by following the drama as it unfolds, by participating in the spectacle.

Is a theory of *univers concentrationaire* conceivable? Can men conceive of themselves as living in a society where the agents of public order not only withhold security from their subjects but are also themselves unrestrained perpetrators of violence? Is it possible consciously to pose the problem of sociation in a society where the organizers of public order are determined to destroy their subjects physically? I do not think so, because men are unable to visualize living in a "society" where they are not expected to survive physically, and sociologists cannot contemplate a theory of human motivation that could make such a self-destructive society possible. I do not believe that we will ever reach the point where a sociology of *univers concentrationaire* can be written successfully. The creation of a theory of this kind of society would represent the ultimate triumph of man's intellect over his conscience.

Where should we place the present study then? In effect, it is not a study of a *univers concentrationaire*. Rather, it aims to demonstrate, or, more modestly, to illustrate, the impossibility of imposing a model of *univers concentrationaire* on a society. I have tried to stress factors that ultimately would lead to the emergence of alternative forms of collective life, that is, to a new, substitute society, as a response to an attempt at unlimited exploitation by a conquering power.

COMPRESSIBILITY OF SYSTEMS

Under the pressure of the German occupation, as we have seen, the resources of Polish society were drained and the overall performance of the system drastically curtailed. The question that logically comes to mind is: how much "reduction" can a social system endure? How much change, imposed from the outside, causes the destruction of a system rather than its alteration? Is there a point beyond which a social system cannot be further compressed without disintegrating?

One is led in this way to a set of classical questions asked by functionalist sociology: What are the necessary functional requisites of a social system? What are its minimal functional imperatives? I prefer not to devise an arbitrary list of such requisites. Instead, I would simply posit that there are some such minimal conditions (functional requisites) that must be fulfilled for a social system to continue in existence. We may then inquire into the characteristic dynamic of social change being generated whenever social systems are brought by some circumstances to a point where those minimum requisites necessary for their continuing operation are put in jeopardy. For that purpose I propose to borrow from Morgenstern's (1966) discussion of compression of economic systems.

Morgenstern's analysis evaluates performance of an organization in a changing environment. More specifically, he is interested in what happens to an organization when its environment becomes increasingly hostile and exerts growing pressure (compression) on the organization. There are some characteristic moments in the interaction between an increasingly compressing environment and an increasingly resistant social system. Specifically, says Morgenstern, the kernel of a social system "begins to appear if further compression in the same direction brings about a *discontinuous* contraction of the performance of the remaining part of the system" (Morgenstern, 1966:193). Until the kernel is reached, compression of the system may produce a continuous decline in its performance, or there could be no reduction at all.[1] But "when the kernel has been reached, total vulnerability of the remaining type of organization prevails" (Morgenstern, 1966:193).

How does a system's resistance to the gradual increase in compression develop? In any social system, to "trim the fat," to "eliminate outer layers," or to arrange substitutions requires expenditures of energy, because the system will *resist*, if for no other reason than inertia, all those processes of compression. Can the gradual increase of external pressure (compression) bring about the complete elimination of the system? Will a steady increase in compression yield a continuous decline (change) in performance? Morgenstern's answer is that the system's performance will decline steadily under pressure, but only until the kernel is affected. At that point it will remain unchanged for some time and then drop discretely to zero. Thus, for all appearances, the *resistance of the system is different in the immediate vicinity of the kernel.*

More specifically, it seems that when compression of the system succeeds in eliminating all outer layers, leaving only

[1] Compression may be the result of damage, but it may also be produced artificially in order to set free resources "consumed by the expandable layers of the system" (Morgenstern, 1966:196).

294

the kernel, the resistance of the system to further compression increases; further increase in pressure at that time does not affect performance significantly until the final breaking point is reached. A more elaborate theoretical justification for these observations can be provided by reference to two concepts well entrenched in our habits of thinking: the concept of inertia, and the concept of functional equivalence or substitution.

Inertia points toward the phenomenon of any system's resistance to change. In terms of the relationship between performance and compression (that is, as far as behavior of any social system in an environment is concerned), it posits that a given value of performance, for example, P_{10}, corresponds to a *set* of values of compression, $C_{10} + dC$. The increment dC represents inertia; it tells us that if we increase compression from C_{10} by less than dC, the system, because of inertia, will not contract. Some variations in an environment will have no visible impact on a system's performance. Thus, owing to inertia, contraction will not be a smooth, continuous process but rather a process of sharp, discrete discontinuities.

The concept of substitution, or functional equivalence, permits us to evaluate the dynamics of change of increments dC_i necessary in order to bring about reduction of performance from any given performance level P_i to the next below it, P_{i-1}. I suggest that those increments of compression dC_i will be increasing as the level of performance on which compression is applied goes down. Ultimately, dC_i will reach its maximum value as we reach the kernel, that is, the P_0 level of performance of the system, demonstrating that resistance increases as the system is gradually stripped of its resources.

The idea behind this proposition is simple: as compression gradually eliminates the resources of the system, forcing its contraction, it will affect functions that are vital and the levels of performance of those functions, which are judged as barely adequate. At that level—and there is an

295

abundance of historical evidence to illustrate this point (Olson, 1963)—the system will resist further decline in performance, not out of inertia alone, but because it will also try to reallocate what is left of its resources and opt for, or invent, a number of functional equivalents, that is, substitutions. Faced with oil shortages, an auto industry may change its production profile and promote smaller cars; confronted with water shortage, a population may shut off fountains and shower only once a week; encountering a food shortage, a society may limit the variety of foodstuffs it produces and consumes and grow mostly potatoes, which have the highest caloric yield per unit of cultivated land. In the areas of transportation, hygiene, and caloric intake, significant "reduction of performance" will not be noticed; yet the system will do with less oil, less water, and reduced imports of foodstuffs (should artificial shortages in these areas be the main components of "compression" applied from the outside). One can think of innumerable substitutes that a system will generate to cope with all sorts of shortages and compressions.

As each successive reduction of performance will bring about less satisfying conditions of life, more ingenuity, energy and social initiative will be channeled into the search for substitutes in order to avert further deterioration of the conditions of life. Thus, as the level of performance goes down, each successive reduction will require "more" compression. As the index (i) approaches zero—the level of "survival" performance, P_0—the increment dC_i increases. It reaches its maximum at the survival level: resistance of a system to further compression is greatest when it has been stripped to the kernel.

What transpires as a correlate of this analysis is the hypothesis that the most rational allocation of resources within a system will take place in times of most acute shortages. This hypothesis is indeed very plausible. At such a time there will be little dispute about priorities; information about available resources will be easiest to evaluate because there will be fewer resources than at other times; waste will be most carefully avoided; and no normative constraints as to the most efficient application of resources will be likely to hinder the freedom of action. Fighting for survival, the system will adopt the principle that "the end justifies the means," and therefore it will be capable of the most rational allocation of its resources, without discarding many efficient applications that at other times would be judged "improper." In general, the idea of propriety will gradually disappear from the system as shortages become more and more acute. In other words, as compression increases, so does normlessness in the system.[2] At the survival level the system will be normless, and human beings most likely will become amoral.

Throughout this study I have argued that the purpose of German occupation policies was to exploit Polish society to the point of literally destroying it. The Germans tried not only to "trim the fat," but they also set up a system of demands (level of compression) that had to affect the kernel of Polish society. But, as we have just learned, resistance to compression increases dramatically in the immediate vicinity of the kernel, and this paradigm should explain, at least in part, the seemingly unique phenomenon of the complex Polish resistance to German occupation.

Here one more observation may help in understanding why the Poles resisted the Germans so vigorously. The explanation follows from a typology of human groups that allows us to distinguish between two broad categories: those groups in which one acquires membership, and those in

[2] This diagnosis is not intended as a moral condemnation, although it leads to conclusions about morality. It should be taken as a strictly sociological proposition with a classic's authority behind it: from Merton's (1938) famous article we have learned to associate innovation with rejection of established norms of conduct. In that sense, a degree of normlessness is a necessary concomitant of substitutions.

which membership is ascriptive. All human associations may be said to fall into one of these two categories.[3] The distinction is that in order to be admitted to a group of the first type, one must express a desire to join and sometimes fulfill certain specific requirements, while membership in a group of the second type is automatic. Conversely, renunciation of membership in an ascriptive group is difficult, often impossible; it may require some sort of ritual, and it is psychologically traumatizing. To put it briefly, in ascriptive groups there is a ritual of departure connected with resignation from membership, while in the other type of human associations there is a ritual of admission connected with acquiring membership.[4]

With reference to this typology, one may immediately formulate an observation: it follows from the definition of categories here introduced that it is particularly difficult to dissolve a group based on ascriptive membership. There is a threshold of a symbolic nature at the point of dissolution that to some extent accounts for strong resistance against pressures aimed at definite dissolution, that is, against the destruction of such a group. Or, while there is a *variety of substitutes* potentially available as satisfactory alternatives

[3] "We note here the distinction of two principles, which clearly indicate a basic differentiation of the sociological significance of groups generally, no matter how much practice may mix them and make the difference lose some of its sharpness. On the one hand, there is the principle of including everybody who is not explicitly excluded; and, on the other, there is the principle of excluding everybody who is not explicitly included" (Simmel, 1964:369).

[4] Which human associations belong to the category of groups with "acquired" membership and which to that of "ascriptive" membership is, to a degree, historically determined. Until the nineteenth century, high or low birth determined one's ascriptive membership in Europe more than, perhaps, even nationality. Today, the nation-state has become the main frame of reference for ascriptive memberships, although not the only one: family is another; race, in certain parts of the world, still another. On the other hand, there is a multitude of groups with acquired memberships: for example, voluntary and professional associations.

for the fulfillment of needs provided for through affiliation in acquired-membership groups, there are practically *no substitutes* for the fulfillment of needs provided for through ascriptive-membership groups. Apparently, acquired-membership groups are instrumental; ascriptive-membership groups, on the other hand, are consumatory, that is, they are values in themselves.

In conclusion, it appears that a system cannot adjust by developing substitute structures or goal orientations, neither at the point when the kernel is affected, nor when pressure is applied against ascriptive-membership groups. In such circumstances it either resists successfully or is destroyed.[5]

RECAPITULATION

The German effort to colonize Eastern Europe indicated, it seems to me, that even a readiness to use all the instruments of coercion available to the government of a modern state without restraint is not a foolproof guarantee of the success of comprehensive social engineering. In order for it to succeed, at least two components must be present in addition to the capability and willingness to use coercion. The first one I would call "token justice."

Token justice, as I define it, resembles justice only superficially. It does not necessarily add moral justification to the imposed rule, but at the same time, it preserves an important component of justice: calculability. In a scheme of comprehensive social engineering a *gradation* of repressive measures must be established and maintained to counteract infractions of the new order. This is necessary, not so much in order to maintain a pretense of the fairness of the new regime, but to raise, by comparative standards, the cost of all-out opposition.

Second, if terror is used, that is, if the objective is to pro-

[5] In the words of yet another economist, "the voice option is the only way in which dissatisfied customers or members can react whenever the exit option is unavailable" (Hirschman, 1970:33).

mote revolution rather than to prevent a counterrevolution, the final project of the future society, its promise, must be articulated in terms understandable and attractive to the population subjected to terror. People will not be terrorized into promoting a revolution if they have reason to believe that there will be no place for them in the society the revolution is intended to introduce.

From this perspective one immediately recognizes the importance of support from a collaborating group. Its existence is a vivid example, almost a proof, that the project of the new society being implemented is not a death warrant issued against the subjugated population. A government that collaborates with the invader will always claim that but for its actions things would be much worse, that conditions would further deteriorate. In the least favorable circumstances, when they are not capable of mitigating the occupiers' demands, collaborationists are still in a position to alleviate the plight of the subjugated populace: having an intimate knowledge of their society, they may redistribute burdens in a manner least harmful to the society. "If we give them what they want," collaborationists will argue, "we will be better off as a collectivity than if they exact the same levy by themselves. It is so because we know where the resources are and we care for the welfare of our society. Thus we can redistribute burdens in a way that will spare vital functions and institutions."

When there is collaboration, there is always an opportunity to articulate a theory of "lesser evil." "Let us conform to the new rule," it states, "in order to be able to save and preserve as much as possible." But people gradually lose the sense of what it is that they are trying to "save" for, and their attitude, instead of being instrumental, becomes routine and an end in itself, since it assures their self-preservation and, not infrequently, their comfort. Finally, collaborationists' "expertise" can prove, in a sense, much more effective than the occupying power in suppressing organized

300

resistance. Collaboration gives an occupier an unparalleled opportunity to penetrate a society with his agents.

Many people who in different circumstances would never consider this alternative might, for self-preservation, reluctantly join the collaborationists under the pretense that someone else might do it anyway and that society will be better off when they do so because they will carry out "good works" that others, more cynical or subservient, would not care to pursue. Every collaborationist will, to some degree, seek such a justification, and the collaborating apparatus will become the source of an ideology of "service," "true patriotism," and "sacrifice." That collaboration was originally a consequence of a disaster, military occupation and defeat, and thus a sad and unwelcome necessity, will gradually be forgotten. Increasingly, under the growing pressure of dissatisfaction within the society or from a national liberation movement, collaboration will be more militantly paraded as a patriotic duty.

The emergence of a collaborating government affects, as well, the time perspective of the occupation. As former leaders ally themselves with the occupier, people's expectations of a temporary and brief occupation will be undermined. Visible local support lends the occupation an aura of stability and permanence. Some collaborationists may secretly work for the downfall of the new regime, and their motivation to join the collaborating group may have stemmed from the belief that as insiders they would be capable of damaging the regime most effectively.[6] As a rule, however, collaborationists will not be allowed to proclaim publicly their doubts about the chances for the new regime's survival. Quite the contrary. Their task, as assigned to them by the occupiers and as they see it themselves, is to bring about "normalization and stabilization." What they do is designed

[6] There is a hero in the Polish Romantic literature, Konrad Wallenrod, who joined the Teutonic Order for similar reasons. The Polish term *wallenrodyzm* is used to designate such an attitude.

to prevent the public from entertaining the notion that the conqueror will soon be defeated. And this is crucial, because the expectation of the short duration of an occupation creates a widespread climate of support for active and passive resistance against the occupier. Thus, for example, the increasing in-fighting among segments of the German occupation administration, the periodic shifts in policy direction, and the lack of any systematization in enforcing ill-defined rules of the occupation all contributed to the creation of an atmosphere of an interim and transitory rule and helped to perpetuate the Poles' belief that the German occupation would soon come to an end.

In order for a people to stand against a state, it is indispensable that they believe in its prompt disintegration. Man feels helpless when faced with the monstrous power of a modern state, and he would be foolish to think that anything he is capable of doing might possibly bring its downfall. But if he can be persuaded that it is a paper tiger, a colossus with clay feet, whose demise is imminent and unavoidable, he will joyfully join the ranks of gravediggers.

Finally, an atmosphere of relative stability and normalization creates conditions in which the middle-of-the-road attitude of "wait and see" becomes popular. In itself this attitude may be a formidable buffer against a potential resistance movement.

As I have noted above, the prewar political arrangements in Poland and the goal of unlimited exploitation pursued by the German occupiers prevented the latter from either finding collaborators or creating an atmosphere of relative "normalization" in the country. However, if not collaboration, then what? I have tried to show that the alternative to collaboration is not necessarily resistance. Accordingly, we must note that in spite of formidable pressures to split Polish society into villains and heroes, it is nevertheless possible to identify during the war a distinct, one is tempted to say an "apolitical," role: that of the expert. The expert's outward neutrality is respected by both the occupier and the national liberation movement. Because his services are valuable to both sides, neither group pressures him severely into either outward subserviance or open defiance. Therefore, I should modify the argument concerning stratification of Polish society during the occupation by noting that it contained a distinct, although numerically small, group of experts who enjoyed more protection, more security than any other group. Their relative security was a significant differentiating factor in a society where security was the most sought-after commodity. In that bitterly antagonistic society the experts held, so to speak, the middle ground between the occupiers and the occupied.

In my analysis of Polish society under German occupation, I have pointed out numerous processes of substitution.[7] They indicate how a society reacts against potentially destructive threats, and how it neutralizes antagonistic relationships or transforms them into cooperative ones. The most obvious mechanism of substitution that I have singled out is corruption. By means of corruption, normative and calculative modes of involvement were superimposed on the alienative mode and provided for some social solidarity between the occupiers and the occupied. If it were not for corruption, there would not have been any persuasion in Polish society, only coercion. Subsequently, we saw other mechanisms of substitution: the influx of real experts into the auxiliary administration, the growing importance of redistribution (middlemen) as a source of income at a time when production was tightly controlled and utilized almost exclusively by the occupier, the entrenchment of social interaction in the principle of loyalty. And, finally, the most spectacular substitution of all; the emergence of an underground state, an underground society. My intention has been to show that resistance should not be conceived mere-

[7] For a masterful application of the concept of substitution to the study of society, see Aleksander Gerschenkron's (1962) essays on economic history.

ly as a political-military movement but, rather, as a complex social phenomenon.

Resistance, as the mode of solidaristic response of the Polish society to the German occupation, was deeply rooted in Polish historical tradition. This was its strength and its weakness at the same time. Inquiry into the past revived the tradition of active resistance and insurrection and the conviction that national identity and sovereignty can be preserved and restored through sacrifice. At the same time, the organizational framework within which resistance was conducted turned out to be the familiar structure of political institutions that expressed social plurality, that is, the pattern of "communities," as they emerged during the brief moment of freedom in prewar Poland. However, as the dominant theme of the nineteenth-century tradition was the preservation of national substance, while politics in the independent Poland of 1918-1939 was continually preoccupied with the emotionally explosive issue of nationalism, the solidaristic response of Polish society during the occupation was limited by divisive lines of ethnicity. A sense of "community" had not been forged across nationality lines in Poland in the recent past, and this was revealed dramatically when the society was subjected to the ruthless regime of occupation.

The political composition of the underground state, and the organizational framework within which the society's initiative for resistance was formed, was a reproduction of the Polish political map existing before the May 1926 coup. Looking at the composition of the underground establishment, one can hardly believe that during the last ten years of Polish independence Sanacja was the sole arbiter in Polish politics. During the occupation, when efforts by the Poles to reestablish authority within their own society could rely only on voluntary compliance by the citizens themselves, social plurality, which years ago had been translated into a pattern of political allegiances, brought to life the same organizations as before. Deutsch's (1966:78) observation that although "governments can modify communities . . . in rare and favorable situations, . . . on the whole it is the communities which make governments" finds confirmation in a most striking fashion in Poland.

It is puzzling to see the ghost of a complex, democratic polity reemerge from the political obscurity to which it had been confined for a decade under the Sanacja regime. I am inclined to look at this spectacle as something more than merely another peculiar episode in the history of a strange country and to suggest that what we observe in the General-gouvernement during the Second World War is an early case of, as I would like to call it, a democratic revolution. By this name, I refer to a recent process of political transformation that with increasing frequency captures our attention: the restitution of pluralistic democratic polities in countries subject to authoritarian rule.

Just as the totalitarian revolution in Italy, Germany, China, Russia, or Eastern Europe was the most characteristic and most important process of political transformation for the first part of the twentieth century, so the democratic revolution—on the Iberian peninsula, in India, in Greece, in Czechoslovakia for a while, in Egypt perhaps—is for the second part of the century. It has but barely begun.

Authoritarian governments, particularly those that were introduced by a totalitarian revolution, find themselves in a serious predicament. For they are, figuratively speaking, cut off from their own societies. Insulated by powerful bureaucracies that are interested primarily in self-perpetuation, they know less and less about the true nature of the interests, aspirations, fears, and preferences of the existing and newly forming social forces in the complex modern societies over which they rule. By imposing an ostensible uniformity and obedience they do not prevent social initiatives from developing and various group interests from being pursued. Rather, by denying legitimacy to this authentic social plurality they induce interest groups to manipulate the system by feeding it with slanted information in order

305

to extract from it favorable rulings and force them to circumvent the existing institutions, to articulate outside of the officially sanctioned establishment. Consequently, with the passage of time, the authorities have a completely distorted representation of reality, and, as I have argued in Chapter III about the German administration in the GG, they cannot do anything about it because accurate information regarding important resources in such a society is simply *not available*.

One could perhaps argue that this matters little; after all, despotic governments are by definition not supposed to be troubled by their inability to read and therefore satisfy the preferences of their subjects. But in truth, a government needs information about public preferences and resources, not only in order to cater to public tastes, but also in order to manipulate the public. And this is the reason why the social vacuum in which an authoritarian government finds itself is so incapacitating: such a government cannot even plan to reform itself because it is incapable of predicting the consequences of any reforms. It is paralyzed by having lost the capacity to foresee the consequences of its actions; it can only *respond* to breakdowns because it has lost the ability to anticipate.

I believe that we shall continue to see many authoritarian regimes succumb to democratic revolutions whereby societies or, as Deutsch said, "communities," will once more reassert themselves against governments. I have attempted here to analyze an early episode of this most important and still emerging social process.

Bibliography

ARCHIVES AND COLLECTIONS

Biblioteka Polska (Polish Library), London
Hoover Institution Archives (HIA), Stanford University
    Polish Government Collection (PGC)
Hoover Library (HL), Stanford University
    Polish Underground Collection (PUC)
Instytut Historyczny Imienia Generała Władysława Sikorskiego
(General Sikorski Historical Institute) (GSHI), London
    Kolekcja Prezydium Rady Ministrów (PRM)
    Kolekcja Kota (no. 25)
    Unnamed Collection (A)
Piłsudski Institute of America, New York
Studium Polski Podziemnej (Underground Poland Study Trust),
London
    General Collection
    Kancelaria VI. Oddziału

MANUSCRIPTS

Czapiński, Władysław. 1942. Zagadnienie urzędnicze: organi-
zacja doboru wyższego personelu urzędniczego administracji
publicznej. Prepared for Biuro Prac Administracyjnych, Lon-
don. Stanford: Hoover Library.
Ronikier, Adam. N.d. Pamiętnik Adama Ronikiera prezesa RGO.
London: Biblioteka Polska.
Zimand, Roman. 1974. Od 12 w nocy do 5 rano nie spałem.
Próba lektury.

UNDERGROUND PRESS

Biuletyn Informacyjny
Głos Warszawy
Głos Wolny

Jutro
Kraj
Orka
Placówka
Płomienie
Pobudka
Polska Ludowa
Prawda
Prawda Młodych
Przez Walkę do Zwycięstwa
Reforma
Robotnik w Walce
Rzeczpospolita Polska
Sprawa
Sprawy Polskie
Wiadomści Polskie
Wolna Polska
Wolność
WRN

Books, Dissertations, and Articles

Abel, Theodore. 1951. "The Sociology of Concentration Camps." *Social Forces* 30:150-155.

Arendt, Hannah. 1965. *Eichman in Jerusalem: A Report on the Banality Of Evil*. New York: Viking Press.

Armstrong, John. 1963. *Ukrainian Nationalism*. New York: Columbia University Press.

Baldensperger, Fernand. 1968. *Le mouvement des idées dans l'émigration française 1789-1815*. 2 vols. Repr. ed. New York: Burt Franklin.

Barton, Allen H. 1970. *Communities in Disaster*. New York: Doubleday and Co.

Bartoszewski, Władysław. 1961. "Konspiracyjne piśmiennictwo kulturalne w kraju w latach 1939-1945." *Twórczość* 10:81-102.

———. 1973. "Tajny ruch wydawniczy w Warsawie w latach 1939-1944." In *Studia Warszawskie*, Vol. 17, *Warszawa lat wojny i okupacji: Zeszyt 3*, pp. 384-396.

———. 1974. *1859 dni Warszawy*. Cracow: Wydawnictwo Zank.

————, and Dobroszycki, L. 1968. "Prasa ruchu oporu w Polsce 1939-1945. Stan badań i postulaty." In Pracownia Historii Czasopiśmiennictwa Polskiego XIX i XX wieku PAN, ed., *Historia prasy Polskiej a kształtowanie się kultury narodowej*, 2:53-67. Warsaw: Państwowe Wydawnictwo Naukow (PWN).

————, and Lewin, Zofia, eds. 1969. *Righteous Among Nations: How Poles Helped the Jews, 1939-1945*. London: Earlscourt Publications Ltd.

Becker, Howard. 1968. *Through Values to Social Interpretation*. New York: Greenwood Press.

Bendix, Reinhard. 1962. *Max Weber: An Intellectual Portrait*. New York: Doubleday and Co.

Bergmann, Felix. 1935. *La Pologne et la protection des minorités*. Paris: Librairie L. Rodstein.

Berliner, Joseph S. 1957. *Factory and Manager in the USSR*. Cambridge, Mass.: Harvard University Press.

Black, Donald J. 1971. "The Social Organization of Arrest." *Stanford Law Review* 23:1087-1111.

Blaschek, Dr. 1965. "Reisebericht über meine Dienstreise zur Regierung nach Krakau vom 21 bis 26.VIII.1942." *Biuletyn Głównej Komisji do Badania Zbrodnii Hitlerowskich* 15:126-163.

Bloch, H. S., and Hoselitz, B. F. 1944. *Economics of Military Occupation*. Chicago: University of Chicago Press.

Bloch, Marc. 1961. *Feudal Society*. Chicago: University of Chicago Press.

————. 1969. "The Empire and the Idea of Empire Under the Hohenstaufen." In Bloch, *Land and Work in Medieval Europe*, pp. 1-43. New York: Harper and Row.

Bojarski, Wacław. 1942. "O nową postawę człowieka tworzącego." *Sztuka i Naród*, 1. Reprinted in Zdzisław Jastrzębski, ed., *Konspiracyjna publicystyka literacka 1940-1944*, pp. 47-52. Cracow: Wydawnictwo Literackie, 1973.

Bracher, Karl Dietrich. 1970. *The German Dictatorship*. New York: Praeger Publishers.

Breslauer, George, and Dallin, Alexander. 1970. *Political Terror in Communist Systems*. Stanford: Stanford University Press.

Brochwicz, Stanisław. 1940. *Bohaterowie czy zdrajcy? Wspomnienia więźnia politycznego*. Warsaw: Wydawnictwo Nowoczesne.

Broszat, Martin. 1965. *Nationalsozialistische Polenpolitik, 1939-1945.* Frankfurt and Hamburg: Fischer Bücherei KG.

Brzozowski, Stanisław. 1937. *Legenda Młodej Polski.* Warsaw: Wydawnictwo Instytutu Literackiego.

Buczek, Roman. 1970. "Organizacja i Polityka Stronnictwa Ludowego w latach 1939-1945." Ph.D. dissertation, Polski Uniwersytet na Obczyźnie, London.

Bühler, Josef, ed. 1943. *Das Generalgouvernement—seine Verwaltung und seine Wirtschaft.* Cracow: Burgverlag G.M.B.M.

Camus, Albert. 1951. *L'homme revolté.* Paris: Gallimard.

Coser, Lewis A. 1956. *The Functions of Social Conflict.* Glencoe, Ill.: Free Fress.

———. 1968. *Continuities in the Study of Social Conflict.* 2d ed. New York: Free Press.

———. 1974. *Greedy Institutions: Patterns of Undivided Commitment.* New York: Free Press.

Dąbrowski, Jan, ed. 1946. *Kraków pod rządami wroga 1939-1945.* Cracow: Drukarnia Uniwersytetu Jagiellońskiego.

Dallin, Alexander. 1957. *German Rule in Russia.* London: Macmillan and Co.

Davies, Norman. 1972. *White Eagle, Red Star: The Polish Soviet War, 1919-1920.* New York: St. Martin's Press.

Deutsch, Karl. 1966. *Nationalism and Social Communication.* Cambridge, Mass.: MIT Press.

Das Deutsche Führerlexikon. 1934. Berlin: Verlagsanstalt Otto Stallberg.

Dobroszycki, Lucjan. 1962. *Centralny katalog polskiej prasy konspiracyjnej 1939-1945.* Warsaw: Wydawnictwo MON.

———. 1963. "Zaginiona prasa konspiracyjna z lat 1939-1945." *Najnowsze Dzieje Polski: Materiały i studia z okresu II wojny światowej* 7:173-198.Warsaw: PWN.

Dołęga-Modrzewski, Stanisław. 1959. *Polskie Państwo Podziemne.* London.

Drozdowski, Marian. 1963. *Polityka gospodarcza rządu polskiego 1936-1939.* Warsaw: PWN.

Du Prel, Max F. 1942. *Das Generalgouvernement.* Würzburg: Konrad Triltsch Verlag.

Duraczyński, Eugeniusz. 1966. *Stosunki w kierownictwie podziemia londyńskiego, 1939-1943.* Warsaw: PWN.

————. 1970. "La structure sociale et politique de la resistance anti-hitlerienne en Pologne 1939-1945." *Revue d'histoire de la deuxieme guerre mondiale* 78, no. 4:47-66.

————. 1974. *Wojna i okupacja.* Warsaw: Wiedza Powszechna.

Durkheim, Emile. 1897. *Le Suicide. Étude de sociologie.* Paris: F. Alcan.

Etzioni, Amitai. 1961. *A Comparative Analysis of Complex Organizations.* New York: Free Press.

Fainsod, Merle. 1958. *Smolensk Under Soviet Rule.* Cambridge, Mass.: Harvard University Press.

Ferrero, Guglielmo. 1942. *Principles of Power.* New York: G. P. Putnam's Sons.

Fogelman, Charles, and Parenton, Vernon. 1959. "Disaster and Aftermath: Selected Aspects of Individual and Group Behavior in Critical Situations." *Social Forces* 38:129-135.

Fox, Paul. 1924. *The Reformation in Poland.* Baltimore: Johns Hopkins University Press.

Frank, Hans. 1970. *Okupacja i ruch oporu w dzienniku Hansa Franka.* Edited by L. Dobroszycki et al. 2 vols. Warsaw: Książka i Wiedza.

Frohlich, Norman, and Oppenheimer, Joe. 1974. "The Carrot and the Stick: Optimal Program Mixes for Entrepreneurial Political Leaders." *Public Choice* 19:43-61.

Garliński, Józef. 1971. *Politycy i żołnierze.* 2d ed. London: Odnowa.

————. 1975. "The Polish Underground State." *Journal of Contemporary History* 10:219-259.

Gay, Peter. 1968. *Weimar Culture: The Outsider as Insider.* New York: Harper and Row.

Gebethner, Jan. 1965. "Relacja o Komitecie Obywatelskim i Straży Obywatelskiej." In *Cywilna Obrona Warszawy we wrześniu 39r,* edited by Stanisław Płoski et al., pp. 177-181. Warsaw: PWN.

Gerschenkron, Alexander. 1962. *Economic Backwardness in Historical Perspective: A Book of Essays.* Cambridge, Mass.: Belknap Press of Harvard University.

Grudziński, Edmund. 1959. " 'N' 'Drapacz.' Propaganda Okręgu Warszawskiego AK wśród Niemców." *Najnowsze Dzieje Polski: Materiały i studia z okresu II wojny światowej* 2:43-107. Warszawa: PWN.

311

BIBLIOGRAPHY

Halévy, Élie. 1938. *L'ère des tyrannies. Études sur le socialisme et la guerre*. Paris: Gallimard.

Halicz, Emanuel. 1965. "Doświadczenie powstania styczniowego w ujęciu naczelnych władz hitlerowskich." *Wojskowy Przegląd Historyczny* 10, no. 3 (35):356-368.

Hernas, Czesław. 1974. "Złota wolność (notatki do interpretacji)." *Teksty* 16:1-11.

Herzog, Leon. 1962. "Czy Hitler chciał utworzyć buforowe państewko polskie? Na marginesie pracy Czesława Madajczyka 'GG w planach hitlerowskich,'" *Wojskowy Przegląd Historyczny* 7, no. 4 (26):295-316.

Hillebrandt, Bogdan. 1973. *Konspiracyjne organizacje młodzieżowe w Polsce 1939-1945*. Warsaw: Książka i Wiedza.

Hirschman, Albert O. 1970. *Exit, Voice and Loyalty: Response to Decline in Firms, Organizations and States*. Cambridge, Mass.: Harvard University Press.

Hoffmann, Stanley. 1974. *Decline or Renewal*. New York: Viking Press.

Homze, Edward L. 1967. *Foreign Labor in Nazi Germany*. Princeton: Princeton University Press.

Horak, Stephen. 1961. *Poland and Her National Minorities 1919-1939*. New York: Vantage Press.

Huntington, Samuel. 1970. "Social and Institutional Dynamics of One-Party Systems." In *Authoritarian Politics in Modern Society: The Dynamics of Established One-Party Systems*, edited by S. Huntington and C. Moore, pp. 3-47. New York: Basic Books.

International Military Tribunal (IMT). 1947-1949. *Trial of the Major War Criminals Before the International Military Tribunal*. 42 vols. Nuremberg.

Iranek-Osmecki, Kazimierz. 1971. *He Who Saves One Life*. New York: Crown Publishers.

Ivanka, Aleksander. 1964. *Wspomnienia skarbowca 1927-1945*. Warsaw: PWN.

Janion, Maria. 1975. "Wojna i forma." *Polityka*, February 1, pp. 1-14.

Janowski, Andrzej. 1972. "Okręg stołeczny Stronnictwa Narodowego. Dzieje Organizacji 1939-1944." In *Studia Warszawskie*, Vol. 10, *Warszawa lat wojny i okupacji: Zeszyt 2*, pp. 167-211.

312

Jasiński, Józef. 1965. *Z dziejów polskiej spółdzielczosci spożywców podczas II wojny światowej.* Warszawa: Spółdzielczy Instytut Badawczy.

Jędruszczak, Tadeusz. 1961. "Stanowisko społeczeństwa i opozycji wobec powstania Obozu Zjednoczenia Narodowego." *Najnowsze Dzieje Polski: Materiały i studia z okresu 1914-1939* 4:191-210. Warsaw: PWN.

Jonassen, Christen. 1951. "Some Historical and Theoretical Bases of Racism in Northwestern Europe." *Social Forces* 30:155-161.

Kamenetsky, Ihor. 1961. *Secret Nazi Plans for Eastern Europe: A Study of Lebensraum Policies.* New York: Bookman Associates.

Kenig, Marian. 1965. "Fragment relacji dotyczący Robotniczych Batalionów Obrony Warszawy." In *Cywilna Obrona Warszawy we wrześniu 39r,* edited by Stanisław Płoski et al., pp. 207-229. Warsaw: PWN.

Kennan, George F. 1968. *From Prague After Munich: Diplomatic Papers 1938-1940.* Princeton: Princeton University Press.

Kersten, Krystyna, and Szarota, Tomasz, eds. 1968. *Wieś Polska 1939-1948.* 2 vols. Warsaw: PWN.

Kirk, Dudley. 1946. *Europe's Population in the Interwar Years.* Geneva: League of Nations.

Kirkpatrick, Clifford. 1946. "Sociological Principles and Occupied Germany." *American Sociological Review* 11:67-78.

Kisielewski, Tadeusz, and Nowak, J., eds. 1968. *Chleb i krew. Moja wieś w czasie okupacji. Wspomnienia.* Warsaw: Ludowa Spółdzielnia Wydawnicza.

Kluke, Paul. 1955. "Nationalsozialistische Europaideologie." *Vierteljahrshefte für Zeitgeschichte* 3:240-275.

Kłosiński, Tadeusz. 1947. *Polityka przemysłowa okupanta w GG.* Poznań: Instytut Zachodni.

Koehl, Robert L. 1957. *RKFDV: German Resettlement and Population Policy 1939-1945.* Cambridge, Mass.: Harvard University Press.

———. 1960. "Feudal Aspects of National Socialism." *American Political Science Review* 54:921-933.

Korboński, Stefan. 1968. *Fighting Warsaw: The Story of the*

Polish Underground State 1939-1945. New York: Funk and Wagnall.

———. 1975. *Polskie Państwo Podziemne*. Paris: Instytut Literacki.

Kornhauser, William. 1959. *The Politics of Mass Society*. Glencoe, Ill.: Free Press.

Kot, Stanisław. 1960. *Georges Niemirycz et la lutte contre l'intolerance au XVIIe siècle*. The Hague: Mouton.

Kotula, Franciszek. 1959. "Czy były próby utworzenia proniemieckiego rządu po klęsce wrześniowej." *Najnowsze Dzieje Polski: Materiały i studia z okresu II wojny światowej* 3:73-80. Warsaw: PWN.

Krawczyńska, Jadwiga. 1971. *Zapiski dziennikarki warszawskiej 1939-1947*. Warsaw: Państwowy Instytut Wydawniczy (PIW).

Kubijovych, Volodymyr. 1975. *The Ukrainians in the General-gouvernement, 1939-1941*. Chicago: Mykola Denysiuk Publishing Company.

Kukiel, Marian. 1970. *Generał Sikorski—żołnierz i mąż stanu Polski Walczącej*. London: Instytut Polski i Muzeum im. gen. Sikorskiego.

Kula, Witold. 1947. "Życie gospodarcze ziem polskich pod okupacją." *Dzieje Najnowsze* 1:139-160. Warsaw: Instytut Pamięci Narodowej.

Kulski, Julian. 1964. *Zarząd miejski Warszawy 1939-1944*. Warsaw: PWN.

———. 1968. *Stefan Starzyński w mojej pamięci*. Paris: Instytut Literacki.

Landau, Ludwik. 1962-1963. *Kronika lat wojny i okupacji*. 3 vols. Warsaw: PWN.

Leff, Nathaniel H. 1964. "Economic Development Through Bureaucratic Corruption." *American Behavioral Scientist* 8:8-14.

Lerner, Daniel. 1951. *The Nazi Elite*. Stanford: Stanford University Press.

Lewandowska, Stanisława. 1973. "Niektóre problemy działalności legalizacyjnej konspiracji warszawskiej." In *Studia Warszawskie*, Vol. 17, *Warszawa lat wojny i okupacji: Zeszyt 3*. Warsaw: PWN.

Lijphardt, Arend. 1968. *The Politics of Accommodation*. Berkeley: University of California Press.

Linz, Juan. 1964. "An Authoritarian Regime: Spain." In *Cleavages, Ideologies and Party Systems*, edited by Erik Allardt, and Yrjo Littunen, pp. 291-341. Helsinki: Academic Bookstore.

Lipiński, Karol. 1973. "Problem młodzieży współczesnej," *Płomienie* 7 (1944). Reprinted in Zdzisław Jastrzębski, ed., *Konspiracyjna publicystyka literacka 1940-1944*, pp. 183-194. Cracow: Wydawnictwo Literackie.

Lipset, Seymour Martin. 1967. *The First New Nation*. New York: Anchor Books.

Łukasiewicz, S. 1958. *Okupacja*. Warsaw: PIW.

Lyttelton, Adrian. 1966. "Fascism in Italy: The Second Wave." *Journal of Contemporary History* 1:75-100.

McMullen, M. 1961. "A Theory of Corruption." *Sociological Review* 9:181-201.

Madajczyk, Czesław. 1961. *Generalna Gubernia w planach hitlerowskich. Studia*. Warsaw: PWN.

———. 1964. "Cele wojenne Rzeszy po podboju Polski." *Wojskowy Przegląd Historyczny* 9, no. 4 (33):196-205.

———. 1970. *Polityka III Rzeszy w okupowanej Polsce; okupacja Polski 1939-1945*. 2 vols. Warsaw: PWN.

Marks, Stephen R. 1974. "Durkheim's Theory of Anomie." *American Journal of Sociology* 39:329-363.

Mastny, Vojtech. 1971. *The Czechs Under Nazi Rule: The Failure of National Resistance*. New York: Columbia University Press.

[Marciniak, Florian]. 1962. "Sprawozdanie naczelnika Szarych Szeregów do KGAK oraz naczelnika komitetu harcerskiego w Londynie," *Najnowsze Dzieje Polski: Materiały i studia z okresu II wojny światowej* 6:285-315. Warsaw: PWN.

Marczak-Oborski, Stanisław. 1967. *Teatr czasu wojny. Polskie życie teatralne w latach II wojny światowej 1939-1945*. Warsaw: PIW.

Mellon, Stanley. 1958. *The Political Uses of History*. Stanford: Stanford University Press.

Merton, Robert K. 1938. "Social Structure and Anomie." *American Sociological Review* 3: 672-682.

Michel, Henri. 1972. *The Shadow War: European Resistance 1939-1945*. New York: Harper and Row.

Miłosz, Czesław. 1972. *Prywatne Obowiązki*. Paris: Instytut Literacki.

315

Milward, Alan. 1965. *The German Economy at War*. London: University of London, The Athlone Press.

————. 1970. *The New Order and the French Economy*. Oxford: Clarendon Press.

Młynarski, Feliks. 1971. *Wspomnienia*. Warsaw: PWN.

Montesquieu. 1964. "Considerations sur les causes de la grandeur des Romains et de leur decadence." In Montesquieu, *Oeuvres Complètes*. Paris: Edition du Seuil.

Morgenstern, Oskar. 1966. "The Compressibility of Economic Systems and the Problem of Constants." *Zeitschrift für Nazional-ökonomie* 26:190-203.

Nałkowska, Zofia. 1974. *Dzienniki czasu wojny*. Warsaw: Czytelnik.

Namier, Lewis. 1964. *1848: The Revolution of the Intellectuals*. New York: Doubleday and Co.

Nietyksza, Bronisław. 1972. "Warszawianka." In *Studia Warszawskie*, Vol. 10, *Warszawa lat wojny i okupacji: Zeszyt 2*, pp. 299-318.

Nye, J. S. 1967. "Corruption and Political Development: A Cost-Benefit Analysis." *American Political Science Review* 61:417-427.

Oberschall, Anthony. 1973. *Social Conflict and Social Movements*. Englewood Cliffs, N.J.: Prentice-Hall, Inc.

Olson, Mancur, Jr. 1963. *The Economics of the Wartime Shortage: A History of British Food Supplies in the Napoleonic War and in World Wars I and II*. Durham: Duke University Press.

————. 1965. *The Logic of Collective Action*. Cambridge, Mass.: Harvard University Press.

Orlow, Dietrich. 1968. *The Nazis in the Balkans*. Pittsburgh: University of Pittsburgh Press.

————. 1973. *The History of the Nazi Party*. Pittsburgh: University of Pittsburgh Press.

Parsons, Talcott. 1942. "Some Sociological Aspects of the Fascist Movements." *Social Forces* 21:138-147.

Pasternak, Boris. 1958. *Doctor Zhivago*. New York: Pantheon Books.

Pawłowicz, Henryk. 1961. "Komisariat cywilny przy dowództwie obrony Warszawy we wrześniu 1939." *Najnowsze Dzieje Pol-*

ski: Materiały i studia z okresu II wojny światowej 5:153-180. Warsaw: PWN.

Paxton, Robert. 1972. *Vichy France.* New York: Alfred A. Knopf.

Pełczyński, Tadeusz, et al., eds. 1970-1976. *Armia Krajowa w Dokumentach 1939-1945.* Vol. 1: *Wrzesień 1939–Czerwiec 1941.* Vol. 2: *Czerwiec 1941–Kwiecień 1943.* Vol. 3: *Maj 1943–Lipiec 1944.* London: Studium Polski Podziemnej.

Petit annuaire statistique de la Pologne 1939. 1939. Warsaw: Publication de l'office centrale de la statistique.

Piłsudski, Józef. 1903. *Walka rewolucyjna w zaborze rosyjskim. Bibuła.* Część I. Kraków: Wydawnictwo Naprzodu.

Z Pola Walki. Cele i drogi podziemnego ruchu robotniczego w Polsce 1939-1942. 1943. London: Nakładem Nowej Polski.

Polonsky, Antony. 1972. *Politics in Independent Poland 1921-1939.* Oxford: Clarendon Press.

Pospieszalski, K. 1958. *Documenta Occupationis.* Vol. 6. Poznań: Instytut Zachodni.

Próchnik, Adam. 1957. *Pierwsze piętnastolecie Polski niepodległej.* Warsaw: Książka i Wiedza.

Pużak, Kazimierz. 1977. "Wspomnienia, 1939-1945." *Zeszyty Historyczne* 41:3-196. Paris: Instytut Literacki.

Radford, R. A. 1945. "The Economic Organization of a P.O.W. Camp." *Economica*, n.s., 12:189-201.

Regulski, Janusz. 1965. "Relacja o organizacji i działalności Straży Obywatelskiej w Warsawie we Wrześniu 1939r." In *Cywilna Obrona Warszawy we wrześniu 1939r*, edited by Stanisław Płoski et al., pp. 341-353. Warsaw: PWN.

Ricoeur, Paul. 1969. *The Symbolism of Evil.* Boston: Beacon Press.

Roberts, Walter R. 1973. *Tito, Mihailovič and the Allies 1941-1945.* New Brunswick: Rutgers University Press.

Rybicki, Stanisław. 1965. *Pod znakiem lwa i kruka.* Warsaw: Instytut Wydawniczy Pax.

Rzepecki, Jan. 1971. "Organizacja i działanie Biura Informacji i Propagandy (BIP) Komendy Głównej AK." *Wojskowy Przegląd Historyczny*, 16, no. 2 (57):128-155; 16, no. 3 (58):136-160; 16, no. 4(59):147-171.

Santoro, Cesare. 1931. *Through Poland During the Elections of 1930.* Geneva: Albert Kundig S.A.

317

BIBLIOGRAPHY

Schapiro, Leonard. 1969. "The Concept of Totalitarianism." *Survey* 73:93-115.

Schelling, Thomas C. 1963. *The Strategy of Conflict*. New York: Oxford University Press.

Scott, James C. 1972. *Comparative Political Corruption*. Englewood Cliffs, N.J.: Prentice-Hall.

Shibutani, Tamotsu. 1966. *Improvised News: A Sociological Study of Rumor*. New York: Bobbs-Merrill Co.

Simmel, Georg. 1964. *The Sociology of Georg Simmel*. Edited by Kurt H. Wolff. New York: Free Press.

Skalniak, Franciszek. 1966. *Bank Emisyjny w Polsce 1939-1945*. Warsaw: Państwowe Wydawnictwo Ekonomiczne.

Śliwiński, Artur. 1965. "Relacja o powstiniu i działalności Komitetu Obywatelskiego podczas oblężenia Warszawy." In *Cywilna Obrona Warszawy we wrześniu 39r*, edited by Stanisław Płoski et al., pp. 393-397. Warsaw: PWN.

Smelser, Neil J. 1962. *Theory of Collective Behavior*. New York: Free Press.

Sorokin, Pitrim A. 1943. *Man and Society in Calamity*. New York: E. P. Dutton and Co., Inc.

————. 1945. "War and Post-War Changes in Social Stratifications of the Euro-American Population." *American Sociological Review* 10:294-303.

Speer, Albert. 1970. *Inside the Third Reich: Memoirs*. New York: Macmillan Co.

"Sprawozdanie referatu zawodowego wydziału bezpieczeństwa MSW o stanie bezrobocia w Polsce," (Tajne, 2.VI.1936). 1961. *Najnowsze Dzieje Polski: Materiały i studia z okresu 1914-1939* 4:211-238. Warsaw: PWN.

Stolarz, Jan. 1965. "Powiat Węgrów w walce z okupantem," *Najnowsze Dzieje Polski: Materiały i studia z okresu II wojny światowej* 9:95-142. Warsaw: PWN.

Streng, Heinz. 1955. *Die Landwirtschaft im Generalgouvernement*. Tübingen: Studien des Instituts für Besatzungsfragen.

Strzelecki, Jan. 1974. "Próby Świadectwa." In Strzelecki, *Kontynuacje (2)*, pp. 5-70. Warsaw: PIW.

Swanson, Guy E. 1971. *Social Change*. Glenview, Ill.: Foresman and Co.

Szacki, Jerzy. 1965. *Kontrrewolucyjne paradoksy*. Warsaw: PWN.

Szafrański, Jan. 1960. "Straty Polsky w II Wojnie Światowej." In Zachodnia Agencja Prasowa, *Straty Wojenne Polski w Latach 1939-1945*, edited by Roman Nurowski, pp. 34-61. Poznań: Wydawnictwo Zachodnie.

Szarota, Tomasz. 1972. "Jawne wydawnictwa i prasa w okupowanej Warszawie." In *Studia Warszawskie*, Vol. 10, *Warszawa lat wojny i okupacji: Zeszyt 2*, pp. 140-166.

————. 1973a. *Okupowanej Warszawy dzień powszedni*. Warsaw: Czytelnik.

————. 1973b. "Inteligencja Warszawska." In *Studia Warszawskie*, Vol. 17, *Warszawa lat wojny i okupacji: Zeszyt 3*, pp. 261-303.

Szczepański, Jan. 1970. *Polish Society*. New York: Random House.

Szcześniak, Antoni, and Szota, Wiesław. 1973. *Droga do nikąd. Działność organizacji ukraińskich nacjonalistów i jej likwidacja w Polsce*. Warsaw: Wydawnictwo MON.

Szturm de Sztrem, Tadeusz. 1965. "Fragment wspomnień dotyczący Komisariartu Cywilnego przy Dowództwie Obrony Warszawy." In *Cywilna Obrona Warszawy we wrześniu 39r*, edited by Stanisław Płoski et al., pp. 389-392. Warsaw: PWN.

Tarnogrodzki, Tadeusz, and Tryc, Ryszard. 1966. "Polskie organizacje konspiracyjne w kraju w latach 1939-45." *Wojskowy Przegląd Historyczny*, 11, no. 4(40):250-274.

Terej, Jerzy Janusz. 1971. *Rzeczywistość i Polityka. Ze studiów nad dziejami najnowszymi Narodowej Demokracji*. Warsaw: Książka i Wiedza.

Tocqueville, Alexis de. 1856. *L'Ancien Régime et la Revolution*. Paris: M. Levy Frères.

Tokarzewski-Karaszewicz, Michał. 1964. "U podstaw tworzenia Armii Krajowej." *Zeszyty Historyczne* 6:17-44. Paris: Instytut Literacki.

Torzecki, Ryszard. 1972. *Kwestia ukraińska w polityce III Rzeszy (1933-1945)*. Warsaw: Książka i Wiedza.

Treugutt, Stefan. 1974. "Napoleon Bonaparte jako bohater polskiego romantyzmu." *Teksty*, 17, no. 5:37-44.

Trunk, Isaiah. 1972. *Judenrat: The Jewish Councils in Eastern Europe Under Nazi Occupation*. New York: Macmillan Co.

Trzebiński, Andrzej. 1942. "Pokolenie liryczne i dramatyczne." *Sztuka i Naród*, 5 (1942). Reprinted in Zdzisław Jastrzębski, ed., *Konspiracyjna publicystyka literacka 1940-1944*, pp. 53-66. Cracow: Wydawnictwo Literackie, 1973.

Ulam, Adam. 1973. *Stalin: The Man and His Era*. New York: Viking Press.

United States, Chief of Counsel for Prosecution of Axis Criminality. 1946. *Nazi Conspiracy and Aggression*. Washington, D.C.: United States Government Printing Office.

Uziembło, Adam. 1950. "Podziemie." *Kultura*, no. 1(27), pp. 3-33. Paris.

Walicki, Andrzej. 1970. *Filozofia a mesjanizm—studia z dziejów filozofii i myśli społeczno-religijnej romantyzmu polskiego.* Warsaw: PIW.

Wandycz, Piotr S. 1969. *Soviet-Polish Relations, 1917-1921.* Cambridge, Mass.: Harvard University Press.

Weber, Max. 1968. *Economy and Society*. New York: Bedminster Press.

Weinberg, G. 1964. "Hitler's Image of the U.S." *American Historical Review* 69:1906-21.

Weingrod, Alex. 1968. "Patrons, Patronage and Political Parties." *Comparative Studies in Society and History* 10:377-400.

Weinstein, Jan. 1967. "Władysław Studnicki w świetle dokumentów hitlerowskich II Wojny." *Zeszyty Historyczne* 11:3-91. Paris: Instytut Literacki.

Werner, Andrzej. 1971. *Zwyczajna Apokalipsa—Tadeusz Borowski i jego wizja świata obozów.* Warsaw: Czytelnik.

Wilbur, Earl. 1945. *A History of Unitarianism.* Cambridge, Mass.: Harvard University Press.

Witos, Wincenty. 1963. "Listy Witosa do H. Libermana z lat 1937-1939." *Najnowsze Dzieje Polski: Materiały i studia z okresu 1914-1939* 6.

————. 1965. *Moje Wspomnienie.* Paris: Instytut Literacki.

Worsley, R.H.M. 1942. *Europe vs. America: Implications of the New Order.* London: Jonathan Cape.

Wroński, Tadeusz. 1974. *Kronika okupowanego Krakowa.* Cracow: Wydawnictwo Literackie.

Wyka, Kazimierz. 1959. *Życie na niby.* Warsaw: Książka i Wiedza.

Zaremba, Zygmunt. 1957. *Wojna i Konspiracja.* London: B. Świderski.

320

Żarnowski, Janusz. 1961. "Zagadnienia ideologiczno—programowe w uchwałach XXIV Kongresu PPS w 1937r." *Najnowsze Dzieje Polski: Materiały i studia z okresu 1914-1939* 4:101-133. Warsaw: PWN.

————. 1976. *Struktura społeczna inteligencji w Polsce w latach 1918-1939.* Warsaw: PWN.

Zawodny, Janusz K. 1962. *Death in the Forest: The Story of the Katyń Forest Massacre.* Notre Dame, Ind.: University of Notre Dame Press.

Zink, Harold. 1949. *American Military Government in Germany.* New York: Macmillan Co.

Znaniecki, Florian. 1952. *Modern Nationalities.* Urbana, Ill.: University of Illinois Press.

Zweig, Ferdynand. 1944. *Poland Between Two Wars.* London: Secker and Warburg.

Index

AB-Aktion, 47
agrarian reform, 15, 16; anti-minority bias of, 19
agriculture: administration of property by Liegenschaftver-waltung, 94, 95; contribution to GNP, 99; debts, 95; inter-war surpluses, 93; and price scissors, 16; unrest in 1930s, 17
AK. *See* Home Army
AL. *See* People's Army
alcoholism, 104, 160; spread of, 105
America, in Nazi plans, 40
Anders, Władysław, and the Katyń massacre, 86
anti-Semitism, 124, 140, 184-185
Antoni, Emissary. *See* Iranek-Osmecki, Kazimierz
Arbeitsamt, 107; corruption of, 80; Ukrainians in, 189
Arendt, Hannah, 63
Armstrong, John, 188
Association of Revenge (ZO), 285
atomization, 115; under coercion, 199; of Polish society, 150, 177; and the underground, 235
Austerlitz, 122
Austria-Hungary: and Poland in the 19th century, 11; Polish collaboration with, before World War I, 128
authoritarianism: and collaboration, 121, 122; concept of, 21; predicament of, 305, 306; in prewar Poland, 27, 28; of

Sanacja, 171; and tradition of resistance in Poland, 231
authority, 30, 32, 60, 61, 91, 129, 177, 201, 228, 264, 268, 304; based on coercion, 199, 202, 203; and collaboration, 117, 119, 121, 125, 126; Frank and, 64, 67; the Führer-prinzip, 46, 88; legitimization, 14, 29; loss, 136, 167; under patrimonial domination, 207; search for, 259, 265, 266, 274, 287; Starzyński and, 216; vacuum, 135, 137, 167, 215, 260, 261
auxiliary local administration, in the GG, 45, 119; armed attacks on, 161; certificate of employment in, 80; differentia-tion into urban and rural, 132; dilemmas of employees, 135; employment in, 134; and normative orientation, 138
auxiliary local administration, rural, 141; and compulsory quotas, 143; as a hostile force, 143; Jewish, 185; manpower needed in, 132; as mediator, 148; replacement of, 142; skills needed in, 142; Ukraini-ans in, 189, 195; visibility of, 142
auxiliary local administration, urban: as distributor of serv-ices, 142; expertise, 132; normlessness, 137; profes-sionals in, 173; and wages and cost of living in Warsaw, 101; in Warsaw, 52

telligentsia in the underground
in, 237; outside assistance to
underground in, 241; war
casualties, 84; *Warszawski
Głos Narodowy* on, 289;
workers in Germany, 81; and
Z.A.M., 151
Frank, Hans (Governor General),
46, 48, 50, 51, 53, 56, 63, 67,
83, 85, 134, 161, 162, 210;
and alienation of work, 115;
attitude toward Poles, 64; and
Baudienst, 109; and the black
market, 155, 156; career, 60;
conception of legal state, 62,
63; dilemmas of GG's administration, 89, 90, 91, 99; and
forced labor, 78, 80; and
Judenrate, 125; and Kruger,
59, 64, 65, 68; and lack of
cadres, 55; and living conditions in GG, 102; and mass
executions, 82; memorandum
to Hitler, 61, 81; negotiations
with Himmler, 66; and
NSDAP, 57; in Nuremberg,
133; and Polish intelligentsia,
74; and property rights, 94;
relations with the police and
SS, 62, 63, 65, 66, 87; and
resettlements, 71, 72; resignation, 65; and security breakdown, 163; and Sonderdienst,
65, 66; state of emergency
and, 107; and Ukrainian Central Committee, 186; on Warsaw, 221; and the Wehrmacht,
68, 69
freedom: "golden," 6; ideal of,
7; loss of, 9; Napoleonic wars
and, 6; in 1939-1944, 240
French Revolution, 34, 35
Frohlich, Norman, 206
Front Morges, 275

Führerprinzip, 30, 46, 52, 67,
88, 91; and centralization, 51

Galicia, 45, 53, 95, 133, 134;
attached to GG, 187; and food
quotas, 107, 133; under the
Hapsburgs, 5; loyalism in, 5;
nationality of wojts and mayors,
141; and Stanczycy, 128, 134;
Ukrainian local administration
in, 95, 198; Ukrainian schools,
19
Garliński, Józef, 136, 243
Gay, Peter, 14
Gazeta Polska, 24
Generalgouvernement (GG), 3,
43, 44, 50, 67, 79, 87, 91, 100,
143, 153, 159, 163, 182, 187,
199, 221, 222, 305, 306; administration versus police and
SS, 59, 64-66; administrative
manpower, 54, 56, 208; administrative setup, 46, 47, 51,
52, 53; agricultural surplus
before the war, 93; alienation
of work, 115; appointment of
Government Delegate in, 287;
apportionment of resources,
89; Bank Emisyjny in, 139;
and collaboration, 122, 124,
125, 126; collective action in,
226; collective responsibility
in, 210; conditions for collective protest in, 230, 231; conditions of work in, 107; and
corruption, 147, 151, 155, 174;
creation of, 48; and economic
exploitation, 92, 93, 98; economy of, 103; employment of
Poles and Ukrainians in, 133;
finances of the underground,
242, 248; fiscal measures in,
96; food deliveries in, 102, 105,
106, 107; and Germanization,

LIBRARY OF CONGRESS CATALOGING IN PUBLICATION DATA

Gross, Jan Tomasz.
Polish society under German Occupation.

Bibliography: p.
Includes index.
1. Poland—History—Occupation, 1939-1945.   I.   Title
DK4410.G76   943.8'05   78-70298
ISBN 0-691-09381-4